TWINSPIRATION

TWINSPIRATION

*real-life advice
from pregnancy through
the first year*

Cheryl Lage

TAYLOR TRADE PUBLISHING
Lanham | New York | Boulder | Toronto | Oxford

Published by Taylor Trade Publishing
An imprint of The Rowman & Littlefield Publishing Group, Inc.
4501 Forbes Boulevard, Suite 200
Lanham, Maryland 20706

Distributed by National Book Network

Library of Congress Cataloging-in-Publication Data

Lage, Cheryl, 1964–
    Twinspiration : real-life advice from pregnancy through the first year /
Cheryl Lage. — 1st Taylor Trade Pub. ed.
        p. cm.
    Includes bibliographical references.
    ISBN-13: 978-1-58979-280-7 (pbk. : alk. paper)
    ISBN-10: 1-58979-280-7 (pbk. : alk. paper)
1. Twins. 2. Multiple pregnancy—Popular works. 3. Multiple birth—Popular
works. 4. Infants—Care. I. Title.
    HQ777.35.L34 2006
    649'.1'0242—dc22

                                                                    2005019672

∞™ The paper used in this publication meets the minimum requirements of American National Standard for Information Sciences—Permanence of Paper for Printed Library Materials, ANSI/NISO Z39.48–1992.

Manufactured in the United States of America.

Contents

Part III: Preparation and Anticipation

Part IV: At Last, the New Generation

Part V: Navigation and Coordination

Foreword

We brought our twin daughters home, and 8 weeks later I began a busy full-time career as a pediatrician. I faced the challenges of raising twins at home and advising new and expectant parents of twins on the obstacles they faced medically, psychologically, and emotionally. I, too, combed the bookstores for advice on my own little ones. I found few books with practical advice on twins. The books that I did find that mentioned twins seemed outdated or too superficial on the most important topics relating to raising them. Even medical school had hardly covered the real-world issues specifically related to multiples. It seemed the only way to do it was to roll up our sleeves and jump right in! This book helps change that.

My twins are now 9 years old and 2 other children have since joined them (one at a time, not a second set of twins!). I see many sets of twins in my office and frequently do prenatal interviews with couples expecting twins. I see these wide-eyed families awaiting twins, anxiously preparing for their double blessing. They, as myself before them, do not know what to expect before, during, and after delivery of their twins. After reading Cheryl's personal account of raising twins, I believe she has captured the practical aspects of having twins, which will benefit those families facing the same twin issues. Cheryl's *Twinspiration* brings a real-world "in the trenches" approach to bringing up twins that other texts fail to address. She recognizes the real differences between raising twins and raising a single child.

I have been on both sides of the fence with twins: the personal experience at home and the medical experience of twins before birth, in the hospital, and in the office. *Twinspiration* carries much merit in bringing a practical everyday reality to raising twins, great factual information, and an awesome bit of humor—which we all need every day. I will without reservation recommend this book to parents approaching a new life with twins. And I feel certain you will find comfort and confidence in her success story. We're raising twins, and you can too!

Dr. Lora Christian, M.D.
Pediatrician

Acknowledgments

How's that song begin? "Let's start at the very beginning . . . a very good place to start." Clearly, my earliest and most profound ideas of what motherhood should be come from my own Mama, so abundant gratitude and love go her way first. My entire family has been so very understanding and supportive during the adventure of getting this text completed, my thanks and love to you all.

To Kay Coates, Craig Sanders, Rachel Lower, Connie Correia Fisher, Dr. Carol Livoti, Bruce and Susan Lindeman, Pam and Todd Hervey, and Ann Douglas who so willingly plowed through the manuscript, read sample chapters, offered suggestions, shared perspectives, and composed "early reviews," thank you. I'm truly in your debt.

To the twin parent friends who have been so encouraging and supportive on my website www.twinsights.com, and to the many e-friends I have made via twin parenting message boards, multiple thanks and please stay in touch. Undoubtedly, we have plenty of twin parenting tribulations and triumphs to share in the years ahead.

Dr. Richard Rinehardt, how pleasant you made my months of pregnancy! Whenever folks ask about what they should seek in a plural pregnancy physician, I merely recite the qualities you possess with such personality and grace. For ushering my twosome into the world, you will always hold a place of honor in my heart. Thank you.

Once our darling duo arrived, how blessed they were, and how blessed we were as parents, to have the reassurance and pediatric expertise of Dr. Lora Christian. I wish everyone reading this had the opportunity not only to read her words, but also to benefit from her kindness, empathy, and pediatric acumen.

Erin Reel, dear Erin Reel, the title of "agent" sounds so distancing and über-professional. While of course you are consummately professional and skilled at what you do, what I have come to treasure more is your ever-bolstering support, confidence, and friendship. From the faith you exhibited by taking this text on, to the passing along of toddler togs; from your tenderness in early editing, to our shared enjoyment of quoting semiobscure song lyrics and simultaneously craving delivery pizza—how thankful I am that our connection transcends the mere agent/client relationship. As far as literary agents (and girlfriends) go, I think Horatio Sanz speaks for me, "You da best in da biz!" I acquired an agent, but found a friend. Thank you, E.

Speaking of confidence and faith, appreciation galore to all the crew at Taylor Trade Publishing. To Mandy Phillips, thank you for your initial belief in this book. To Rick Rinehart (is it a strange coincidence your name bears uncanny resemblance to the man who brought my twins into the world?) and darling, dutiful Dulcie Wilcox, your patience with my neophyte questions and enthusiasm about this book has been appreciated more than you could know. To Katherine Smith and Jen Linck, thank you for all your publicity efforts to get this book into the hands of those who are seeking it. To Piper Furbush, thank you for designing such a beautiful, touching cover. To Jason Proetorius, thank you not only for your editorial skills, but also for your thoughtful encouragement.

When I became friends with my husband, Scott, I knew I was a fortunate gal. When I married him, it was obvious my life was blessed at least twice that of the average gal's. Who could have known, or dared even hope, that together we'd be twice blessed again in this same lifetime. How grateful I am to God, and my in-laws, for conceiving this incredible man, husband, and father and how grateful I am to him for his unflinching patience, support, humor, and love. Without Scott's "Double Daddy's Perspectives," this book would be woefully incomplete. At the risk of sounding a bit too Jerry Maguire, without him, my life would be woefully incomplete. Scott, I cannot thank you enough for the incredible joy and sense of wholeness that you have brought to my life. You are my absolute love. You have my heart today, and for always.

At the end of the day, this book wouldn't be possible without Darren and Sarah, my beloved twinspirations. Here's hoping this book helps other twin parents experience the joy and love you have both brought, and continue to bring, to my life.

Twintroduction

If you are anything like me, as soon as you got the exciting news you were expecting not one, but *two* babies, you rushed out to the local bookstore and scanned the shelves for books on twins. A few good ones are out there . . . but that is the key word, few.

Most texts on pregnancy and life with baby offer a token chapter on the "multiple birth," but no nitty-gritty, firsthand information. Most twin-based books are written by doctors with lots of medical explanations, definitions, causes, and horrifyingly, reasons to panic . . . such a sad few (I counted one) supportive-style books from true-life twin mommies who had "been there, done that," and done it recently.

Once I knew twins were on the way, I wanted an intimate, real-world account . . . no-holds-barred, from the discovery of twin-pregnancy segueing straight into day-to-day life with two newborns. The hormonally intensified questions were swirling away in my mind: What is a twin pregnancy like? What if this is my first pregnancy? What symptoms can I expect? Is bed rest automatically prescribed? What is twin labor like? Are twins always born via C-section? Will the babies have to stay in the hospital longer than I will? How will my partner deal with everything? Will we sleep at all after they come? What about breastfeeding? Is it possible to truly prepare? How much is this going to cost? What do we really need to have? Will we ever have sex again? Will we want to? How can we raise two happy individuals at the same time? Will I have enough hands/eyes/energy? How crazy is it? How wonderful is it?

The good news? Honestly, having twins is incredible. Clichéd as it sounds, you won't trade it for the world.

More good news? Your pregnancy and first years of your babies' lives are likely the most rewarding challenge you will ever face. Key word: challenge. But, aren't most things worth doing a challenge? Aren't most truly *fun* endeavors a challenge? Jump in, my sisters, and enjoy the ride. Guess what? You can even steer to some degree.

Trepidation, Seeking Information

What?! There Are Two Buns in the Oven?

To be entirely truthful, new mommy bliss blurs some of my early prenatal doctor's office visits; but I remember well and am sure you remember pretty vividly the moment you discovered you had two "in there."

For my husband and me, during our first OB-GYN pregnancy confirmation visit (at six weeks), the ultrasound showed a second, smaller sac our doctor was convinced would be reabsorbed into my uterus. At the time, we were unfamiliar with the phrase or phenomenon "Vanishing Twin Syndrome."

Doctors now believe as many as one in eight pregnancies begin as multiple gestations, but for whatever biological reason, result in single baby/singleton births. Prior to the proliferation of first trimester ultrasounds, the "vanishing twin" (who often "disappears" in the first 12 weeks) was rarely discovered. In our modern medical times, prenatal technology advances have enabled doctors to estimate that Vanishing Twin Syndrome occurs in 21 to 30 percent of multiple pregnancies. Now please, before you allow that seemingly large percentage number to tailspin your twin-pregnancy hormones into panicky overdrive, flip the statistics. Of twin pregnancies 70 to 79 percent result in twin births—a pronounced, landslide majority. Start directing your mind-set to focus on the "positive" percentages early in your twin pregnancy;

you will find yourself *far* more relaxed (better for you, better for your babies) than if you allow yourself to obsess over each and every "possibility" of twin pregnancy complications.

Back to our "diagnosis": my beloved OB-GYN entreated us not to grieve over the "lost" (described in my medical records as "degenerating") twin . . . that if we had done our first ultrasound later in my pregnancy, we'd have never known of his or her existence.

Since we hadn't even entertained the possibility of having twins prior to that first appointment, and no "hope" was projected for a viable second baby in utero, we took to calling our healthy baby "Elvis," since The King had a twin who didn't make it. (Okay, so we were a bit morbid, but you get a little edgy from early hormones. Your life is changing pretty rapidly. Levity betwixt partners is really helpful during pregnancy, and once the babies arrive. However humor manifests between you and your partner, maximize it.)

Imagine our surprise when we went back for our next visit at eight weeks, and saw two healthy-looking little hearts beating. I'll never forget my husband, Scott, pointing at the monitor and asking wide-eyed, "What's *that*?" After the rounds of congratulations from the doctors and nurses, my husband and I were left in the exam room.

Dumbfounded. Stupefied. Overjoyed. So much so, that after an undetermined period of time in the clearly needed room, a nurse tapped on the door with a courteous, "Is everything okay?" It was. We were okay. All four of us.

II

Expectation

3

So You Are Extra Knocked Up: The Early Days of Twin Pregnancy (The First Trimester)

Some moms-to-be have no idea of their twin pregnancy until they actually see the two infants via ultrasound. Other women suspect they must be carrying twins because of the intensity of the traditional symptoms.

Other than a missed menstrual cycle, a symptom equally experienced whether you are bearing a singleton or septuplets, what are some of those "traditional" symptoms of early pregnancy that you may experience to an elevated degree?

Nausea

Affectionately referred to in pregnancy circles as "morning sickness," the hormonally instigated queasiness can occur any time of the day. In its most insidious incarnations, it is an around-the-clock reminder of your pregnant state. Plenty of twin-expectant women are afflicted with a double dose. Amazingly, considering my gastronomical response to just about every stimulus, my mild tummy-dizziness was a factor in only the very early morning hours for only the first 2 to 3 months.

When you find yourself feeling super sick, the temptation is to avoid sustenance altogether, both solids and fluids. Don't. Many women are shocked to discover that putting something in their upset tummy actually has the effect of holding it in place.

If you are victimized by the most notorious of pregnancy symptoms to a doubled degree and as a result are losing rather than gaining weight, stay in close contact with your OB-GYN. From seasickness wristbands to safe prescription anti-nauseals, your doctor has a variety of options to consider for your case.

Fatigue

Exhaustion is a tough characteristic to quantify to those who are not personally experiencing it.

As soon as you discover you are pregnant, you may find yourself super sensitive about others' perceptions, fearing it will appear you are milking your newly pregnant status . . . especially with symptoms like exhaustion that cannot be medically diagnosed.

For the next 9 months, forget concerns about your personal reputation. Remember two babies are counting on you to care more for yourself and their development than for what the office gossip might say on the elevator. Keep your feet up. Lie down when you can. Take off work when you know you should. You do not want to be a martyr at your babies' expense. If you are tired, your body is telling you something. If you are bordering on comatose, two other little bodies are adding their input.

A twin-expectant mommy-to-be's body is literally doing *twice* the gestation of her singleton-carrying colleagues. If you find yourself full of physical energy in your first trimester carrying twins, please call the authorities and the local news station. I have not heard of even one twin-pregnant woman who did not feel wiped out in the first trimester . . . and maybe the second, and the third. . . .

Breast Tenderness

Your breasts may typically be tender with your monthly cycle. The first trimester of pregnancy ushers your breasts even further toward their ultimate biological calling. The discomfort of descending the stairs bra-less provides an early reminder of your mammaries' direct connection to motherhood.

Your breasts will be evolving in ways you can't anticipate unless you've been twin-pregnant before. Make sure you always have at least one well-fitting, supportive bra. Since your bra-size will be increasing at a rate just shy of implants, don't overinvest in any single transitional size.

Heightened Emotions

Suppose it is no coincidence how many pregnancy symptoms parallel those of a stereotypical menstrual period. Magnify those factors exponentially when multiples are on board.

Before you were pregnant, your emotions might have seemed erratic on a monthly hormonal basis. With twin infants in utero, your hormones will be in a perpetually animated state for the duration of your pregnancy . . . and for quite some time after the babies arrive.

Excuse yourself for the tearful response to the baby with puppy commercials. Excuse yourself for the sudden affinity for repeats of Little House on the Prairie. Excuse yourself for bursting into uncontrollable sobs when you cannot decide what to eat for lunch. Excuse yourself for weepiness when someone comments on your blessed state. Excuse yourself for reacting more intensely to your lunch dilemma than your gratefulness for the babies on the way.

You are okay. You are normal.

Real-world, life-altering changes are occurring in your life. You don't even need hormonal fluctuation to spur the tears with that level of life intensity, but alas, the hormones want to add to the melee. Share your concerns and feelings with your partner, friends, family, clergy, and therapist if needed. Overcommunicate, regardless of how silly you feel, rather than undercommunicate. Perhaps most important, try to keep your humor about your transient and frequently ridiculous outbursts. After all, they are transient.

Sense of Smell

For those who are visually impaired, their other senses are more keenly attuned than those of us who are fully sighted. Nature protects individuals who may be at risk by making them more fully receptive to their surroundings via other sensory methods.

As a mom-to-be carrying two individuals who might be at risk from unperceivable elements in their surroundings, get ready for your sense of smell to escalate to bloodhound caliber. Smells (and some would contend tastes) that have danger intertwined are sensed with incredible clarity very early in twin pregnancies. I could smell popcorn burning in a microwave across the office-building floor. Residual propellant fumes stood out more than the fragrance of perfumes in department stores. The distinct aroma of the permanent magic markers in our business shipping department compelled me to leave the room.

The scents of certain food items midpreparation that previously appealed may now cause revulsion, or worse, nausea. Get your nose out of the neighborhood and again realize your accentuated olfactory awareness is temporary.

Weight Gain and "Showing"

In a clear majority of instances, women expecting two (or more) will put on pounds and appear to "show" pregnancy earlier than if expecting one. For moms who are not of "advanced maternal age" and as a result do not have many first trimester appointments with their OB-GYN, twin pregnancy may actually be explored as a possibility when early weight gain and belly-size grow beyond the singleton norms.

By-products of Burgeoning Blood Flow

You may find yourself asking, "Is it hot in here?" in what others declare are chilly rooms. When rising to your feet after a significant time at rest you may find yourself feeling faint. You may find your chest, inner elbows, and backs of your knees suddenly have visible vein patterns resembling road maps. When taking a deep breath, you may feel a tingling "asleep" sensation in your fingers. The increasing volume of blood circulating through your body (and the two growing infants') as well as swiftly swelling tissues may result in all of those physical manifestations. On the flip side, enjoy it when people tell you that pregnancy agrees with you. Your rosy cheeks will be a testimony to your circulatory superiority!

Achiness

Whereas most expectant moms can escape the first trimester without ligament stretching achiness, as a twin-expectant mom, you may experience it before the end of these early weeks. Sit down. Lie down. Drink lots of water. You *will* get some relief. Rub your belly and let your twins know you can feel them growing!

You may feel so altered by your twin-pregnant and symptom-rich first trimester that you assume your expectancy is obvious to all. You do have a decision to make: To tell, or not to tell . . .

Whether you share your news before the completion of your first trimester or after, when you do decide to reveal your twin-expectant condition, the excitement is unbounded. Matching stuffed animals, pairs of unisex onesies, and the generous well-wishes start coming in twofold. So do the shared stories of twin (and singleton) pregnancies and births gone well, and not so well. The camaraderie of motherhood seems to activate a birth-story-revelation reflex in any woman who has experienced labor and delivery. Thankfully, many moms who've "been there" are courteous enough to remember their expectant-mommy audience and approach the honest (no one wants sugar-coated) recounting of their personal tales with encouraging emphasis on the joyous end result(s). Others unfortunately take the more sensationalistic approach and describe in lurid (and embellished) detail the graphic tale of their friend's brother-in-law's second wife's awful experience in birthing her baby.

Start learning to treat the unwelcome commentary of others lightly. You will hear much more when your twins are born. With your sensitivity and emotions so linked to your children on the way, it is easy to overreact to comments that should be ignored with a dismissive smile.

Since you are expecting twins, here are a few aspects of preparation you may elect to address in this first trimester, as opposed to procrastinating.

Borrow or invest in maternity clothes. Twin moms-to-be get bigger, faster.

Get at least one book that reveals the week-by-week progress of your babies' physical development. Your twins will grow at virtually the same rate as a single baby in utero, so the text need not be specifically composed with twins in mind. We took great delight marking each week of pregnancy completion by consulting our two books and learning what our twins had grown/developed/accomplished in the past 7 days.

Discovering major progress in the babies' sizes and neurological maturity tended to blur the maternal discomforts of the preceding week, helping me "no pain, no gain" my way through the times of inordinate unpleasantness.

Enroll in prenatal classes and schedule shower dates sooner than if you were expecting a single baby. Bearing in mind that twins arrive on average 3 weeks early, back time your pregnancy classes and celebrations by at least that margin. For example, if singleton-pregnant women tend to take classes and have baby showers at the start of the third trimester, you should set a goal for doing the same activities midway through your second trimester. You want to be able to comfortably get to and from your classes and to enjoy your shower(s). As your pregnancy progresses, even if you aren't placed on bed rest, from week 20 or so onward, you may slowly begin to curtail your outings and physical activities.

Decide when you will need to quit working. Granted, you may have to adjust the date if medical reasons dictate; but discuss with your doctor a feasible, healthy time to stop participating in the daily grind, even if your pregnancy proceeds complication-free. Each day at work I was committed to leaving things in a way so that if for any reason bed rest was prescribed, a coworker could step in, decipher exactly what the status was with my clients, and take over if need be.

Familiarize yourself with the indicators of preterm labor. Not to be pessimistic, but prepared. Red flags of warning include: uterine tightening/contractions (like a fist squeezing) every 10 minutes or more often; a noticeable increase in the discharge from your girl parts; intensified ache in your lower back; some vaginal bleeding or spotting; diarrhea; or just a feeling "something isn't right." Unfortunately, every single one of those "red flags" can occur to some degree at any time in your pregnancy. If you think for a minute your symptoms may indeed be preterm labor, don't give a second thought to calling your doctor. As a matter of fact, it is irresponsible *not* to call. Your doctor's job is to guard you and your babies' health. He or she cannot do the job effectively without your active and caring compliance. Far better to be reassured via your doctor's phone-diagnosis, or even to go in and be released for a "false labor," than to take unnecessary and unhealthy risks.

While I was in my first trimester, the *Today Show* had a report declaring a new study had determined that morning sickness was an added assurance of a healthy pregnancy. I had morning queasies but never threw up. My pregnancy with two surely couldn't be very healthy.

Wrong. So if you *are* upchucking constantly, try to view it as a good sign. Albeit unpleasant, but temporary.

You haven't even felt queasy? Don't let the news media panic you. If you don't experience every typical symptom, you don't need to be alarmed. Chances are you and your babies are just fine . . . and very fortunate.

My most pronounced early symptom? Absolute, incapacitating, total exhaustion. Exhaustion that made me want to lie down on the asphalt walking to my car in the parking lot. Exhaustion that allowed me to sleep while my husband and his contractor friends literally knocked down a wall in our house. Surely something was weird with my pregnancy to be so tired, so early on. Wrong.

Worry tends to be a universal symptom of early pregnancy. You have not only yourself to be conscious of now but two babies depending on you. Your hormones are kicking into a heretofore-unknown level, and all the legendary dangers of the "first trimester" are swirling about in your brain. No doubt with good intentions, Chicken Littles are giving you admonitions on every physical activity you undertake, every morsel you put in your mouth, and every book you read. Listen to your doctor. Listen to your partner. Listen to the family and friends you trust. Sift through it all; then, listen to your own body and your gut. You don't know what your body and gut are saying? Relax. Take it easy. My guess is that's what your body and gut are saying anyway. Statistically, you and the babies have better-than-Vegas odds of making it through the coming months with flying colors.

| 4 |

Paranoia and the Plural Pregnancy

Whether real or ridiculous, legitimate or ludicrous, myriad malcontentious specters haunt the newly expectant mother. When not one but *two* excruciatingly vulnerable infants in utero are fully dependent on mom's discretion and restraint for their well-being, that's intimidating pressure. Hormones wreak havoc with pregnant women, and twin-toting moms-to-be often experience double their share of the anxiety. As soon as you begin showing (and you will show earlier than if you were only expecting one), everyone will have words of caution. Many of the day-to-day elements of life prepregnancy may now strike inordinate fear in the heart (and uterus) of the doubly pregnant woman. So, how do you decipher between well-documented warnings, and well-intentioned wives' tales?

Your ultimate arbiter should always be your OB-GYN. Ideally, he or she has got the most up-to-date studies and medical references in mind or within reach for any and all of your questions. Which brings up an important point: when in doubt, *ask!* Don't be embarrassed about asking a "stupid" question; remember that ignorance is *not* blissful when you have gnawing curiosities robbing you of valuable relaxation time. The biological fortitude required to gestate two infants as well as keep you semiupright and functioning is boggling. Don't sacrifice a single modicum of your energy stressing about a question your doctor may take 10 seconds to answer.

Here's a far from all-inclusive listing of some valid, and some not-so-valid, causes for thinking twice when you're twice as pregnant.

Alcohol

Prior to the discovery of Fetal Alcohol Syndrome/Fetal Alcohol Effects in the early 1970s, an occasional glass or two of wine was thought to be perfectly safe for consumption by a pregnant woman. Since no medical organization has yet been able to determine just how much consumption is "safe" when pregnant, why chance it? Especially since you have two infants who will likely already have lower birth weights by virtue of the fact they have a wombmate. Abstain in the interest of safety.

Air Travel

When I was 9 weeks pregnant, we flew. I was assured the metal detectors were not harmful. The flight itself didn't have me concerned. However, after the fact, I learned many folks don't recommend air travel for mothers carrying multiples. Most airlines do not allow women pregnant with a singleton to travel after 36 weeks . . . just in case of early labor. After 24 weeks most OB-GYNs will put the "no-go" on travel for twin-pregnant moms-to-be. In honesty, after you get to a certain size, travel by air or by car sounds pretty unappealing. Check with your doctor before any out-of-town journey.

Twinternet Overload

Research is not a bad thing. As a matter of fact, I'd encourage you to sleuth out some text and online references whose perspectives you espouse. However, overindulging into in-depth exploration of every possible syndrome, difficulty, and complication affiliated with twin pregnancy and birth will keep you in a perpetual state of panic and angst. Know your limits. Turn off the computer if you are starting to experience paranoid palpitations each time you log on. Find supportive, positive sources of valid twinformation. Your pluperfect authority should be members of your own medical team, as they are the most informed and most-familiar with your unique twin pregnancy.

Aspartame

The Food and Drug Administration says the calorie-free taste enhancer is totally safe. My OB-GYN assured me that aspartame is the most-researched substance in FDA history; and it has continually come up clean. Prior to my plural pregnancy, my daily consumption of Diet Coke/Diet Pepsi and aspartame-sweetened coffee was easily enough to fill a bathtub. In my personal manifesto, I've consistently pooh-poohed the conspiracy theorists who are convinced the artificial sweetener manufacturing contingent is powerful enough to sway not only the U.S. government but even the most-reputable establishments of higher learning. Alas, as soon as I learned I was pregnant, I could no longer bring myself to even sip my heretofore beloved beverages of choice. Far from repulsed by the refreshments, it seems the anti-Aspartame-antagonists had somehow managed to instill a measure of subconscious apprehension. Prepregnancy, it was worth risking for me alone but not for my brood of buns in the oven. Gave it all up cold turkey. Go with your own gut on this one.

Cigarettes

The warnings on the packs specifically addressing the dangers for pregnant women and their children should motivate you to alter your smoking behavior; if not forever, at least for the duration of your pregnancy. Ask your doctor for support systems available to you in coping with a forced "rapid-quit" if you are currently a smoker.

Secondhand Smoke

Unpleasant when not pregnant, and more risky from a health perspective when you are. With the heightened sense of smell you will experience when you're in a family way, it may be thoroughly intolerable. Avoid it whenever possible.

Hot Showers

In your nonpregnant state, a hot shower may have relaxed you and soothed your aches, pains, and stresses. Unfortunately, along with saunas, hot tubs, electric blankets, fever associated with illness, and hardcore exercise, anything that raises your internal body temperature significantly is ill-advised and potentially dangerous during pregnancy.

Dental Appointments

You can certainly get your teeth cleaned while pregnant, but be sure to let your dentist know you are expecting before you even sit in the seat. X-rays (dental and otherwise if avoidable) are a pregnancy no-no. Do expect your gums to bleed more than normal owing to your increased buns-in-the-oven blood flow.

Pesticides

Not just the kind used for agricultural crop-dusting, but even the milder varieties for killing fleas on Fido, mosquitoes in the backyard, and roaches or ants in the home, all are potentially dangerous to the pivotal neural development of babies in the first trimester, and to a degree beyond. Personally, I'd avoid anything that ends with "-cide" during a plural pregnancy! If a treatment of sorts is a must in your residential or occupational environment, evacuate the premises for a suitable window of time before returning.

Household Renovations

You have not one, but *two* babies on the way. Seems like just the right time to take care of those home improvements you've been considering. Heaven knows, you want to paint the nursery. Once the babies come, those opportunities for home beautification, and the financial flexibility to do so, may seem very limited. Wonderful! Go ahead and start. You, the doubly encumbered, just need to be out of the house for the span of time needed. With the demolition of old walls and erection of new ones, your home may be a temporary hotbed of exposed lead paint, asbestos, and solvents. Don't take chances. Stay with friends or family while major home modifications are underway. Once everything is completed, you can do murals with water-based paints in the nursery.

Massage and Yoga

Before signing up for a massage or yoga class (or before continuing the strain of yoga you currently practice), make sure the type you are subscribing to is deemed appropriate for a pregnant woman. First and foremost, ask your obstetrician if you are a candidate for participation in either option. If he or she gives you the okay and you are confident you will be fine, don't be shy with dispensing details. Let your masseur or

yoga instructor know you are carrying multiples. They may be unwilling to chance your participation in their offerings. Respect their concern for your (and your babies') well-being. Many pregnant women experience unparalleled relaxation and a sense of increased fitness and flexibility if they make use of a prenatal massage or prenatal yoga class. Just make sure you don't take unnecessary risks.

What are the risks anyway? In massage, the risk occurs with the stimulation of "danger zones" (the webbing between fingers and toes is rumored to start labor), abdominal stimulation is often uncomfortable for mom as well as babies, and the use of potentially unsafe oils can pose another potential threat. For yoga, certain styles of yoga are almost guaranteed to increase your body temperature to 102 degrees plus—a definite no-no in pregnancy. Likewise, certain positions are not advisable for a pregnant (much less, *plurally* pregnant) woman. Please do your research before mounting the massage table or unrolling your yoga mat.

Herbal Remedies, Teas, and Aromatherapy Oils

Just because a substance is "natural" does not inherently imply "safe" or risk-free. As a matter of fact, most of our modern prescription medicines (and plenty of recreational drugs) are descendents of centuries-old herbal remedies. Most homeopathic practitioners will accurately attest that herbs possess tremendous power and can be highly effective in treating just about every affliction. As such, while you are pregnant (or breastfeeding), do not make use of any natural/herbal concoction without first ascertaining its guaranteed safety with your OB-GYN. ("Guarantees" with some herbal elements can be tricky as most are unregulated by the FDA. Use extra care and caution.)

Junk Food

Not necessarily a dangerous factor, as much as a far less-healthy option . . . especially when what you are ingesting will nourish two developing babies. For those experiencing extreme food aversions or intensified nausea with their twin pregnancy, my nondoctoral advice would be to eat what you can. No doubt the doctors of whom I speak would not want to go on record, but I know personally of at least two instances where OB-GYNs have told twin-pregnant moms-to-be to eat Big Macs, Baskin Robbins, whatever high-calorie foodstuffs they could "keep down." Listen to your doctor's suggestions and use the discretion appropriate for your special situation.

Hair Dye/Manicures/Tanning Beds/Botox Injections

Many of the cosmetic processes we incorporate into our prepregnancy routine are of questionable and undocumented safety when it comes to the potential impact on a growing, developing baby . . . in your case, *babies*. Although you may be feeling particularly unattractive, try to trust the old saying, "A woman is never more beautiful than when she is pregnant."

Honey

Absolutely verboten for infants under the age of one (as it can contain botulism spores), most medical folk will agree that a mommy-to-be's maternal body filter can weed out any danger to her dual boarders. For me, the fact that there is actually a warning printed on the label declaring its potential danger to newborns scared me out of eating any for the duration of my pregnancy. You may feel absolutely fine with it . . . talk to your doctor and make your own decision.

Microwave Ovens

Research has indicated that the vast majority of microwaves have adequate protection against "leaks." Err on the side of safety, and if you use a microwave, and I sure did, don't stand in front of it or alongside it while it's in operation. Heck, go in the other room!

Aerosol Fumes

About 10 weeks into my twin pregnancy, immediately following my daily around-the-head orbital spray of hair shellac; I went into a panic. That smell! Those fumes! My poor developing babies' brains! Surely it was the equivalent of my wee infants sniffing glue. A frenzied call to the doctor's office assuaged my fear. Excessive fume inhalation is certainly not advisable; but the likelihood of pronounced neural damage from my hair spray habit was unlikely. Mommy's bodily processes do indeed serve as a semi-filter for your babies' well-being. You will find yourself amazed at the heightened sensitivity of your sense of smell (and sometimes taste) during your pregnancy. No doubt nature is manipulating sensory overdrive to keep you away from potentially baby-harming elements within your environment. Medical assurances aside, I switched to an unscented pump hair spray.

Prescription Drugs

Read the enclosure in any prescription or over-the-counter medicine and you will be amazed at the proliferation that indicates "not for use if you are pregnant, breastfeeding, or thinking about becoming pregnant." If they haven't provided one already, ask your OB-GYN for a list of suitable-for-use-during-pregnancy drugs. Many pregnant women, with multiples or otherwise, elect to "tough it out," even when a medicine is "approved" for use. Go with your gut. Stay in close touch with your doctor who should be able to provide you with a spectrum of options to minimize your discomfort in your months of pregnancy.

Changing Kitty's Litter Box

Do you hate cleaning Fluffy's litter box? Then pregnancy is your dream rationale for passing off the job to someone else. Toxoplasmosis is a dangerous infection contracted through contact with cat feces. (It can also be contracted via eating undercooked meat.) Keep your pet out of food preparation and consumption areas, always wash your hands after petting the cat, and wear gardening gloves if your cat is ever outside, defecates, and buries the feces shallowly. Reptiles may also be carriers of toxoplasmosis, so have your partner clean the iguana's area as well. (Never let newborns or toddlers under five touch or pet a reptile for the same reason.)

Advanced Maternal Age

You cannot change your age. Look at the bright side; if you are of "advanced maternal age," you automatically qualify for more ultrasounds and special care. Combine that with the fact you are carrying multiples, and you are set for medical reassurances (typically on your insurance's tab) whenever you need them. Enjoy the benefit of your years!

Sex

We were assured that sex was not a significant risk while we were expecting our twins. Yet somehow, the fact that a good friend's doctor had encouraged her to have sex to "start up" a past-her-due-date labor seemed in conflict with the fact that I was attempting to gestate the twins and postpone labor as long as possible. Maybe this is a bit personal, but I was too apprehensive to engage in the deed while doubly knocked up. Even though my libido was definitely increased in my second trimester, the fear of accidentally spurring early labor as a result of succumbing to the urge squelched my lust sufficiently.

Whether it was my portly appearance, the untouchable holiness of pending motherhood, or perhaps even a congruent sense of apprehension, my husband was equally resigned to sexual abstention for our pregnancy period.

Unlike our physician, numerous doctors negate the idea of intimate relations while expecting two or more. Each baby-bearer has a different physical condition and history. Your doctor, your partner, and you should make a team decision regarding your individual case.

Food Factors

Egad. Seems like all sorts of the goodies (and baddies) we consume in a nonpregnant state possess dangers galore for little ones in utero. As always, use your doctor as your official referee. Ask for his or her list of foods to avoid during your pregnancy and while breastfeeding. To supplement or reinforce that list, here are some debated, some deleterious, and some downright dangerous foodstuffs:

- Undercooked meats, eggs, sushi, or seafood (salmonella/ toxoplasmosis/bacteria)
- Soft cheeses or anything made with unpasteurized milk (brie, camembert, etc.)
- Deli meats and hot dogs (nitrates and listeriosis danger if insufficiently cooked)
- Pâté
- Caesar salads and restaurant "homemade" mayonnaises (raw egg use)
- Soft-serve ice cream or fast-food milk shakes (bacteria in rarely cleaned machines)
- Artificial sweeteners
- Coffee, soda, chocolate, tea (all conveyors of caffeine—a pregnancy no-no)
- Tiramisu (alcohol and chocolate tag-team)
- Liver (rich in vitamin A—an excess of which is potentially dangerous)
- Swordfish, shark, mackerel, tilefish (mercury content)
- Unwashed vegetables and fruits (pesticides and bacteria)
- Raw sprouts (salmonella)

- Tuna (consume only in strictly limited quantities—mercury content)
- Shellfish

From all sides, pregnant women are assailed with warnings to avoid heretofore-harmless (and maybe even enjoyable) indulgences. Before you allow the incessant barrage of "helpful" advice overwhelm you, remember the inherently good intent behind the liberally dispensed information overload. The general population wants only the best for you and your babies, and subsequently they want to contribute whatever they can to ensure you and the twins have the absolute optimum chances of full-family health. So when the fifth person apologetically approaches you with warnings as you attempt to enjoy a "questionable" lunch item in the mall food court, smile graciously and fight the defensive urge to pull out the latest research from Johns Hopkins declaring the safety of Cinnabons.

You may feel marvelously liberated when your doctor okays exposure to a mismaligned and highly craved food or practice. However, even when items are "doctor-approved," you as a multiple-mom-to-be may still feel uneasy. When it comes down to erring on the side of safety, always take approvals under advisement, but go with your own rapidly expanding gut.

While your gut seems to be expanding rapidly, conversely, time seems to pass lugubriously for the first two trimesters (through approximately week 27). Why? Largely because the preponderance of widely circulated statistics on preterm labor possibilities keep twin-moms-to-be counting the days toward the mile markers of infant viability and life-systems development.

Dreaded repercussions of most plural pregnancy paranoias can be circumnavigated through maternal awareness and restraint.

Frustratingly, avoidance of preterm labor, the consummate plural pregnancy paranoia, is not entirely in your control. Genetics, the fact that you are carrying multiples, and other factors outside of your realm of influence play a role. However, you and your doctor(s) may take measures to minimize your potential for delivering your twosome before their designated time. If you experience symptoms of preterm labor, your doctor will base his or her course of action on what gives you and your twosome the greatest likelihood of extending your pregnancy to term. Hospital stays, administering of pregnancy-prolonging, labor-slowing drugs, a cerclage (small "stitch" to stabilize a compromised cervix), steroid shots administered to develop the babies' lungs in utero in case of early delivery . . . , all are common methods employed by OB-GYNs to protect and care for the twin mommies and babies entrusted to their care.

Upon learning of a multiple gestation, most twin-pregnant women find themselves paranoid considering the probabilities of forced bed rest, certainly the most-prescribed prolonger of plural pregnancy. Depending upon your caregiver, some OB-GYNs will prescribe bed rest (modified or strict) as a preventative measure, regardless of whether or not you are experiencing complications. Women expecting triplets or more are almost universally placed on bed rest as their pregnancies progress.

If bed rest is prescribed for you, retain a big picture perspective. Bear in mind the duration is finite: it cannot extend beyond 9 months. Even if you are placed on mandatory, fully hospitalized bed rest for the remainder (or entirety) of your pregnancy; that commitment of time, however frustrating, is a small investment giving your twins every opportunity for minimal to no life-impacting complications from premature delivery. Bed rest will give your twins every opportunity to "stay in" longer. Don't let the potential prescription add a bit of worry to your plurally pregnant plate.

The Double Daddy Perspective

It's important to know that as a man, you will lose the battle against too much information. Your wife will be busy cramming her brain with every wives' tale, urban myth, and Internet half-truth regarding twin pregnancies. You can tell her that people for centuries have given birth to twins, long before the invention of the Internet and Barnes & Noble, but that doesn't matter. Just keep reminding yourself that a multiple pregnancy is inherently risky and therefore brings with it twice the paranoia of a single pregnancy. And most important, that her irrational worrying comes from love. Then, after you remind yourself of this, unplug her computer.

True confessions time: What were my personal pregnancy paranoias? Despite all my proselytizing efforts toward positive mind-set, what apprehensions continued to resurface throughout my twin pregnancy?

Paranoia #1

That each baby would select his or her own individual birth route. I wasn't afraid of a C-section. As a matter of fact, early in my pregnancy,

I naively preferred the idea. I wasn't necessarily afraid of a vaginal birth either. What I did not want was to have two areas of postpartum recuperation. Like in so many other aspects of plural pregnancy, the statistics are in your favor. An exploration of informal twin mommy websites revealed the cases of dual-direction twin delivery hover around 10 percent. Flipping the stats of course reveals that 90 percent dodge the double escape route. Ultimately, I came to grips with the fact that even if I did fall within the percentage of those women whose babies took divergent paths, in all likelihood it was an unavoidable medical choice made in the interest of our three-person collective well-being. My trust was thrust doctor-ward, and I tried to put fear-inducing possibilities out of my mind.

Paranoia #2

That at any given time, one baby or the other wasn't doing well in utero. With two babies in belly, inevitably the comparisons between your children start before they are even born. As soon as I started feeling the babies move, concerns followed that one was moving more than the other and subsequently was "healthier." If one baby was particularly active, and the other not-so-much-so, what was going on? What if superactive sibling calmed down dramatically, and then both were calm simultaneously? Could that be okay? Nonsynchronous hiccups. Both have hiccups, and they aren't in time with one another . . . are they oxygen deprived, and unequally so? How can one be kicking strongly and the other be totally immobile when they are in such close proximity to one another? Thankfully, in a twin pregnancy, ultrasounds are plentiful and frequent. The reassurance provided by seeing two sets of working active organs while feeling no "movement" was always welcome. I'd have been thrilled to have an ultrasound machine strapped to me 24–7. Between exams, I did eventually learn to take solace in the reminder that although the twins were sharing a uterine duplex, they were still unique individuals with differing physical personalities. If you ever find yourself unduly paranoid about disparate levels of twinactivity, go ahead and call your doctor. Stress reduction is always a positive prescription.

Paranoia #3

That the late-in-pregnancy (30 weeks plus) seemingly perpetual vaginal discharge was one (or the other) twin's water sac leaking. All the prenatal class discussion of how once the water sac is broken, the baby(-ies) need to be born within 24 hours in order to prevent unhealthy infection struck a danger chord with me. I had two of everything in a very limited space. With the cramped quarters (I could feel what must have been my daughter's feet on my shoulder blades) and the mental visual of two highly squished water balloons being poked, prodded, and compressed by two babies seeking every spare bit of space, I surmised the water sacs were fighting a losing battle for survival. Plus my panties (and liners) were in a state of constant saturation. Again, with the weekly visits to the OB-GYN, who verified the sacs were stable and sufficiently sealed, I found some much-needed reassurance. The actual content of sundry fluids soaking my britches may never be pinpointed. What I do know for certain is that it was neither of the twins' water breaking, or even leaking. Like the concerns arising from varied levels of movement, ask your doctor to check your twins' water/fluid whenever your stress reaches an apex.

Although paranoia is an unavoidable symptom of plural pregnancy, do what you can to remain calm and relaxed. Entrust your medical team to do the job for which they are qualified: to care for you, to prolong your pregnancy, and at your pregnancy's conclusion, to deliver two healthy babies.

5

The Coming Months
(The Second Trimester)

From the moment you learn of your pregnancy, you start calculating not only the babies' due date (which of course your doctor typically helps you determine) but other key mile markers to expect throughout your pregnancy. For me, the completion date of the first trimester was circled in red on the calendar.

As Twin Pregnancy Week 13 concludes, you can expect some of those dastardly symptoms characteristic of the first trimester to diminish, and perhaps even, disappear. Never fear, you won't be bored. New bodily changes await you as you and your babies progress into your next phase. This chapter provides a peephole into what you may expect as your second trimester arrives.

Most of the pregnancy books you'll read will predict a resurgence of energy and vigor beginning in your second trimester. Personally, I wasn't quite as catatonic in the second trimester as I was in the first, but by no means was I ready to embark on any dance routine. Twin pregnancy is going to be a drain on your body. GET REST. The good news is, the onset of your second trimester does bring some reassurance that your pregnancy is going according to plan. Your twin pregnancy has an even greater likelihood of working out A-OK. That fact alone should help you relax a bit.

With the onset of your second trimester, you may start experiencing symptoms of pregnancy you never realized *were* symptoms of pregnancy. Things no one warns you about. In my case, projectile nosebleeds. Apparently, not uncommon for women carrying two babies. As a pending mom of twins, you have an inordinate quantity of blood your body is pumping to you and two others. You may spring a leak every now and then. If you leak from the vagina however, do call your doctor. At 13 weeks, right when I thought I had made it through the first trimester "danger zone," I experienced some very mild bleeding. In all likelihood, it's no cause for alarm, but blood in your condition is something you need to tell your doctor about. The doctors on call tend to be very reassuring if it's off-hours, and the bleeding isn't copious. We went in the next morning for a look-see and thankfully, all was well.

If the bleeding is more than a few drops, your doctor or a doctor on call may want to see you sooner rather than later. Don't automatically assume the worst. Let your doctor(s) do their job, and don't self-diagnose yourself into a dither.

Keep your stress to a minimum if you bleed a bit. Twins weigh a little heavier on your cervix (and all your gal parts) and a broken blood vessel occurs with greater frequency in twin pregnancies than with singletons. Of course, my wonderful husband, who had to calm down a shrieking banshee with her pants at her ankles and a wad of pink-tinged toilet paper in her hand was fairly confident all was well, but having the doctor back him up calmed me down significantly.

The Double Daddy Perspective

Not being a woman and not being pregnant with twins, the man must realize that he has absolutely zero credibility on any medical matters with the mother-to-be. So as a man, remember that your best friend is the Doctor's On-Call phone number. She'll never believe even the most common sense, level-headed explanation of any pregnancy-related discomfort until she hears it from a doctor or a nurse. Just cut to the chase, dial the number, and hand her the phone. Because after all, can you really blame her?

Speaking of weighing heavier on your girl parts, at some point, even as early as week 12, you may start to feel some unexpected pressure on your pelvis. Initially for me, it felt as though I was on the brink of needing to pee, like a heavy, full bladder, but further back. Eventually, it felt similar to the weight of two duckpin bowling balls (or regulation if you go 37 to 40 weeks). If you walk, jog, or work on your feet, take extra care, and listen to your body. Be straightforward with your OB-GYN about your typical daily routine. Certain activities may need to be curtailed, modified, or eliminated altogether to minimize the stress/health risk to you and the twins. Your cervix has got a daunting job to do, truly double duty; so give it a break.

Get off your feet when you can. Elevate your feet when you can. Lie down when you can. Exercise is important, but so is keeping those babies in there cooking as long as they can. Talk to your doctor about how to stay fit and healthy during your pregnancy. Bag the dieting, put figure-consciousness aside and remember two lives are counting on you to use sensible judgment. Believe me, you will get plenty of exercise after your babies arrive. And if that isn't good enough, if you breastfeed twins, many doctors recommend you intake an additional 1,600 calories each day. Additional. On top of what you would normally eat. If you breastfeed through the first year, your challenge will be to keep weight on.

Speaking of food, let's touch a bit on the legendary cravings of pregnancy. First and foremost, if you are nauseated, my layperson's advice is to eat what you can keep down. Personally, I think there are way too many scare tactics on what you should and should not eat during pregnancy. Obviously, caffeine, alcohol, and cigarettes are off-limits. Some lesser-known no-nos are sushi, rare meat or eggs, honey, fast-food milk shakes, soft-serve ice cream, and mall-style frozen yogurt. All of those normally safe for adult consumption items can pose a threat to babies in utero. Bacteria that adult systems can handle may be too challenging for the developing wee ones. Don't take unnecessary chances. Discuss pregnancy food safety, and consider developing a diet plan, with your OB-GYN.

In the instances where you are confronted with a questionable, un-doctor-approved food item, use your best judgment. You may be wise to err on the side of safety, and abstain.

There are all sorts of anti-nitrate/organic-only/aspartame-free proponents out there, and if you and your doctor feel that's the way for you to go, fantastic. On the flip side, if you wake up one morning, and rather than your daily breakfast of fresh fruit and bran flakes, you are craving a hot dog, don't condemn yourself for caving in. Especially if it is the yummy kind that only 7-Elevens and gas stations sell—the ones that spin in their own grease for hours prior to being embraced by an enriched flour laden, moderately soggy bun. Let's not forget about fast-food double cheeseburgers: two babies, two patties, two slices of cheese. Coincidence or kismet? You make the call.

Let me put it this way; you won't be alone. You'd be hard-pressed to find a doctor who will say with conviction that an occasional diversion from the perfect pregnant woman's diet will harm you or your babes. Just keep the major strays "occasional," and keep your OB-GYN appraised of your intake.

For me, and a lot of other women I have spoken with, more common than food cravings are food aversions. Lemonade? Get it away! Chicken, normally a favorite, revolted me. I could eat it in a salad, but not in breast form. You'll no doubt hear tales of pregnant women retching when even smelling coffee or bacon.

The good news is your old favorites will probably taste good once again when your wee ones arrive.

Okay, there's no way I could let the phrase "breast form" slip by without mentioning another delightful and second trimester intensifying pregnancy symptom: mutations of the breast. All the books out there seem to claim your areolas will darken and expand. They'll expand, but they may or may not darken. Don't freak out either way. Your breasts are entities (en-titties?) unto themselves now. Let them do their thing. No one warned me that you wake up one day and it looks like a swarm of nonitchy mosquito bites surround your nipples. They're called Montgomery glands, no cause for alarm, and they are part of the breasts-as-dairy-fountains package.

Likewise, no one warned me that you will awaken one day to discover your nipples are pointing downward. Ready for easy baby sucking access.

As I am sure all my former coworkers will attest because they watched me succumb to the urge, your growing, pendulous bosoms will itch all over. This, I learned, was the skin stretching. It'll pass once they've gotten as big as they're going to. You'll be overwhelmed by the need to just grab and scratch them. Go ahead. No one is going to begrudge a soon-to-be mom of twins anything. Your belly may itch the same way. Scratch at will. Well, at least until the bottom of your belly is so big it looks like you are scratching the private area below. Then, use your discretion.

All that skin expansion can cause the dreaded stretch marks we hear so much of on infomercials claiming to have a cure. You may get them; you may not. But considering all the stretching your belly will need to do to accommodate two, the odds are not in your favor. They may not be the most attractive reminder of your buns-in-the-oven state, but they are a small price to pay for the prize.

Ditto, hemorrhoids. You may get them; you may not. But, it is pressure on that rectal area that causes the dastardly inconvenience. The weight of your uterus, your two babies, potentially two placentas and sacs of amniotic fluid is an impressive amount of pressure. By the end of the second trimester, twin-pregnant women have often gained 20 to 25 pounds, often 10 to 15 more than their singly pregnant pals. Doctors recommend that women carrying twins gain a total of 35 to 45 pounds over the duration of their pregnancy. Obviously, you may gain even more. If the added weight alone wasn't significant enough to increase your chances of getting hemorrhoids, if you are fortunate enough to have your babies vaginally, you put tremendous push-pressure on everything "down there" during the labor process. I won't pussyfoot around the subject; I got them late in pregnancy. The labor process exacerbated them. They are not comfortable, but certainly nothing to fear. You may walk a little funny, but that will happen anyway.

Waddling during pregnancy is totally normal, and will probably affect you earlier than your pals who are in a family way with a single baby. Your center of gravity is changing, and your walk will have to change, too. As your babies get bigger, they will try to find every accommodating bit of space they can. So if you think aching sciatica is something only granny suffers from, think again.

You may wake up one day as I did, with a shooting pain traveling down your groin to thigh with each step on your left leg. (It can happen on your right, too.) Waddling and limping is comical to behold, even when you are the one doing it. While it is tremendously uncomfortable, it may go away as mysteriously as it arrived. Those babies can shift at any moment and relieve the pressure.

However, like the bleeding we talked about earlier, mention it to your doctor. Some sciatic pressure can be so severe; it can cause your leg to give out. Again, use your good judgment. Don't take unnecessary risks. If you think you may tip over, or worse, fall down the stairs, get off your feet. Ask for help.

Which brings up another "fall prevention" topic: the night-teeters. Before you were pregnant with twins, if you woke in the night to pee, you probably just rose from bed as expeditiously as possible and trekked to the bathroom. In your pregnant-with-twins state, it is not so easy. As you get bigger and the massive blood supply expands, going from lying down to sitting up can dramatically decrease the blood flow to your brain, if done too quickly. Hence, the night-teeters. If you're not careful, night-teeters can lead to passing out, so be careful. Push yourself up slowly. Sit on the edge of your bed a bit, take some deep breaths, and gain your bearings before getting to your feet.

Of course, when it is toward the end of your pregnancy, moving at all in bed is a challenge. You will no doubt develop a strategically arranged pillow placement system that allows you to get some comfort and rest. There are lots of stories out there of women who have spent their last pregnant months in La-Z-Boy recliners. I managed to stay in a traditional bed throughout my pregnancy, laying on my left side as doctors recommend for optimum blood circulation. (True confessions: Sometimes I laid on my right side. We all made it A-OK.) The collection of pillows used to facilitate my sleep went (1) between my knees, (2) in the small of my back, (3) under the side of my belly, (4) under my head, and (5) embraced in my arms. Understandably, you may, as I did, try and talk yourself out of late-night trips to the bathroom just to avoid the production involved. Forget it. You will need to go, resign yourself to it.

Go you will. Often. Especially, when it's least convenient. Despite the temptation to drink less in efforts to reduce bathroom visits, do your best to down the ever-recommended 64 ounces of water a day. You can and should include your milk intake in the daily 64-ounces-of-liquids goal. Caffeinated teas (herbal does not mean caffeine-free), coffee, and obviously, alcohol, need to be avoided altogether. But whatever you do, don't cut down on your water/fluid intake trying to minimize your restroom visits. You'll just get dehydrated, and you'll still feel the urge to pee. Drink up.

While we're potty-talking, throughout your twin pregnancy, and particularly in the later months, discharge of many textures and viscosities may appear in your sexy maternity panties. Let your doctor know if it ever looks bloody or is so prolific that you feel your water may have broken. Chances are, you'll just be oozy. Panty liners are a great thing. Consider changing your panties if that's preferable. Whatever you do, do not use tampons! For your health and the babies', let the ooze and air flow.

Other orifices down there may also be problematic. Most women I know, myself included, ran the gamut of the poo-density spectrum.

From the "prenatal-vitamins-are-creating-hard-to-pass-nuggets" to the "late-in-pregnancy-there's-no-room-in-my-inerds-for-anything-to-stiffen-runs," you will have a vast array of bowel-movement styles awaiting you. Don't sweat any of them. They'll all pass—literally.

Amidst this extensive list of what may, but should not, be interpreted as "negative" symptoms, there are some undeniable positives.

Weight gain (within reason) as not only an acceptable but an encouraged thing. How long have we waited for that? A life-long, and typically self-denying, Pop-Tarts lover, I reveled in the consumption of not one, but both succulent pastries on an almost daily basis. (You're right. Pop-Tarts, delicious though they may be, weren't the healthiest breakfast option. When I gained eleven pounds in one month, it was pretty easy to determine the culprit. Although weight gain is certainly expected, my OB-GYN gently reminded me to be a bit more "occasional" with the double Pop-Tarts fests.)

The legendary, but real, pregnancy glow. It's true! You, as a double-baby bearer, are likely to absolutely ignite with it. Caused by the increased blood flow to the skin, you literally should have twice the glow of your pregnant with single-baby pals. Twincandescence. Enjoy it. Consider having your picture taken.

Abundant help. People will bend over backwards (and they'll need to because you certainly can't) assisting you with heavy doors, lifting even the lightest of loads, making meals, whatever they can do to help. Let them. Accept assistance graciously, remembering the times you have helped others in a similar state.

Weeks of potential relief from chronic conditions/discomfort. As difficult as it seems to believe, in many cases, mine included, the hormonal upheaval of pregnancy (intensified in twin pregnancy) often minimizes or soothes the day-to-day physical imperfections of your prepregnancy life. My prescription-drug-requiring allergies? Nary a symptom during my pregnancy . . . especially welcome since my prescription was not approved for use while knocked up or breastfeeding. Equally absent was my chronic knee/joint pain. Remarkable, since the discomfort is typically exacerbated with even the slightest weight gain, and I piled on 45 pounds in short order. A friend who suffers from fibromyalgia experienced her longest absence of symptoms during the months of her pregnancy. Clearly no guarantees exist, but you may find yourself relieved of some of your usual conditions as a result of your "babies on board" state.

The joy of rubbing your growing belly. You've seen people throughout your life lovingly caressing a tummy large with child. Now's your chance. You have two babies in there that can feel your touch and hear your voice. Massage them, sing to them, read to them. Their birth will be a face-to-face meeting with a very special someone they already know through their other senses. Encourage daddy to do it, too.

6

Tests, Ultrasounds, and Probes

Oh my. Twin-pregnant women are automatically categorized as amidst a "high-risk pregnancy." If you are over 35, you are of "advanced maternal age"; you are automatically categorized as a "high-risk pregnancy." If you have sought fertility treatments due to difficulty achieving or maintaining a pregnancy, you will likely be categorized as a "high-risk pregnancy." In the twenty-first century, growing numbers of women are falling not only into the first group but often into two or even all three groups. Subsequently, twin pregnancy is resplendent with tests, ultrasounds, and probes. Amidst the cavalcade of pokes, prods, and cavity invasions, keep your eye on the prize. Remember that the medical team's persistence in monitoring both mommy and twins is a reflection of their commitment to the successful completion of your pregnancy and healthy delivery of your twins. On the rare occasion there are anomalies in your test results; find reassurance that early discovery facilitates early treatment, even perhaps eradication, of potential dangers. In spite of the anxiety preceding each of the various procedures, an unanticipated benefit is the uncanny reassurance when results come back "normal." No better time to take a nap . . . your relaxation potential is very high.

As we all remember from our school days (and maybe recurrent nightmares), one of the most anxiety-provoking aspects of "test day" was the inability to foresee what the test would require. Since you won't be graded on your performance, consider these twin-pregnancy tests "open book."

Here's your cheat sheet.

The OB-GYN "First Visit"

At this appointment, you may or may not learn that you are expecting two. Typically, in the pregnancy confirmation visit, some very basic early statistics and tests are conducted. The appointment will usually involve an early ultrasound/gestational dating (along with an estimated due date), an in-depth discussion of personal medical and family histories (daddy-to-be should definitely attend this appointment), a pap smear and pelvic exam, a determination of mommy-to-be's blood type and RH factor, a check for Rubella (German measles) immunity, a check for hepatitis and HIV antibodies, a check for sexually transmitted disease(s), blood work, weight, and urine cultures.

You can expect to get to know your obstetrician very well in the coming weeks/months. Our records reveal a full fourteen-visit dance card prior to our twins' delivery, with the visits becoming more frequent as the plural pregnancy progresses (one of our visits was an impromptu, doctor-on-call-prescribed, first-thing-in-the-morning pop-in to assuage panicky twin-mom-to-be after a late-night bleeding episode at 13 weeks).

If you haven't already begun taking them prior to pregnancy, your OB-GYN will prescribe prenatal vitamins for you to take the duration of your pregnancy (and for the duration of your nursing window if applicable). Some doctors encourage an increased dosage for twin-expectant moms; others recommend the standard one vitamin per day. Ask if you have concerns about taking too much or too little. Morning sickness afflicted moms may find the iron-rich vitamins intensify the already queasy status of their digestive systems. As with every aspect of your medical situation, be 100 percent honest and forthcoming with your doctor. There may be alternative doses or types of vitamins that don't worsen already unpleasant symptoms.

You may have some aspects of your past (or present) that you do not share openly with family, friends, or even your doctor. For the sake of your soon-to-arrive children, and for the integrity of your relationship with their father, do not keep any secrets regarding your medical and/or psychological history from your doctor. Your collective family health will be better for the open airings and admissions. You will feel better, too.

Ultrasounds/Sonograms

Carrying two babies will earn you the rights to numerous prenatal viewings of your children, especially if you are over 35. As a matter of fact, we were so spoiled by the seemingly every appointment surveillance sessions, that at 27 weeks when we were only given the opportunity to *hear* their heartbeats and given no opportunity to actually *see* the fetal flickers thumping away, I was somewhat downhearted . . . and surprised. When I asked if we'd be able to see our twosome, the nurse looked at me with the disdain of a parent on Christmas Day when the children are seeking yet more presents after an overindulgent glut has already been opened. Earlier generations, younger moms-to-be, and women pregnant with singletons receive a very limited number of ultrasounds. Enjoy (and appreciate) the spectator privileges your double-baby bearing status will afford you.

A review of my pregnancy medical records reveals no less than eight ultrasounds—three of which occurred on what my husband and I affectionately referred to as the "NASA ultrasound," the high-definition, perinatologist (high-risk pregnancy specialist) equipment. God bless science.

Our first ultrasound was of the transvaginal variety. Trust me, you don't see this type of ultrasound depicted on television sitcoms! A handheld, condom-enrobed curling iron-size probe is thankfully well-lubricated and inserted into your vagina—sending visual images to a monitor for you and your doctor to enjoy. Not at all painful, just kind of awkward and unexpected. As pregnancy progresses, the transabdominal ultrasound replaces his transvaginal cousin.

If you aren't familiar with how an transabdominal ultrasound is actually performed, you as the pregnant lady will lie down semirecumbent on an examination table, a gelatinous clear blue-green pastel colored goo (sometimes chilly) is squirted upon your bare, burgeoning belly, and a wand (called a transducer) is rubbed around the surface transmitting images from your uterus to a monitor screen.

You will likely have your first perinatologist-administered comprehensive plural fetal screen transabdominal ultrasound somewhere around 20 weeks. (We had three perinatologist exams paired with über-ultrasounds.) Measurements will be taken of the babies' heads and abdomen circumferences, leg bone lengths, assessments of the organs: the chambers of the heart, stomach, kidneys, bladder, and genitalia. You will be asked by your medical team if you do or do not wish to know the gender of your babies. If you do not want to know, be sure to be vocal. Certain views on the high-tech equipment will make it challenging to avoid an accidental revelation. (On the lesser-definition equipment, you will have a hard time deciphering what you are looking at, even if you do get a full fetal crotch perspective.)

AFP/AFP-3 (or Triple Screen)

Administered between weeks 16 and 18 of your pregnancy, this test uses your maternal blood (non-uterine invasive) to measure levels of alpha-fetoprotein (AFP) (the triple screen also measures human chorionic gonadotropin/hCG and unconjugated estriol). When a woman is not pregnant, there is no alpha-fetoprotein in her blood at all, since it can only be created/produced by a fetus or its yolk sac. By weeks 16 to 18, you likely already know if you are expecting twins. However, some women (especially younger mothers-to-be who have fewer ultrasounds and fewer "early" visits to their OB-GYNs) have actually learned of their multiples-in-tow status through this very test. High levels of the protein can indicate more than one fetus producing the protein. Likewise, a high AFP level may cause a re-assessment of the progress of the pregnancy; it could be further along than originally predicted or estimated. Unfortunately, high levels can also be an indicator of potential spina bifida or other neural tube defects in the developing infant(s). Low AFP levels may reflect a possibility of Down's syndrome or other chromosomal anomalies.

Try not to panic with the AFP or triple screen, if you elect to have the process done (it is an optional prenatal test). Bear in mind the "test" is a *screening*. Results are not a confirmed diagnosis. False "positives" indicating an increased risk for defects are common, adding anxiety to already overstressed multiple-moms-to-be.

So what are the benefits of having the AFP or triple screen? Clearly the majority of the screening results come back "normal," easing some apprehension for mom-to-be. (Important to note: all birth defects are not "revealed" via these screenings, but eliminating a wide spectrum of possibilities does provide an opportunity to exhale.) If the results are questionable, a secondary level of testing can be administered to ascertain a greater sense of the initial screening's accuracy. If indeed an anomaly with either baby is discovered, thanks to the screening, you have the incredible possibility of performing beneficial prenatal treatments, as well as the time to prepare for any necessary neonatal treatments.

Honesty time: Awaiting the results of this screening was one of the most challenging and stressful times of my plural pregnancy. Those days were filled with mental images of how we would cope with whatever abnormalities might be revealed by the screening. To top it off, my husband was out-of-town on business during the week we imagined we'd receive the results, allowing my hormonally charged state of apprehension to run amok without the balance of a realistic perspective. When my colleague beeped my desk to tell me my gynecologist (not just his office) was on line #2, my heart stopped. Surely, that could not be a good sign. Little did I know, our doctor makes a practice of delivering the results himself so that he can elaborate and answer any questions. If you are leaning toward the anxious side amid your twin pregnancy, it might be worth asking who will call you and when they will call you with the testing feedback.

Results of this screening are given in a 1: _____ ratio format, meaning a 1 in _____ chance that your babies will suffer from either a Down's syndrome risk or an open spina bifida risk.

Your doctor will inform you as to what a "normal" ratio for each of these risks is based on your maternal age.

If your results show either or both of your babies have an increased "risk," it is important to remember that increased risk does *not* equal a definite presence of a pending birth defect. Think about what those results truly indicate: a 1 in _____ chance of the defect. Depending upon your situation, along with your partner's and doctor's input, you may elect to have a more definitive diagnostic test done, such as amniocentesis. Of course there is risk involved with the diagnostic tests. You need to determine what you are willing to risk for your peace of mind, or what course of action you would take upon verification of the birth defects present.

Ideally, your pregnancy will fall within the vast majority; and these results will provide welcome reassurance that all is progressing well and normally with your growing infants.

You may understandably elect to waive all voluntary screening and diagnostic tests (other than ultrasound) in the interest of "taking things as they come." Again, be honest and forthright with your doctor, and decide accordingly.

Amniocentesis and CVS (Chorionic Villius Sampling)

Both amniocentesis (done between weeks 16 and 18) and CVS (done between weeks 10 and 12) are typically offered to women over the age of 35, who are more at risk for carrying a baby with a chromosomal abnormality. Both tests involve the extraction of samples (either of amniotic fluid from the sac in the case of amniocentesis or of a placental sample in the case of CVS) either via a needle (amnio) or a thin tube catheter (CVS). Both tests do carry a risk, however small, of spontaneous miscarriage. Noninvasive, no-risk ultrasounds (prior to CVS) and the equally noninvasive, no-risk AFP-3 Triple Screen (prior to amniocentesis) are encouraged prior to embarking upon either risk-carrying test.

Many doctors are reluctant (or understandably unwilling) to perform the "riskier" prenatal tests in a multiple gestation pregnancy. Others are confident of their ability to administer the tests with minimal risk.

Take some time in discussion with your medical team, as well as your partner, to thoroughly explore the potential amnio/CVS benefits and the potential amnio/CVS dangers before making your decision on whether or not to take either of these tests as part of your twin-pregnancy prenatal treatment.

Almost ironically, if your twins are diagnosed with twin-to-twin transfusion syndrome (TTTS—see the glossary for the definition), amniotic fluid reduction through amniocentesis can be lifesaving. How fortunate we all are to be twin moms in this medical age!

Cervical Checks

From week 24 on, you can expect your obstetrician to do a manual (with his or her fingers) check of your cervix at each appointment. As twin-pregnant women have dual pressure placed on the cervix (membrane holding the twins "in"), your doctor needs to confirm the status of your cervix earlier than with a single-baby pregnancy. Any early effacement (thinning of the cervix) or dilation (opening or shortening of the cervix) needs to be discovered early, so that if bed rest (easing pressure on your cervix by taking gravity out of the equation) needs to be prescribed, it can be.

Your doctor will probably alert you, but be forewarned. Some spotting is not unusual after a cervical check. In the interest of safety, let your doctor know if the postexam bleeding is more than just a spot or two.

Glucose Tolerance Test—(or more aptly described, the test to detect gestational diabetes)

Usually administered between weeks 24 and 28 of your pregnancy, you may be directed to fast the 12 hours preceding your glucose tolerance test. If your doctor forgets to direct you to do so, let me suggest you schedule your test for first thing in the morning, so that will not be as challenging. Many friends of singletons warned me of the "vile," heinously sweet liquid you are directed to consume to begin this prenatal test. Imagine my surprise when I thought it was delicious! Blood will be taken before you drink the sugar solution, and incrementally afterward, for a testing span of up to 3 hours. Using your blood samples, your blood sugar levels are measured to determine if the hormonal fluctuation and additional strain placed by two developing babies have sent your pancreas into a state of insulin-creating inadequacy. Twin-pregnant women do develop gestational diabetes more often than singleton-pregnant counterparts. The test is nothing to fear, just time-consuming as you allow your body time to "combat" the sugar overload. Bring some reading material, and try to relax. If indeed you do learn you have gestational diabetes, early detection is invaluable. Take comfort in the fact that your doctors are well-versed in how to adjust your prenatal care accordingly. After your twins are born, your pancreatic functions will most likely return to normal, and no further diabetic treatment will be needed.

Non-Stress Test

In singleton pregnancies, this test is not necessarily a prenatal requirement . . . often given only if a mother has carried the baby beyond the projected due date, or if there are other factors that warrant a check in on the baby's status or stress level in utero. Twin-expectant moms are given a NST as a facet of routinely prescribed prenatal care. For the NST, similar to your ultrasounds, you will lie down on the exam table, and monitors will be placed strategically on your abdomen to monitor the harmonious fetal heartbeats. If one or both babies are sleeping, you may be asked to drink a sugary (stimulating without caffeine) beverage to kick the twins into action. Sometimes an audible stimulus is employed to get a movement response from your twins. As mommy, you indicate with the pressing of a button when you sense the babies are moving.

Our non-stress test was surprisingly stressful. Administered at 34-plus weeks, I was pretty large with children. When escorted to the exam room, I was asked to recline on the exam table, await the doctor's arrival and further instruction. Thrilled at the direction to lie down, I heave-ho'ed my super-sized self atop the table and stretched out flat on my back. Big mistake. Within seconds, I broke out into a cold sweat. Ever-grateful for my husband's presence, I asked if it was inordinately hot in the exam room. When Scott verified it was actually cool in the room, I could see his eyes open wide with concern. Apparently I was bright red. Suddenly, I felt more nauseated than I had at any point prior in the pregnancy. Feeling woozy and about to throw up at any minute, I began to become concerned that this excruciatingly uncomfortable multilevel sensation was my unfamiliar experience with the onset of labor. Scott dashed out and returned in seconds with the doctor. Who calmly said, "You're okay, Cheryl. Roll over to your side and sit up a little." Instantly, I felt relief. The weight of the babies, placentas, amniotic sacs et al. had grown substantial enough that if placed directly over my vena cava and spine (as it was when lying flat on my back), the pressure was enough to cut off my circulation. Adrenaline had kicked in, and caused the excessive discomfort reaction.

Needless to say, after that jolt, our twins needed no supplemental stimuli to respond appropriately when their monitors were placed for their non-stress tests!

Fundal Height Measurements

Fundal height was a phrase I had never heard prior to my pregnancy. The phrase refers to the distance between your pubis bone (the hard bone bump right below your pubic hair line) and the top of your fundus, or the more commonly used term, uterus. Using a tape measure, your obstetrician will measure that distance in centimeters while you are reclining on the exam table at each appointment.

In a healthy, normal singleton pregnancy, the number of fundal height centimeters directly corresponds to the number of weeks a woman is pregnant. In the very early weeks, for a young mother-to-be, an extra long fundal height might merit an ultrasound to ascertain if multiples might be expected.

In the final weeks of a multiples pregnancy, twin-moms-to-be often find a tangible medically documentable explanation for their extreme discomfort when they realize the comparative magnitude of their fundal height to a singleton pregnancy at the same stage week-wise. For example, at right around 32 weeks, I was measuring 40 centimeters in fundal height—the full-term size for a singleton pregnancy—but ideally I had 8 more weeks to go. Twin-moms-to-be who are bed rested (and even some who aren't!) sometimes measure upwards of 44-plus centimeters at their time of delivery. Try to keep a big picture perspective: while your enormous maternal size may be gruesomely uncomfortable, it is a *temporary* state that benefits your twosome greatly, potentially for a lifetime.

Hemoglobin (Blood) Checks

With two babies requiring nourishment to grow, often absorbing some of mommy's nutrition supply, maternal anemia (iron deficiency) is a frequent by-product of twin pregnancy. Since anemia can be a contributing factor to preterm labor and delivery, your doctor will want to keep an eye on your iron stability. He or she will offer options for keeping your red blood cells thriving while you nourish your twins.

Blood Pressure Checks/Weight Monitoring/Urine Checks

Each visit to your obstetrician will incorporate a blood pressure check, a weight check, and often a urine check, especially in the latter weeks. Early in my pregnancy, I remember thinking, "Gosh, I hope I can always remember not to pee before the morning appointments," assuming I'd be unable to muster enough output for a viable specimen otherwise. Wrong. As the pregnancy progressed, with the voluminous quantities of water you're directed to consume combined with the bladder pressure applied by two gestating twins, you'll pee-pee prolifically. The doctors are looking for sugars or proteins dropped in your urine, either of which can indicate a need for closer attention to your pregnancy. Likewise, high blood pressure or dramatic weight gain (or loss) may alert your doctor to perform additional status checks. Try to keep your alarm to a minimal, whatever tests are deemed necessary. Your medical team wants to know any and every aspect that may have an impact on your (or your babies') health. Be an accommodating and appreciative patient.

A "test" that twin-mom-to-be should consider self-administering early in her pregnancy is *a personal state-of-mind probe.*

From earliest childhood, women formulate perceptions and beliefs about what they anticipate life will be like as a new mother. Prior to even becoming pregnant, you developed opinions and convictions on many aspects of pregnancy and child-rearing. You may have vociferously condemned the use of disposable diapers; declared you'd never want to know the sex of your baby in utero; proclaimed you'd never get an epidural. Those toddler "leashes"? Never!

Typically, those mental images, and subsequent declarations, are hinged on the assumption of a singly arriving newborn. With two on the way, take the time to reassess, reevaluate, reconfigure, or reinforce your previously held ideas. Certainly many of those questions should be addressed in tandem with your medical team and your spouse/partner; but you personally should spend some time in contemplation. Waiting until your children are born to rethink, and on occasion reverse, your viewpoints may place undue maternal pressure on you at a sleep-challenged, emotionally overwrought time. You may be able to translate your visuals and goals into a twin pregnancy, birth, and family life; if so, wonderful! But, don't view yourself a failure, if in the interest of medical safety; you decide to forego your non-hospital/midwife-only/drug-free birth plan.

School tests were given to gauge our academic progress, confirm our preparedness for future challenges, and imbue us with the confidence to move forward in life successfully. In truth, your prenatal testing is not all that different. But how can you "study" or prepare? Follow your doctor's orders. Ask questions when you have them. Eat nourishing foods. Drink gallons of water. Get adequate (bordering on excessive) rest. Breathe deeply and often. Your interim "grades" and dual diplomas will reflect your commitment.

7

A-Child, B-Child: He-Child, She-Child
(The Third Trimester)

No, not a new Dr. Seuss book, it was our ultrasound-revealed birth order. Your "A-Child" is the one closest to the exit ramp. "B-Child" is the next in line. Now, if you are very organized, not to mention clairvoyant, you may have already named the folks queuing up in your belly. If not, get used to "A-Child" and "B-Child." The robotic neutrality of the monikers may actually provide you with some incentive to come up with names. Especially if you feel you are projecting a better "grade" onto one child over the other. Sometimes I am convinced that the prevailing trend toward unisex names is a direct result of the desire to dodge the A and B, all the while maintaining the "surprise" of gender at birth. You are having not one, but *two* babies. Enough surprises already! Feel free to guiltlessly find out what apparatus you are dealing with in there. As a multiple-birth pregnancy, you will no doubt qualify for more high-tech ultrasounds than your single-baby pals. It's going to be pretty darned hard to "keep it a secret." Obviously, you need to do what you and your hubby want to do. I'll just say it was great knowing ahead of time. Plus you have the fun game of temporarily assigning gender-specific famous duo names to the babies. You'll find all sorts of occasions to get a giggle out of them. For instance, "Honey, I didn't sleep at all last night. Fred and Ethel were jumping on my bladder." Substitute A-Child and B-Child into the preceding sentence and it's no fun at all. Although, you are limitless in your assigned pair names if you keep their genders a "mystery," so have fun either way!

Regardless of what you call them in utero, there's a very special feeling that comes when you are told in the later months of your pregnancy that "A-Child" is head down. Ideally, shortly thereafter, "B-Child" will assume the position, too. Pregnancy is 9 months crampacked with laughter and miracles. Yeah, yeah, I hear you. There might be nausea, diarrhea, hemorrhoids, uncomfortable sleep, and the like. Choose to focus on the laughter and miracles.

On average, twins are born 22 days earlier than their friends who are born solo. In terms of weeks, which the bulk of pregnancy milestones are measured by, that is more than 3 weeks preceding your estimated due date (EDD). Many preparatory aspects for single baby arrival are procrastinated to the last weeks of that third trimester. Since you have two babies en route, who have a greater likelihood of arriving earlier, address those necessary "must-do's" earlier in your pregnancy.

What are some of the tasks you'll feel better having under your maternity support belt?

Car Seats in Vehicle(s)

Decide where you want the car seats placed in your vehicle(s) (be sure to check out "Maneuvering Multiples" for suggested placement), and go ahead and get them securely put in now. Many fire stations provide the service of installing infant car seats as a courtesy to confirm the seats are in safely and correctly. If you choose to take advantage of your local heroes' generosity, be sure to call the local firehouse first to determine if they indeed offer their services. We were directed to our city's station (not surprisingly the one closest to BabiesRUs), where the officers are specially trained in how to affix the bases to vehicles. One of my first "twins are special" moments came as a result of pulling into the station with our two car seats to be installed. As I waddled across the parking lot, carrying a seat in each hand, the fireman grinned his congratulations before I even was in speaking range. Since you cannot leave the hospital with your twins until your car seats are safely mounted in your vehicle, go ahead and tend to this task early.

Name Selections

As little girls, most of us composed exotically glamorous and über-masculine sounding names for our future offspring. Oddly enough, when the need arises to select names to last a lifetime for your children on the way, the implications are a bit greater. My previous criterion of how the name would look on a movie marquee or on the cover of *Sports Illustrated* suddenly seemed less important than if it was a name other kids could easily make fun of, or if it made the transition from child to adult gracefully.

Many twin parents, in a desire to affirm their twins' connectedness, decide upon a set of alliterative or rhyming names. Other parents seek to reinforce individuality from the onset of their babies' lives and decide upon a pair of audibly unassociated names.

When perusing the cavalcade of baby name books, don't forget to pair the potential first and middle names with your surname. Our last name (pronounced Log-ee), didn't mesh well with first names like Lucy, Ruby, or Lincoln. Of course a whole new spectrum of fun (albeit, cruel) "would be" names came to mind: Pecan Lage, Yul Lage, and a personal favorite, Bumpona Lage, just to name a few.

Enjoy the giggles with the babies' daddy; but for the love of your twins, don't choose your children's names on the basis of their humor factor.

We generated a two-columned paper "short list" of names we both liked and continued to add to the list (and strike from the list) for the duration of my pregnancy. I could excuse our indecision by stating we "wanted to meet the babies first" before selecting their names, but that is only partially true. Largely, the final decisions remained unmade because we kept bandying about different pairings of first and middles without any sense of "Eureka! That's it!" until after they were born.

Drafting Members of Your Support Team

Have your parents or in-laws already declared they will come and help in the first days with your twins? Let them know you are counting on them, and set up a loose schedule.

Since you will need significant help, see if you can stagger the visits from the new twin grandparents, allowing for a lengthier window of help coverage, rather than doubled up help for a shorter time frame. What about sisters? Brothers? Friends? Neighbors? Book club pals? Church friends? Coworkers?

Sit down as parents-to-be and create a list of who you will ask for what type of assistance. For instance, if a neonatal intensive care unit (NICU) stay is a part of your first days as twin parents, you could ask your neighbors to keep an eye on your house, pick up your newspapers, check your mail, or walk your dog on the occasions no one is home for lengthy periods of time. If twin dad has to leave town for business and the twins are only a couple of months old, consider asking the babies' aunt to stay for a while.

You know best what you can expect from whom; your goal is to get comfortable asking.

Phone List/Chain for Birth Announcement

Far more people will want to know when your babies arrive than you will have the time or energy to call yourselves. Grandparents, siblings, and a few key friends will need to hear from you directly; but allow some of the people who have offered to help "anyway they can" to activate a predetermined phone chain.

Be sure the phone call patrol is given the following information to dispense:

1. Names of the babies, if determined. (If no names have been given yet, the gender[s] of the babies will certainly suffice.)
2. Date(s) and time(s) of the births
3. The babies' weights (and heights if desired)
4. Health status of the twins and mom. Happiness status of dad

In the interest of overinforming as opposed to underinforming the assigned bearer of double baby good tidings, pass along new twin-mommy's room number if one has been assigned, as well as her projected date of discharge. Let the individual making phone calls know whether or not you would like to receive guests.

Basic Nursery Prep

If you plan on commissioning a mini-Sistine Chapel reproduction as your nursery motif, you'd better start far earlier than your third trimester! Real world nursery preparation may include any or all of the following: a fresh coat of paint (mommy-to-be should evacuate the premises for that process), setting up and stocking your changing table (with a changing pad, preemie/newborn diapers, wipes, Vaseline or diaper rash cream), plugging in and testing your baby monitors, installing a smoke/carbon monoxide detector, setting up your diaper disposal system, placing a nightlight (not just for the twins' benefit, but so you can have nursery night vision), adorning walls with whatever décor you have selected, stocking drawers with not only the twins' wardrobes but plenty of burpie/spitty cloths and receiving blankets, and last but far from least . . .

Crib(s) Assembly

Anything requiring assembly can be the source of much consternation. Whether you or the babies' daddy puts the crib(s) together, perhaps no visual quite excites the expectant parents more than a fully assembled baby bed built for two . . . or two cribs placed side-by-side. As soon as the precious bedding and mobiles have added the final touch to the crib(s), be ready to have an emotion-spurred twin-mommy-to-be weep-fest! Enjoy it.

Packing the "Hospital Bag"

Whether you learn via a prenatal class instructor, or whether you are informally told by your OB-GYN, in the latter stages of your pregnancy, you will want to have a prepacked bag of items you want with you for the arrival of your twins.

Our "Prepared Childbirth" classes were not taught with pending multiple births in mind, and subsequently, the list we were given with suggested/encouraged items to pack was full of goofy things that we didn't need . . . and actually we were highly amused afterward that we had packed them (for example, vanilla scented candles, which I LOVE, but for crying out loud, there are oxygen tanks in the room! Duh!).

Here are the things we packed wisely, or wish we had:

- Camera
  (with spare batteries or film)
- CDs, and a means to play them
  (ditto on the batteries)
- Pre-paid phone cards
  Hospitals do not permit the use of cellular phones, and the in-room phones cannot accommodate long distance or calling card directed calls.
- Pencil/Pen and paper
  Paper and pencil come in handy more often than you would imagine in the hospital. Scott passed me the names he liked written on a piece of paper immediately following their birth. (Sadly, in the dual neonatal shuffle, that life-impacting and highly sentimentally charged piece of paper was lost.) You may elect to leave some of the flowers, balloons, edible goodies you receive while in the hospital at the nurses' station to prevent serious car overload when going home. Pencil and paper helped me keep track of those first visits and gifts . . . so that maybe by the time the kids turn four, I can fill in their Baby Books.
- Your own gown or robe, if you wish
  Don't wear one for the birthing; it'll just get messy. Save your glamour gown for well-after birth. I just wore the hospital gowns the whole time, and was *fine*, but it's a matter of personal preference and comfort.
- Socks and/or slippers
  (for you, and maybe your partner, too)
- Maternity panties
  The hospital staff will give you some panties. They're odd. You may want your own.
- Your own pillow
- Snacks for daddy-to-be
  (and *you* immediately following birth, as soon as you're allowed)
- Toothbrushes and toothpaste, deodorant, toiletries, hand lotion, cosmetics
  I wished I had packed a razor. It had been a *long* time since I could effectively shave my legs!

- ChapStick/LipBalm or vaseline
  With only ice chips to eat, and all the erratic breathing, your lips get uncomfortably dry
- Going home outfits for you and for the twins
  Pack a maternity outfit for yourself. You'll be much smaller, but not ready to don your regular clothes quite yet. Pack *small* outfits for the babies. I packed two of my favorite coordinated outfits, but they *swallowed* them! The twins will likely be on the small side . . . pack the weeest of togs you can!
- Reading material
  Although an avid reader, I didn't feel like reading much while I was in the hospital. You may want to bring some diversionary literature.
- All your insurance info
- Spare change, pocket money
  (For vending machines, coffee shop, etc.)
- Nursing bras
  Didn't bring 'em; and don't regret it. Just went commando as the kids were tandem nursing so often. You may elect to get used to them as soon as possible.
- Receiving blankets and baby tees
  You cannot take the hospital's blankets. (We were given two clean, but clearly well-used T-shirts, one per baby.)
- A big manila envelope for collecting all the "Baby's First" paperwork
  The "It's A Boy"/"It's A Girl" tags from their in-hospital bassinets, the copies of birth certificates, testing forms and the like. I had brought along a narrow-spine three-ring binder with a pocket to keep them neat and am very glad I did.
- Nursing pillow
  We brought along a Boppy, as we didn't have a twin nursing pillow when they were born. In retrospect, it would have been great to get used to using the twin nursing pillow while the nursing staff was so quick to help. Tote 'em if you got 'em.

Your partner will probably go home a time or two while you're in hospital, so don't fret if you realize there's something you'd like to have after the babies are born. Even if your spouse elects to stay by your side for every minute of your hospital stay, you can always ask friends or family to run to your house, the store, wherever. While you are in the hospital is the perfect time to get used to asking for help when you need it.

Birth ball? Focal point photograph? Aromatherapy oils? To our view, all were useless, frivolous, or worthless once the triplicate collection of monitors were hooked up.

Why would you feel the need to address such a comprehensive list of responsibilities so early in the third trimester of your twin pregnancy? Especially if your multiple gestation is proceeding dreamily with nary a complication, shouldn't there be plenty of time to get things accomplished? Ideally, yes; but with two infants on the way, get used to the idea of taking extra precautions. The heretofore-enjoyed luxury of believing "there is plenty of time" needs to become an element of your plural pregnancy past.

In the final weeks of twin pregnancy, your level of discomfort will increase rapidly. Your ability to easily navigate your unwieldy self in and out of vehicles may be compromised. Your energy level may be reduced to a point where the word "energy" is nonapplicable. Your doctor may wish to put you on some level of modified (or strict) bed rest following any one of the frequent third trimester appointments. The good news is you are nearing the time when you will meet your twins; who I guarantee you will prove worth every Tums tablet you take.

What are those twin-magnified third trimester symptoms you might expect? (Note: Just because a symptom is listed below does *not* mean you will experience each and every one. Better to know what may be a possibility than to be surprised, or worse, scared. Personally, when I was in my most uncomfortable days, I took comfort knowing there were many, many typical twin pregnancy third trimester symptoms I did not encounter. Keep your positive "these days are numbered" focus.)

Loss of Appetite and Weight Loss

Despite the fact that the babies are gaining weight rapidly in the final weeks in utero, you may find yourself uninterested in food altogether and may actually lose weight. Do what you can to keep nutrition flowing in. Your doctor will be monitoring you and the babies relentlessly in the last weeks, so take his or her advice as to how best address and maintain your intake even though you feel perpetually "full."

Less Movement from the Babies

As the babies grow at an astronomical rate, their previously spacious uterine playroom environment affords less and less room for mobility. Since you will be accustomed to virtually constant baby movement, those latter days when both babies are rendered virtually immobile are very disconcerting. Again, stay in active communication with your OB-GYN. Drink lots of fluid. Lie down on your left side often. If you relax, you may be able to detect the twins' movements with greater frequency. For me, it seemed as if only one twin at a time "had room," so only that baby would move. The other would be nerve-wrackingly compacted and still. Then it would flip flop. Those times of protracted stillness were disturbing. Hang in there, and again, keep your doctor in the loop. You may find it reassuring and helpful to chart "kick counts." Ask your doctor for details on what you can expect movement-wise and when. (True confessions: I would occasionally eat a sweet treat to try and kick-start the twins. Within minutes, one, the other, or both would usually respond. Maybe it was just coincidence, but far be it from me to deny myself goodies, with a potential side-benefit!)

Nesting

Mommy bunnies pull the soft downy fur from their own bellies to create a soft, warm, welcoming environment for their babies. Human mommies in the late stages of pregnancy often go into house straightening, decorating, and cleaning (bordering on sterilizing) frenzy. Sadly, many of us twin moms never make it quite far enough along into our pregnancy to truly enact the benefits of the late in pregnancy nesting urge. Those twin moms who do get the urge are often so limited by their size that cowering to clean the dust behind the basement commode is an impossibility. If you are fortunate enough to feel the nesting bug, do take it easy, and let your partner know how fortunate he is.

No doubt my poor husband would have greatly appreciated this symptom in his knocked-up wife.

Heartburn/Indigestion

Many, if not most, twin moms declare heartburn as their greatest nemesis of late pregnancy. Not only are maternal appetites often diminished, but then adding insult to injury, once food is ingested, it doesn't sit well. Talk to your doctor about appropriate antacids, which may, and sadly may not, provide relief. Eating very small amounts throughout the day, as opposed to three square meals, tends to minimize the dreaded effects of heartburn/indigestion. Remember, unpleasant digestive experience is finite in duration and will cease almost immediately after the twins are born.

Veins

The volume of blood coursing through your body, your twins' bodies and their subsistence systems is massive. As if they want some type of acknowledgment for their increased efforts, your veins will be visibly evident in assorted locations all around your body. Some common locales for the circulatory show-boats are the chest, the insides of elbows, backs of knees and calves, inner wrists, tops of feet, and backs of hands. Even your temples may reveal a stressed-looking vein or two. Think of them as a well-earned, nature-bestowed tattoo. The veins may or may not disappear entirely with the births of your twins. The strained rope-like veins on my chest, backs of calves, hands, and feet are gone. The backs of my knees and cleavage veins are still readily apparent. If after your twins are born you find the remaining visible veins seriously diminish your body-image, numerous doctors now offer cosmetic vein reduction services. Consider employing them.

Back, Abdominal, and Groin Aches

You are carrying extra weight; potentially, a great deal of it. Your center of gravity has transitioned. Your exercise (if any) has been limited. Your body is accomplishing something truly amazing, and not without duress. Again, remember the finite duration you will need to endure the discomfort, and the prizes that await you at the finish line.

(Keep your doctor apprised of all your aches and pains. You aren't a whiner; he or she needs to know what's going on. Some sudden shifts in your day-to-day aches can be a portent of the onset of labor. If your back pain becomes severe, or surges rhythmically, let your doctor know immediately.)

Swelling/Edema

Hard to believe that even though you are urinating with relentless frequency, somehow, you are managing to retain water. Faces, fingers, ankles, and feet may blossom into bloated elephantine reservoirs in the latter days of twin pregnancy.[1] Keep your feet elevated as much as you can. Purchase some comfortable support-offering shoes in a larger size. Remove any or all beloved rings before your fingers kielbasa themselves to the point that your rings need to be cut from your fingers. The swelling of narrow passages in your wrists may cause you to experience tingling fingers (especially when you take a big breath) and carpal tunnel syndrome. Elevate your hands when you can. An armchair or recliner can provide a circulatory haven of comfort. Once the babies are born, you will rapidly find your twinflated body parts becoming more and more recognizable. Your dual rewards make this temporary inconvenience seem exactly that, a temporary inconvenience.

Constipation/Diarrhea

The bewildering bowel bonanza continues right until you deliver your twosome. Typically in the days preceding labor, you will have an impressive bout of diarrhea.

Again, when babies arrive; poo perplexities depart.

Linea Nigra

Nature ornaments pregnant women in so many ways! From your navel, vertically down your belly to your pubic hair line expect the appearance of a darkened line of skin. For most women, the line disappears entirely after the babies are delivered. (To me, the line almost seemed to be a directional map pointing the babies to the ideal exit. Remember those old AAA Trip-Tik maps?)

Babies "Drop"

One day you will wake up and the babies will appear both to you and onlookers to have descended. In the weeks preceding the "drop," your expanded breasts will likely rest atop the shelf of your belly. Suddenly, a small space may appear between your tummy and mammaries. You may be able to take a deep breath for the first time in weeks. Do so! You have multiple reasons to celebrate: not only the access to more oxygen but the tangible evidence you won't have to wait much longer to meet your twins.

Vaginal Discharge

The assorted textures and viscosities of discharge testing my late in-pregnancy panty liners were innumerable. Undoubtedly, yours will be too. Talk to your doctor about what to "look out for" or be concerned about; otherwise, try to get used to having perpetually moist knickers.

Sleep Interruptions

In the first 6 months carrying twins, you've likely experienced a bizarre array of hyper-vivid dreams. Now, as your pregnancy draws to its conclusion, you will find yourself waking every couple of hours, almost wide awake. Seemingly, nature is cruelly depriving you of your few remaining nights of uninterrupted sleep. In truth, nature is lovingly introducing you to the frequent wake-ups you'll experience as a mother who needs to feed her children every few hours. Frustrating, perhaps. Amazing and miraculous, definitely.

Skin Tags

Looking like flaccid, flesh-colored dangling moles, these "tags" may appear prior to the third trimester. They may disappear after the twins arrive. They may not appear until after your babies are born. They may disappear, they may not. The skin tags are easily removed by a dermatologist if they persist beyond their welcome. Genetics may dictate whether or not you get skin tags. Overall, they are a benign reminder of your expecting/new mom status.

Butterball Effect

As your baby-filled belly has grown, your navel has gotten noticeably shallower—perhaps even flush with your tummy. Guess what? Toward the end of your pregnancy days, it will pop out like the doneness tab on the Thanksgiving turkey! Don't be alarmed, your belly button will resume its recessed position after your twins are born.

Stretch Marks

Undeniably, you *are* stretched. You may have dermatological documentation to prove it. Like with skin tags, genetics play a role in how dramatically you will experience stretch marks. Not restricted to the belly, stretch marks frequently make appearances on twin-mommy-to-be's breasts and thighs. Various creams, lotions, ointments, and Vitamin E oil reputedly can prevent, or at least reduce, the intensity and permanence of the marks.

Mommy Brain

An underdiscussed aspect of pregnancy, "mommy brain" affects a majority of expectant women, whether they are expecting one or more infants. Throughout pregnancy and particularly in the latter months, a pregnant woman's mind just seems "off" and incapable of performing its most basic of functions. For some, the extent of "mommy brain" is a mere inability to focus. For me, mommy brain manifested itself most dramatically when I could not recall the word for the color "black" (True story, I kid you not.). The phenomenon will not end with the births of your children, but it does eventually dissipate.

Many theories abound about the hormonal causation for the occurrence, which would certainly explain why twin-expectant women declare it more of a universally pronounced symptom than our single-baby pregnant counterparts.

The Double Daddy Perspective

At this stage of the game I felt that my most important contribution was reminding my wife that she was pregnant with twins. I would tell her this, hoping she would go to bed and get the rest she needed. I would tell her this so she would remember why her shoes would no longer fit. I would tell her this so she would stop feeling guilty about all the things she wasn't doing around the house and hopefully . . . go to bed and get the rest she needed.

Shortness of Breath

As a by-product of your third trimester fullness factor (and perhaps even earlier), you may find yourself unable to take a deep breath. The twins are usurping whatever available space they can access. Your poor lungs may not have the room to expand to their full capability. Fear not. As soon as your twins are born, you will be able to take a deep breath of relief figuratively and literally.

Discomfort and Dual Emotions

You are big. You are tired. Day-to-day activities prove difficult. The shortest of car rides border on unbearable. You feel as though you have so much you want or need to do but lack the energy or mental faculties to do anything significant. Pair that plural pregnancy paralysis with an overwhelming sense of joy and anticipation. Each glance at your naked belly reveals the pressure of tiny feet, fists, elbows, knees, bottoms, heads. The twins haven't even been born yet and you already know there is nothing you wouldn't do to ensure their safety and happiness. Each increasingly uncomfortable day for you gives your twosome added strength, health, and a better chance of a complete physical development. Embrace the dichotomy of your physical hyperreadiness to "have those babies" and the emotional/intellectual awareness that the longer your twins "cook," the better off all are. Find peace in knowing that each day, each *minute* of discomfort you endure benefits your children for a lifetime.

Third trimester. The home stretch. As a twin-pregnant woman, expect ambiguous feelings during this final stage. You begin to come to grips with the reality that your perinatologist identified "A" and "B" are truly on the way. You experience magnified personal discomfort and erratic sleep/digestion patterns. Insecurities and apprehensions about premature labor, so frequently a factor in twin pregnancies, lurk in the corners of your seemingly deteriorating "Mommy Brain." Dreaded "bed rest" is often prescribed in these last weeks. Yet in glaring contrast to all the "negatives," your twins are truly on the way. Excitement and joy. Apprehension and elation. Your special "A" and "B." Great things come in twos. Get ready for your "great things."

Note

1. If rather than gradual growth, you experience sudden severe swelling or weight gain, notify your doctor immediately. Instantaneous bloating can be an indicator of potentially serious late-pregnancy complications. Again, remain in active conversation with your caregivers.

III

Preparation and Anticipation

8

Prenatal Agreements

N o, I am not suggesting you consult with a lawyer prior to your babies' births. However, there are numerous areas of extreme significance you and your husband should discuss thoroughly before the arrival of your children. For their sake, and for yours. Here are just a few.

Breastfeeding vs. Formula

Yes, the breasts are yours, but the children belong to both of you. Everyone (even your man) has personal feelings about nursing. The thought of nursing twins can seem particularly daunting. Be open. Share your hopes, fears, and concerns about the process. See if you can arrive at a joint decision. No doubt some men assume that if mommy nurses, he'll get more sleep.

If you do decide to breastfeed, trust me, he won't (and certainly shouldn't) be sleeping through all those middle of the night feedings. With twins, you need a second set of hands to help position the babies on your breasts in the early days. After nursing (or formula feeding), two babies need burping and diapering. The process can move more quickly, and the whole family can try to get more rest, if burping is done simultaneously, rather than in sequence. Your husband will need to fully commit to either feeding option you decide upon. Make the decision together.

You and your husband may decide that formula feeding is a wiser option for your family. *Do not let anyone make you feel guilty about an elective decision to formula feed!* You and your spouse alone are aware of your family's needs and how they are best met. Today's formula manufacturers are incorporating more elements into formula in attempts to mimic breast milk benefits. Formula-fed babies tend to stay fuller, longer. Some pediatricians even recommend adding small amounts of formula to pumped breast milk when breastfed babies are experiencing difficulties in weight gain, or with spitting up.

There are numerous benefits to either feeding option you select. The early days with twins are fraught with enough challenge. The last thing you need is criticism or pressure on how best to nourish your babies.

After your twins are born, you may find you and your partner need to revisit this topic for a variety of reasons. You may have hoped to breastfeed and for some reason, it isn't working for you. You may have decided to formula feed, and now feel you'd like to nurse your twins. Keep those lines of discussion open with your husband. Acknowledge that his feelings toward, and participation in, the feeding process are valid.

Our take (to take or leave): From a health perspective for the babies, we decided to give breastfeeding our best shot. My innate stubbornness (three bouts of mastitis, two outpatient breast surgeries) paid off, and we nursed our twins until their first birthday. Your pediatrician will be able to detail the extensive health benefits to your twins far better than I can, but in that pivotal first year, ours were rarely sick. (Important note: ours were not in a daycare environment, also reducing their exposure to illness.) So rarely, that when they got sick at 13 months, I was wondering if I should have nursed them longer. Doctors assured me, breast milk is wonderful, but if it was a miracle drug/vaccine, adults would still be nursing. Financially, we saved approximately $1,500 in formula costs per baby. From a maternal health point of view, my tummy was for the most part flat within 2 months (breastfeeding causes uterine contractions), and I had lost all pregnancy weight by 3 months. By the 1-year mark, I weighed 10 pounds less than I did prepregnancy. Disclaimer: Much like a Jenny Craig or Weight Watchers commercial, I can't guarantee my results are typical, but they are verifiable for me.

Your Pediatrician

Guess what? Upon arrival at the hospital, you are asked to identify your selected pediatrician. As soon as the babies are outside of your body, your OB-GYN is no longer their doctor. My advice? Ask around. Talk to your friends who are already parents and ask how they like their pediatrician. If you have friends, or even friends of friends, with twins in your area, get their input. Get your short list together, and start calling the recommended practices to make interview appointments prior to your twins' birth.

You and hubby should decide on some key questions to ask ahead of time. Things like:

- Do you have weekend hours?
- Do you have a healthy waiting room and a sick waiting room?
- Do you take our insurance?
- Will I be talking to my doctor typically or a nurse on call?
- Do you have experience with twins and/or preemies?
- What books do you recommend for parents-to-be and new parents? (I'd encourage you to start becoming familiar with the philosophies of various child-rearing experts: Dr. Spock, John Rosemond, T. Berry Brazelton, Dr. William Sears, and the like. You will find viewpoints you like, and those you don't. If a pediatrician suggests a text whose perspective you appreciate, chances are, you will agree later on. Likewise, if the doctor insists T. Berry Brazelton is "the best," and his text is too saccharine to your taste, you will undoubtedly experience differences in opinion later.)

Take notes on the pediatricians' responses. So you like the interviewee, but the reception staff was rude? Not wild about the doctor, but the office is oh-so convenient? Think carefully before finalizing your decision. You already have a child? Do you genuinely like your current pediatrician? Do they have much experience handling twins and/or preemies? Evaluate your situation before just "staying the course."

Nervous that your due date is approaching, and you've yet to "click" with a pediatrician? You've been put on bed rest, and though you trust your partner's opinion, *you* want to meet the pediatric candidates before committing to a decision? The good news is, if you aren't sure you have made your final or right choice when you go to the hospital to deliver, it's not the end of the world. Just declare your preferred doctor at the time, and see how it goes. Although it may be a bit of a hassle, you can always change doctors later.

Our take (to take or leave): Our Prepared Childbirth class leader imparted the wisdom of selecting a pediatrician relatively early in a twin pregnancy. Late pregnancy car travel discomfort and the looming possibility of bed rest are big motivators for pending twin parents to start the pediatrician pursuit earlier than you might if expecting a single child. So, late in our second trimester, we asked friends with children about their pediatricians. We were amazed to discover just how many people are less-than-thrilled with their doctor of "choice." Fully aware that with two young infants (potentially premature) we could anticipate frequent office visits, hubby was determined (I was hormonally hell-bent) to find a pediatrician that we would be happy to see often. After coalescing a fairly substantial list of names, I began making calls. As a stickler for politeness by phone, if the individual answering the phone was less than 100 percent gracious, the doctor's name was immediately removed from my list. No kidding. To my way of thinking, when I'd be calling the pediatric office in the future, I'd likely be stressed enough without having to deal with insolence or disinterest on the part of the front desk staff. Good doctors hire good staff. A few of the doctors on our list were no longer accepting patients. We could quickly remove them from the list as well. Some of the potential candidates' offices seemed too far away from our home. We struck them from the list. Finally, by the beginning of my third trimester, we had scheduled interviews with the three remaining pediatricians.

With our preprinted sheet of questions in hand, we grilled doctor number one. He was thoroughly pleasant, but we weren't bowled over.

On to interview number two. Now fortunately for us, my husband's boss, Angela, has triplets. Her pediatrician fell into the "no longer accepting new patients" category, but she suggested we talk to a partner of his. Her trio had on occasion seen, and liked, a partner in the same practice, a mom of twins herself. After meeting with twin-mommy/pediatrician Dr. Christian, we left the office with literature in hand and smiles on our faces. We made our decision in the parking lot and cancelled our third interview upon arrival home.

For us, chemistry was important. If location were the most important factor, no doubt we'd have selected the third scheduled pediatrician. If longevity of pediatric practice were most important, we'd have picked the first. There are numerous valid factors that go into play when making your decision. See if you and your husband or partner can decide which is most important to you.

Stay-at-Home Parent vs. Daycare

Oooh, this can be a real toughie. Fortunately, my husband and I knew all along how we felt about this issue and were in agreement. Whatever you do, don't just assume you and your spouse feel the same way. Get the subject on the table. Granted, once the babies come, you may change your minds; but by all means, discuss this subject at length beforehand. Try to be open in your discussion, realizing that if a parent isn't going to be the dedicated caregiver, there are a myriad of "daycare" possibilities. Bright and colorful daycare centers seem to be blossoming on every corner. More and more families (when it's financially feasible) are opting for in-home care for their twins, while mom (or dad) works from home. You may consider a nanny or au pair, trained and specialized in child development and care. But rest assured, you will take criticism on this issue whichever course of action you take. The key to remember is that it's your family's decision. Don't feel obligated to defend your position to others. Every family is unique and needs to make its choices accordingly.

If you do feel defensive, make sure it is solely because of other people's lack of understanding and not some deep-seated guilt, regret, or resentment on your part. Make a point to readdress the issue, a few months after the babies are home, once they're in bed. Do you still feel your decision was the right one for you and your family? Be flexible. Be honest. Everything is going great? Wonderful! Make a point to talk about it again in the future. You all are stressed and miserable? You are going broke? Don't be so bull-headed and arrogant that you stick with a choice that is clearly not working for your family. Your children will thank you.

Our take (to take or leave): Scott and I felt and continue to feel strongly about one of us staying home with the twins. Actually, before we even married, we knew we wanted one of us to stay home once we had a child; and that was *before* we knew we'd have two at the same time! When purchasing our home, we took into consideration that we wanted to be able to manage on a single income. We were fortunate in that we had discussed many of the issues surrounding childcare prepregnancy. However, we hadn't pushed the discussion far enough to decide which one of us would be the one to stay home.

Again, don't make assumptions! Fortunately, my husband relented since I was in possession of the feeding apparatus.

So many of my former career colleagues have expressed disbelief that I am "satisfied" as a stay-at-home mommy. Many have responded with an, "Obviously daycare expenses for *two* infants/toddlers would make your return to work almost financially worthless." Let them say or believe what they will. We made a decision that is working beautifully for our family. We *do* make a point to discuss satisfaction "status" often: his, mine, and the twins'. If things change, we are ready to be flexible. But for now and the foreseeable future, we're "satisfied"! More than other areas, I emphatically encourage you to keep communication lines open in this department. Do not get into a prideful "this is what we decided, come what may" rut. "Come what may" could be the dissolution of your happiness, your spouse's, or even your twins'. Talk, and talk often.

Sleeping Arrangements

Will you want two little bassinets in your room? Will you have them in the same crib in their nursery from the first night on? Are you advocates of the "family bed"? There are more sleeping arrangement possibilities (and philosophies) than you can imagine, and with twins it is imperative that you and your partner decide on a course of action prior to that first night home. And, as always, be ready to be flexible.

Think a bit down the road as well. You may want the babies in your room for the first few weeks, and then to co-sleep them in the same crib in their nursery afterward. Perhaps their nursery is right next to your room, and you want them to establish a routine as quickly as possible. Do you and your partner agree about "special instances"? If they're crying, do you soothe them and leave them in their bed? Do you carry them to your bed for the remainder of the night? Do you rock them back to sleep? Try to develop a game plan early on. If mommy and daddy are congruent, the babies will experience consistency. Very reassuring when the whole world is new.

Our take (to take or leave): Here was an instance where we needed to show some flexibility post-"agreement." Our twins' nursery is right next door to our room. So close to our room in fact, that in reality, we probably didn't need a baby monitor in our bedroom at all. Before they were born, we decided our twins would sleep together, in the same crib, in their nursery, from the first night home. Knowing that we'd be feeding them frequently and 'round the clock, we felt we would all be best served to get the nursery established as the nighttime sleep locale.

From the earliest of days, our babies (not unlike their parents) were extremely gassy. Our pediatrician suggested sleeping them with their heads elevated in order to prevent gastrointestinal refluxy, spit-up choking danger. Nothing motivates you to adjust your plan quite like the words "potential choking." Within the first few days of their arrival home, we transferred our predesignated nighttime sleep locale from their crib to their bouncy seats. Now, strategically placed facing the foot of our bed, with even the slightest gurgle, I could reflexively bolt upright and immediately discern nothing was wrong. An unexpected benefit of the modified plan was that the new arrangement allowed us to undertake the night nursings with greater ease. Flexibility pays.

Finances

How are you planning to adjust your household expenditures? Are you dropping one income for a parent to stay home? Will you need to "scale back" your current lifestyle in order to accomplish that? If so, how do you plan on doing it? Are you intending to make use of daycare? How expensive will your selected facility be for two infants? Will you begin savings accounts for them right away? Are you thinking of hiring a nanny or au pair? Do you as parents have life insurance? How much will you be allocating for newborn expenses . . . diapers, formula, pediatrician visits, emergencies?

These are just a few of the questions you need to be thinking about. Try not to let the money part scare you or add to your stress. You will work everything out, but you will need to prioritize your spending with your partner. Be sure to put everything on the table. You'll be surprised at some of the easy and logical ways you can save.

For instance, my husband and I (pre-twins) had a tremendous penchant for magazines; between us, we subscribed to more than eleven. Realizing our "leisure reading" time might be diminished with two infants in the house, canceling the bulk of the magazine subscriptions made great sense, and saved money. Likewise, my husband, though not a massive consumer, did smoke. The pending arrival of the twins provided incentive, health-wise and wallet-wise, to quit.

Talking about your finances before the babies come is a good idea. Sleep deprivation and money discussions don't go well together.

Our take (to take or leave): We knew we'd be sacrificing my income when I stayed home with the twins. Of course, we also knew that the frequency of our weekend excursions, dinners out, movies, and the like would be severely diminished once the twins arrived. A pie graph of our pre-twin household expenditures revealed an inordinate amount of our joint disposable income was exactly that, spent on disposable entertainments. Thus, we disposed of the majority of them. However, please don't think us *too* self-sacrificing. We retained our upgraded cable TV service, knowing our entertainment, when not twins-based, would likely be provided in-house.

Discipline

Obviously, you won't be "correcting" your freshly born infants, but time does fly when you are having fun. Exhausted or not, you will be having fun. Before you know it, you will be seeing behavior you want to discourage. Make sure you and your partner are of the same mind as to what the "no-nos" will be in your household. Make sure you both agree on how correction is to be handled. Will you verbally chasten? Will you ignore negative behavior? Will you distract the wrongdoer? Will you have physical contact?

Consistency is absolutely the key here. Each twin, in addition to receiving their own correction, will usually be witness to their partner's reprimands. In a good and just world, that means they will learn twice as fast from twice the reinforcing observation. After all, babies (and adults) learn via repetition. Your children will repeat the same behaviors over and over to confirm what is acceptable and what is not in your eyes. They may "flip-flop" initiators just to make sure the result is always predictable. If you "allow" a previously "disallowed" behavior even once, they will be incredibly confused. Your previous disciplinary efforts on that issue are now rendered null and void. Don't let your own tiredness "ease" the predetermined consequence.

Keeping your eye on the goal helps. Obviously, we all want happy, well-adjusted, socially responsible children. How we handle the discipline issue directly impacts all three of those key variables.

With twins, your efforts toward appropriate behavior will be twice as effective if handled with unfailing regularity. Whether it is a good behavior receiving a compliment, or a less-pleasant gesture receiving a correction, two children will learn from a single act and result. Of course, the corollary is also true. If you are haphazard and inconsistent in your responses, expect chaos. It's what you will get.

Do not "wait until the discipline situation arises." Please develop your plans for loving correction early, carefully, and together.

Our take (to take or leave): While pregnant, archaic as it may seem to many of you, my husband and I both predicted we'd incorporate gentle, yet corporal, correction in our discipline repertoire. Both spanked rarely, and only for major infractions as children; we felt that with careful accompanying explanation, the "old ways" are often the best ways. Flash forward to the first "punishable" offenses by our twins: surprisingly, even the gentle "attention getting" hand-smack felt grossly wrong. After trying it twice, I stopped. When Scott "tried" it early on, and told me the details later, his recounting of the episode sounded sheepish and confessional. Now from what I hear, when our kids are teenagers, we may out of sheer desperation re-evaluate our dismissal of the method, but for now, no hitting. It's not right for them to do, and it doesn't feel right for us either.

That's not to say I don't use bodily contact frequently throughout the day. Certainly, when one is heading lickety-split toward a potentially dangerous situation, I will quickly grab them to halt advancement. If they are lashing out at each other or me, I will grab the angry hands firmly. Daily, I have rapid, reflexive physical contact with our twins, but sheerly in a preventative way.

So what *do* we do to indicate our displeasure with inappropriate behavior? Exactly what I thought I'd never do, the infamous "time-out." Before the twins' arrival, I thought "time-outs" seemed like the most ridiculous nonconsequence possible, especially the "hug hold" variation. Heck, I'd *try* to get punished if I knew I'd get hugged.

However, when you are little, and having a great time that sadly segues into misbehavior, removal from the fun is horrific . . . at least if the screaming we hear in response is an accurate barometer. The trick is to enact the time-out correctly. In our house, time-outs occur in the crib, upstairs, with all stimuli removed, including mommy. (I have heard arguments against crib time-outs, not wanting to associate "unpleas-antness" with their sleeping environment. To me, when all the blankets, cozies, and fun items are removed from the crib, it's not even the same inviting place. Neither of our twins has ever shown reticence toward their crib as a result of it being the time-out locale.)

Invariably, we are all playing happily, downstairs, when infractions occur. Lazily, I've been very tempted to "not see" the violating act. Take my word. Dodge a punishment that should be administered, and you'll just have to play catch-up later.

Do communicate regularly with your partner so they are alerted to any newly discovered "no-nos." No matter how thoroughly you feel you have discussed this issue with your partner, be ready for the unexpected. For instance, in our house, we never discussed the trashcans as off-limits prior to their births. Who knew they were a source of endless fascination? When Scott arrived home, he was greeted with the story of the day's events, including how we learned that trashcans are a "no-no." Upon my return from an outing, I learned of all sorts of fun play, and how everyone learned that remote controls are a "no-no" that afternoon.

Again, befriend flexibility. Be prepared to assess and re-assess with your fellow warden the efficacy of your disciplinary methods, but don't lose consistency in your response to infractions. Remember, just because the behavior doesn't stop, doesn't mean the twins aren't learning the boundaries you've set.

Spiritual Upbringing

You will be unflinchingly attending to your babies' every physical and emotional need in their first days of life. With pun fully intended, you may elect to religiously attend to their spiritual needs as well. Thoughtfully discuss with your partner your plans for how you will raise your children. Are you and your partner of the same faith or belief system? Do you have a place of worship? Will you select godparents for the children? Will religious rituals (circumcision, baptism, christening, dedication, etc.) be a part of their early lives? Do you and your husband have differing religious or cultural backgrounds? Which faith or philosophy will you pass along? Do you intend to send the children to a faith-based school or daycare? How do you plan on answering some of the tough questions you know are coming? Have you explored, defined, or at least examined, your own beliefs?

None of us know all the answers, but don't use that as an excuse for depriving your children of a spiritual route to explore. Expose them to your beliefs and encourage them to grow in faith and love. Immersion in a faith community gives your children a familiar group of adults and peers who can lavish love on them recklessly. As adults, you will also benefit from the support and encouragement of a spiritual family at this very special, and certainly very blessed, time in your life.

Of course, you may decide church/synagogue/temple involvement is not right for you and your family; but do take the time to discuss your feelings about faith with your partner before your twins arrive. Eventually, your kids will ask you questions . . . have your parental perspective ready to share.

Our take (to take or leave): This particular issue was one of the most challenging for Scott and me to address. Although he and I possess very similar beliefs, prior to the babies' births, we manifested them in very different ways.

After a lengthy, overwrought search, in the years prior to our marriage, I finally found a church community where I felt stimulated spiritually and accepted unconditionally. Scott, fully supportive of my church attendance and participation, was uninterested in church attendance, non-plussed (bordering on repulsed) by the formalized, institutional, liturgical nature of most church services.

With babies on the way, he agreed that as a family, we should participate together in spiritual growth. He and I decided that once the twins were born, he would begin to attend my church. In honesty, it has not been an easy transition for him to make. As open and embracing as our church is, there are still remnants of "old school liturgy/dogma" that rub him wrong. (Well, at least in our church, they are only remnants!)

An unexpected, joyful discovery has been that through participation in an adult creative studies class, together we can openly express our beliefs with others who are also struggling to grow closer to God and each other. Another benefit of our Sunday morning experience is that our church (and most other churches, synagogues, and temples) offers children's nursery or classes during adult classes and services, allowing us to fully participate without the concern of our twins' ebullience disturbing others. The twins love their "class" and church friends.

Our struggles to work through this issue prior to the babies' birth and our promises to re-address it after their birth have paid off. When issues are as emotionally charged and close to the heart as your personal faith, it is very easy to become defensive and hurt when your partner has an equally heartfelt, but differing perspective. This is one of the few topics where tears were actually shed in our attempts to find the right compromise. Please don't wait to talk about how you'll handle this very intimate subject.

Support and Expectations

Take the time with your partner to discuss what you expect of one another in the early days with your twins. Will you both be awake at each and every feed? Will you take turns responding to middle-of-the-night cries? Will you both go to all the well-baby appointments at the pediatrician? Who will do the cooking? (Don't even think about housework!) Will a stay-at-home parent need "days off"? What about groceries and errands? When one (or both) parent(s) returns to work, how will the twins' late-night needs be addressed?

Some twin parents use the "buddy system." On a given night, Baby A is mommy's responsibility; Baby B is daddy's. The next night, they switch up. Obviously, if you are breastfeeding, nursing complicates that particular practice; but you understand my general point. There are plenty of options.

Like just about every other issue involved in twin parenting, flexibility is key. Taking the time to talk about spousal expectations ahead of time just helps prevent those misunderstandings based on false assumptions. Communication, and her close friend, compromise, is often the key. By the way, all these pre-twins talks can be very romantic. You get the chance to see what a great parent your spouse is going to be. It's incredibly attractive.

Our take (to take or leave): In our house, we decided that once Scott went back to work, he would help with the 10 P.M. feeding, then sleep in another room. That way, he could get "real" sleep while I soloed on the 1 A.M. and 4 A.M. feedings. By the time the 7 A.M. nursing was done, he was awake and ready to help burp and diaper before heading out to work. He went to the office fairly well rested; when the babies went down for their daily naps, so did I. We found a way to handle night responsibilities that worked well for us. You may decide on a different method.

Pre-twins, I was a member of a book club and a volunteer tour guide at the state fine arts museum. Scott played bass in a band and often helped a friend with general contracting work on the weekends. We decided those obligations were important enough to each of us, that we'd support each other in maintaining those connections after the twins' arrival. We also agreed to be vocal with each other if we needed "personal" time. Sometimes, Scott even forces me to take some time to myself. (Probably when I start speaking in rhyme . . .)

So what do you think I recommend to you? You got it, flexibility! Start by getting a copy of your date book or calendar from last year. Highlight the groups and events most important to you. Have hubby do the same. Figure out a way to dovetail/shuffle them so you can both maintain some of the personal activities integral to your individual happiness.

Unique Family Issues

Do you always spend Thanksgiving at the in-laws and Christmas with your parents? Does hearing the closing theme to Barney make your hubby's flesh crawl? Is grandpa-to-be a gun collector? Will you not leave the house until your makeup is fully applied and hair done? If the twins are your first children, now is the time to think about the everyday life nuts and bolts that may need to change.

Maybe an alternating host-family holiday schedule can be put into place. Maybe your household will watch Elmo. Maybe safety precautions with grandpa's collection need to be addressed. Maybe you will never leave the house again. Okay, that's extreme, but perhaps you will decide to relax your expectations on personal appearance in the interest of time management.

Or, maybe some of your unique family issues are absolute non-negotiables. That's okay, too. Just determine which scenarios need adjustment and how you will prioritize. Do it for the safety and mental health of your babies, your family, your husband, and last but not least, yourself.

Our take (to take or leave): When Scott and I married, we decided that instead of gifts, each anniversary, we would take a week-long trip to a previously unvisited city in the United States (True confessions: Somehow, we ended up in Las Vegas three times in five years.) With the pending arrival of not only one but two infants, we knew that we would likely alter our anniversary observations. Ordering Chinese in has never been so much fun! Aloha, flexibility.

Obviously, you and your spouse may have other key areas that you wish to delve into prior to your twins' birth. The preceding topics aren't intended to be an all-inclusive list. Consider them a leaping point to spur your own conversation about what may change in your lives upon the arrival of your twins. Please don't feel silly initiating discussion about what you might feel is a "goofy" topic. Plenty of new parents find themselves embroiled in heated conflict regarding the appropriate number of guests for a first birthday party!

Part of the joy of twin pregnancy is the doubly intensified anticipation and preparation. Don't limit your preparation to nursery décor and college savings accounts. Double your time spent in spousal discussion prior to your twins' births, and your potential for sleep-deprived confrontation will be greatly reduced. View it as an investment in "celebration" insurance, and make sure it's a flexible policy.

9

Twice the Bibs, Twice the Cribs, and Other
"You'll Need Twice as Much" Fibs

Believe it or not, even though you have two babies on the way, you don't need twice as much of everything. You won't want twice as much of everything. Unless you live in a mansion, space is about to become a precious commodity in your home.

Now I don't want to mislead you. Some things you will need in double, and that's certainly unavoidable, hence the next chapter. But, your babies will be close to the same size for a while and at virtually the same developmental stage. You won't have to doubly invest in everything right away. Here are some corners you can cut, at least in the early days.

Clothes (including bibs)

Sure, the wee little togs are precious, but they are pricey, too. Even if you have a boy and a girl, so many newborn gowns and onesies are unisex, you can easily get away with one and a half times the clothes recommended for a single baby. Layette "requirements" that baby registries suggest for a single infant are probably enough for two, but you don't want to be doing laundry as frequently as that would demand. Chances are, you won't be buying many clothes for your babies anyway. Shower guests, God bless them, cannot seem to resist the magnetic pull of Gymboree and Baby Gap. No doubt, precious coordinated or matching ensembles en masse will be awaiting your twosome. Your investment will likely be in the less-glamorous attire realm: snap-front T-shirts, plain cotton onesies, and socks. One and a half times the recommended single baby allowance on all apparel. Mark my words, that's enough. Side note: All the baby preparedness books suggest de-tagging and washing all your baby duds in Dreft, and having them in the drawers and closet ready to wear. Yes, you should wash the items first. However, after your baby shower(s), evaluate your gifts and see if you have an overwhelming amount of clothes all in the same size. Babies grow quickly. Too many moms I know washed and prepped all the 0–3-month items, only to have their child(ren) wear the items once, twice, or not at all before outgrowing them. Consider exchanging some items received in the super-small sizes for the next size or two up. The prices are the same for 0–3, 3–6, 9, and 12 months. The gift-giver will be happier if your babies actually get some good from her gift. If the tags are still on, most stores will not require a receipt. So in your zeal to be "ready," do use a bit of thought before washing every gift. I wish I had.

Shoes

Here's a surprise, you don't need *any* baby shoes the first year. Socks in the winter, barefoot in the summer. In fact, many doctors don't recommend shoes at all until the babies begin walking. Unless you have two overachievers, most babies don't walk 10 steps consecutively on a regular basis until 12 months. If your twins receive shoes as a gift, if a relative works for Timberland/Nike/Adidas and passes along some wee samples, fine. But don't feel obligated to invest in shoes for necessity's sake. You don't *need* them.

Cribs

Here's a bigger surprise than the dispelling of "the-babies-need-shoes-myth"; you don't need two cribs. At least not yet. Your twins have already been sleeping together in your belly. Unless you are *much* bigger than most pregnant moms, your uterus provides far more cramped quarters than a single crib. In the early months, the tykes just lie there immobile and cozily swaddled on their backs. There's no risk of them rolling onto each other. No risk of them poking each other, so long as they aren't positioned super close to one another. Lots of pediatricians and NICU units recommend co-bedding twins in the early months. The earliest peer-pressure baby will experience is the example of his or her sibling reminding him or her to breathe by doing it themselves. Some early research claimed sudden infant death syndrome (SIDS) chances were increased by co-bedding; the corollary seems to be the prevailing thought now. Obviously, you need to do what feels right for you, and of course what looks cutest in your nursery, wink wink. Eventually, you will need two cribs. They don't stay still forever, and they will need more space. We slept ours in the same crib for 10 months. At 7 months, when they were getting pretty active, we added a low foam crib divider from www.morethan1.com. (Pretty helpful website, check it out.) When they could dive over that, daddy created a rail-height, padded masterpiece we dubbed "The Great Wall." At 10 months, they could pull up onto the Wall, and giggle in each other's faces. Even though that routine was pretty darned precious, it marked the end of an era. We caved and got the second crib. Our apprehensions about separating them after so long proved ill-founded. With the cribs butted together perpendicularly, they slept all night without a peep the very first night. If you are trying to save a little bit of money at the beginning, or if relatives need an idea for a Christmas present, delaying the acquisition of crib number two may be right for you. If you do elect to wait for Crib #2, you can also hold off on the second round of sheets, bumpers, and mobile. However, if you want coordinating nursery décor, go ahead and register for all the stuff, and keep any second set items you receive in storage until the second crib comes into play.

Changing Tables

Rare is the occasion that both babies need to be changed or even can be changed at the exact same time. Unlike cribs, you will *never* need a second changing table. (However, like many other twin-management accoutrements, you may elect to purchase two if you anticipate needing one upstairs and one downstairs.)

Diaper Genie, Diaper Champ, or Diaper Pail

You're going to have to empty it twice as often, but you don't need a second defecation disposal system. Keep the smell contained in a single location.

Strollers

Here's one we botched it on. You *definitely* will need a double stroller, but you only need one. The sweet gal helping us with our baby gift registry encouraged us to get a single stroller in addition to the double, claiming there would certainly be times when mommy or daddy would be on the go with only one baby. When ours turned a year old, we realized we had used the single stroller exactly twice. In truth, I used it those two times just to use it. Do take a lot of time to select your double stroller. I was convinced I wanted a side-by-side model so both babies could face forward, and neither would be "behind" the other. Daddy said in-line would be wiser, and easier to navigate in and out of doors, through stores, etc. Hands down, he was correct. My suggestion? Treat the stroller acquisition process as you would a car purchase. Explore the floor models fully. Lift the stroller with and without car seats snapped in. Open the stroller from its closed position; and collapse it from its open position. See if you can get a good lifting hold and practice getting it from the floor to the height of your trunk or car/van hatch. (Lifting is something a pregnant woman should do with caution, so make this trip with your partner or a good friend, and consider putting them through the paces.)

Read *Consumer Reports*, and sleuth out customer reviews online. Invest in a model your car seats can snap in and out of; and then as they grow out of their car seats, they just sit in the stroller proper. I guarantee, as long as you're motivated, you'll be mobile sooner.

Diaper Bag

You'll need a big one because you'll be hauling close-to-double supplies; but you'll only need one bag. Make it a sturdy one. Ours has a long enough strap to hang over our stroller handle like a saddlebag. Very convenient. A front pocket can hold my wallet and keys (and lipstick on the rare occasion I am feeling glamorous), so I don't have to haul a purse around, too. Shop around and find one that fits your anticipated needs. Most hospitals give you a complimentary diaper bag per baby, courtesy of the formula manufacturers. They are pretty darned cute, and for short treks (or church nursery-type visits) they may come in very handy.

Playpens

As I am sure you are well aware, opinions on use of the playpen run the gamut. Our twosome love to have the space of their own. To me, the "cage" argument against them is unsound. Heck, a crib is far more cage-like than a playpen. Believe me, there will be waking hours when you need to pee, eat, empty the Diaper Genie, do laundry, etc. Having an area that is safe and fun for your babies is worth its weight in gold.

I certainly wouldn't encourage you to keep them in there for inordinately lengthy periods of time, but with two babies, you will have a need for occasional containment. Whatever you do, don't purchase two playpens. They take up a lot of space, and even though they are collapsible, you'll want to leave it up. If you decide to use one, be sure to get a full-size one. With two babies, they need the space. There are also products on the market called "Supergates" that allow you to create an enclosed space for the babies using snap together walls. If you take issue with the political correctness of a traditional playpen, or if you plain just can't find one you think is big enough, perhaps a Supergate system is for you. You can enclose an amazingly large space by just purchasing more of the snap together pieces. If you have plenty of available floor space, it's ideal. Pack 'n Plays are great for travel, and maybe even for a single child, but way too small for day-to-day twin use. We would recommend getting one, however. They come in very handy. Especially when visiting folks whose homes aren't baby-proofed. You can pop the twosome in for a limited time with some toys, and avoid chasing your babies all around your hosts' home. Likewise, the Pack 'n Play may be a model with a changing table accessory, making it even more practical for times away from home base. Like the second crib, you don't need to make the playpen/Supergate/Pack 'n Play purchase(s) right away. Once they are sitting up well on their own, usually around 7 months, that's the time. Not a bad item to register for if folks are throwing you a shower.

Swings/Exersaucers/Johnny Jump Ups

Again, these are items for the older babies. If you want, you can add bouncy seats to this list, but to me, two bouncy seats were a necessity from day one. You may find you want to invest in two swings, saucers, or Johnny Jump Ups (the springy jumpers you suspend from a doorway) if your babies love them, and you need to soothe or contain them frequently. But, like the playpen, all of these baby (and parent) luxuries consume space. Double sets of all of them are overkill. Consider secondhand stores like Once Upon a Child to get the item(s) you want to audition. If your babies both go crazy over a saucer, then consider the second. Our babies both adored the swing, and we still made do with one. Taking turns is a lesson that can never start too early with twins.

Cameras/Camcorders

People having only one baby invest in these. You are having two; you'll get twice the good out of 'em. You may use twice as much film and videotape, but that is a fairly small dollar item compared with the camera investment.

Bathtubs

Wet babies are slippery. It is preferable to wash one baby with two grown-ups. They can tag-team in the same tub. They can share the same tub toys. I wouldn't suggest they share simultaneous bath times on a regular basis until they are into the toddler stage. If you really want to, once they can sit up efficiently on their own (7 months or so), a double kitchen sink works just as well. Have the camcorder ready for that occasion.

CDs

If you haven't already, go ahead and start playing some of your favorite music to your twins, unless your favorite music comes with the "Parental Warning" labels, then think twice. In utero is not too early. Numerous studies indicate there may even be a benefit to very early exposure to classical music.

Videos/DVDs

Obviously, you don't want to overexpose/addict your wee twosome too early to the TV/video world. However, you will likely find yourself using educational pre-parentally viewed materials sooner than you'd think. In our house, we make use of them when babies are safely contained (playpen, high chairs), and mommy needs a shower. Don't overinvest . . . aim for twice the kids, half the viewing. Financially, you'll have two children maximizing the entertainment provided from a single source.

Books

Personally, I advocate investing in a doubled library of children's books when twins are on the way; not two copies of each specific title, but twice the selection you'd consider for a single child. However, reading material is not an imperative doubling. As they do with musical and visual stimulation, two babies can experience equal entertainment from a single "set." Each family needs to decide its personal "we don't need twice the supply, but we're going to anyway" indulgences . . . this is one of ours.

Vaporizer

If your twins are sharing a nursery, you can dodge purchasing a second humidifier. A vaporizer may seem to be one of those "wait 'til the need arises" types of items, but I'd heartily encourage you to have one (and only one) cool mist vaporizer waiting in the wings. Newborn nasal passages are ever so teensy, and since twins are often teensier than singletons, you can imagine the proportionately narrowed mucus paths. Better to keep the snotties loose and fluid and breathing as uninhibited as possible.

10

Twice the Wash, Twice the "Omigosh," and Twice the Butternut Squash

With twins, there are unavoidable doublings. Try to revel in all of them, especially the "Omigoshes" you'll receive from on-lookers when out and about with your precious babies. Twins are special, and as a mommy of twins, you are, too. When you are purchasing double of the below listed items, try to look on the bright side. At least you will get through each need stage almost simultaneously. Here are the items you'll need in bulk.

Formula/Breastmilk/Baby Food

Two mouths to feed, you can't chintz out here. Breastfeeding *can* work with twins . . . check out the breastfeeding chapters. If you can make it work, it's the healthiest choice for the babies, for you, and certainly for your wallet. If breastfeeding is not the route you decide to go, formula will do the trick just fine.

Most formula manufacturers offer special coupons and deals for parents of multiples. Get on those lists early in your pregnancy. Even if you intend to breastfeed, those companies distribute great developmental information on babies, and you never know. Best to be prepared. Likewise, once your babies are on solid foods, lots of coupons are available to mommies of twins. You'll still need to get double foodstuffs, but you can save a bit here and there.

Diapers, Wipes, and Booty Protective Creams, Salves, and Unguents

What goes in, must come out. Two bottoms, you can't chintz out here either. They need coverage. Many of the predominant diaper manufacturers put coupons in the newspaper regularly and offer coupons to moms of twins. Be forewarned. Even with coupons, the name brand diapers are *much* more expensive than off- and store brands. You can expect each baby to soil or wet 8 to 12 diapers a day for at least the first 2 months. Believe it or not, you *want* that. It confirms your babies are getting enough nutrition. You can do the math. You will go through 960 to 1,440 diapers in your first 60 days alone. We found off-brands (or less popular brands) to be just fine. We used off-brand petroleum jelly with each and every change and rarely had rear rashes. You'll figure out what works best for you. If friends ask what you need for the babies, you need diapers.

Car Seats

You can't leave the hospital without them. They can't share. Our twosome even needed to be "tested" in their car seats for stress prior to being released from the hospital. We have a hysterical photo of our daughter sleeping away in her car seat with electrodes and monitors attached all over her. From what I hear, not every hospital requires this test, but don't be surprised if yours does. For babies under age one, and under 20 lbs., the car seats must be rear-facing. (If your babies reach 20 lbs. prior to their first birthday, they still need to remain rear-facing. You'll then need to invest in "convertible" car seats that can go from rear- to front-facing, and accommodate heavier babies.) Most firemen will install the bases into your vehicle for you, ensuring they are safely and properly in place. Don't wait until late in your pregnancy to get this important task accomplished. Twins *can* and often do come early. Be ready.

Burpie Cloths

After each feeding, each baby will need burping. Often, baby burps travel with spit-up. Hopefully, you will have daddy or a second set of hands burping one baby while you burp the other. You'll need to protect yourselves from the burp cheese.

Even if you are handling burp duty single-handedly (which eventually you will have to) each baby deserves a fresh, cheese-free cloth. There are precious burp cloths out there that coordinate with bibs and outfits. If you get some as gifts, fantastic. For day-to-day and middle-of-the-night use, cloth diapers serve the purpose well. While on the subject of burping, let me digress. When your babies are small, you will probably not burp them over your shoulder as you usually see on TV. For the first 3 to 4 months, until they really get good neck control, it often works best to burp baby while he or she sits on your lap. Hold his or her jaw around the chin in one hand supporting the head, and firmly pat the baby's back with your other hand. We draped the burpie cloth over our hand supporting the head, and put the extra cloth over the leg toward which the baby was facing, just in case. Each baby gets a fresh cloth each burp session. You will need to feed babies approximately 8 times each 24-hour period the first couple of months. Get 20 to 30 cloths and you should be fine. You'll be doing laundry often enough for that to be about right. If you feel you need more, get more. You can always use them for dust-cloths or to mop up mini-messes later. Side note: Not a single book I read indicated when the parent-induced burping should stop. The "after-every-feeding" burping process continued for us until ours were about 6 months, and intermittently after that until they were about 8 months. Ours were exceedingly gassy. Yours may need regular burping for a shorter (or maybe longer) window of time.

Pacifiers-Binkies-Soothers

Two mouths. Both have a suck reflex and are soothed by the process. You'll need a minimum of two. If you plan to breastfeed your babies, some wisdom advocates holding off a bit on introducing the pacifiers until nursing/latching is well established. The phrase "nipple confusion" is one you will hear repeatedly. Personally, I don't believe in nipple confusion where a binkie is concerned. No nourishment flows through a pacifier; give your babies some credit. Now on the flip side, when a fast-flow bottle is introduced frequently prior to nursing/latching becoming well established, that may cause problems getting the babies to breastfeed. Not because they are "confused" between nipples but because the bottle nipple makes it far easier to get big mouthfuls of milk rapidly, and with minimal effort.

Baby Books

They are two children with two distinct sets of achievements to document and cherish. Granted, the babies may be in high school before you get a chance to fill them all in with the notes you've jotted in your poo journal and on notepads, but they each need to have their own book. There are twin sets of baby books out there if you are seeking to coordinate every aspect of their early lives.

High Chairs

Even though you can only place a single spoonful in one baby's mouth at a time, feeding your babies semisimultaneously by alternating bites betwixt the two is far easier than trying to feed them in sequence. Especially if you have one hungry infant watching while his or her sibling is being fed! High chairs serve purposes beyond feeding. They are great containment for finger painting, coloring, and for off-the-floor playing with small toys or books. Some favorite photos of our twins have been taken in their high chairs. Get a pair. You'll be glad you did.

Preparation and Regrouping Time

Two mouths to feed. Two sets of burps to provoke. Two babies to dress. A diaper bag that needs to be prepped to handle needs of two infants. Two car seats to snap in. Two babies to strap into the stroller. Two children to undress and redress at the pediatrician's office. Two cribs to keep in fresh linens. Two booties that need diapering. Two babies to individually hug and cuddle. Allow the extra time you need to do those things that must be done consecutively, one at a time. Attempting to "cram" too much activity into too little time will increase the stress on you, your partner, and your babies.

11

Maximizing Modern Mommy Marvels

Sisters, we are oh-so-lucky to become mommies of twins in this century. How Jacob and Esau's mom did it, I'll never know. At our disposal is an incredible array of resources, tools, and toys to make the daunting task of twin-mommydom easier. (Please note, I did not say "easy," but *easier*.)

One of the first things you should take advantage of while the babies are still in the pressure cooker is the Internet. If you have computer access, you will be able to garner information virtually on a daily basis of where your babies are developmentally. Websites such as www .babycenter.com, www.storknet.com, and www.babyzone.com, all have great tidbits on how quickly baby is growing. They also have links to companies that offer freebies to moms of multiples. Get on those Gerber, Beech-Nut, Similac, Enfamil, Carnation, Heinz, moms-of-multiples lists early! Even if you decide to breastfeed, the formula companies send great info on early life with baby(-ies). For twins, one of the best is www .twinstuff.com. Twins married to twins administer the site, and one of the couples is already parenting twins. You can participate in message boards while you are pregnant, and after. In those months when you are up at all hours (late in pregnancy/early postpartum), there at your fingertips is the wisdom of women who have trodden the same path. Granted, they may not have all the answers, or the answers you want to hear, but there is a tremendous amount of empathy and support. I wish I had discovered it sooner. Another site to check out is www.twinslist.org. This site has links to extensive twin info of all sorts.

You know you are on to something good when women of your mom's generation say, "I don't know how we managed to raise our babies without _____." Here is a short list of new, and some not-so-new, inventions to make you and your babies' lives a bit happier.

Disposable Diapers

Ecologically, they are a nightmare, there's no denying it. Prior to learning of our twin pregnancy, we were fully committed to the practice of cloth diapering. With twins, my idealism went straight into the Diaper Genie. If you do decide upon cloth diapers, my hat is off to you. Do be aware that the cloth diapers do need to be changed more frequently. Twenty-first-century technology has so honed the disposable diaper; the moisture is expeditiously whisked away from your babies' bums, minimizing the opportunity for rash development. (Don't use that as an excuse to change them infrequently!) In the early weeks, especially if you are breastfeeding, you need to determine if enough nutrition is getting into baby by counting the dirty diapers he or she produces. You should have 8 to 12 sullied nappies per baby, per day, the first couple of months. Do the math. We're talking a need for between 960 to 1,440 diapers and subsequent changes in the first 8 weeks alone. I'll say it again, if you go with cloth, kudos to you. Many twin parents have done it with great success; you just need to determine if that is one of your priorities.

Wipes

When my mom told me she and most others of her generation used washcloths, I was absolutely agog. I was under the misguided impression that baby wipes had been around forever. Not only do they wipe baby booty neatly, and sometimes fragrantly, they serve a myriad of purposes. Even once my babies are potty-trained, I am confident baby wipes will still be an active part of my child-raising supply kit. Many moms also swear by the electric *wipe warmer*.

Bouncy Seats

Before our babies were born, everyone said be sure to register for two bouncy seats. What? You have a two-story house? You'd better register for four!

Well, four might have been excessive; we made it A-OK with two. But, we definitely needed two. For us, the bouncy seats became not only a source of consolation during fussy times, but served as a mini-bassinet when our babies needed to sleep with their heads elevated. Guess what? If your babies get a cold, or spit up excessively in the early months, as was the case with ours, your pediatrician will want them to sleep with their heads elevated. Car seats will work, but bouncy seats are as comfy as those hotel beds that vibrate for a quarter. Be sure and get cloth-backed bouncies that envelop or cradle the baby to some degree. Stiff backs are impractical for small babies that are incapable of sitting up on their own. The seats all have a belt system that holds them securely in place, making it a God-send when you need one baby contained happily while you change/console/burp the other. The trick is to remember to turn off the vibrating motion when you extract the baby from the chair. Otherwise, you will be keeping Duracell and Eveready in high clover. (Keep a big stash of size D batteries standing by. It seems most baby accoutrements require size D.) We didn't retire our bouncy seats until our babies could sit up on their own and literally crawl out of them (at about 7 to 8 months). It was a sad day indeed.

Swings

These things are miracle workers. We had a model that went side-to-side as well as forward and back with a mere push and turn of a button. The side-to-side cradle motion worked wonders with ours. As a mother, try not to take it too personally if the swing soothes episodes that your arms may not. The consistent, rhythmic motion combined with a soft clicking sound (some even have music) is often enough to lull even the most stubborn of criers to sleep. You may want to invest in two, but you can certainly make it with one, especially if you have one of the aforementioned bouncy seats. Again, have a stockpile of size D batteries. Our babies were on the small side, and we did not get rid of our swing until they were 10 months old. However, be sure and follow all guidelines that come with your baby adventure products. Safety first, always.

Exersaucers

As soon as your babies have stabilized their heads on their previously incapable necks (usually by 4 months or so), exersaucers can provide entertainment galore. They have the opportunity for all sorts of sight and sound stimulation, as well as motivation to work on eye-hand coordination and standing skills. Do not use the saucers as a sole source of physical exercise. Babies need tummy time to work those necks, arms, and legs. Saucers are a cheery, colorful, non-size D battery-requiring supplement.

Jogging Strollers

Your babies may not be the only ones in need of sight and sound stimulation combined with physical exercise. For all-terrain twin travel and certainly for fitness fan parents, the jogging stroller serves multiple purposes. Available in a broad range of prices, you needn't feel guilty including a jogger on your twin registry.

Monitors

Believe it or not, at some point, you will feel confident enough to leave the babies in a room without you. However, you still want to hear what's going on in there.

Monitors provide you with the reassurance of their soft breathing through the night. More often, they provide the reminder that it's time to eat with soaring red lights corresponding to the ascending decibel level in the nursery. Video monitors are also an option for the modern mommy. Think about that investment carefully. If you can resist the urge to watch your babies dozing peacefully and sleep while they do, consider the purchase. There are certainly times when an "odd" noise through the audio-only monitor caused me to get out of bed and check in the nursery. More often than not, it was a noisy roll-over. A video monitor would have permitted me to look and roll over myself. But, knowing how precious my babies look sleeping, I never would have slept if I could have watched them instead.

Antibacterial Soap

With twins, the last thing you want to be doing between diaper changes is running to the bathroom to wash your hands. Keeping a pump dispenser of antibacterial/no-water-needed soap on the changing table has been really helpful. I also keep a vial in the diaper bag and one in the car. Don't use it on the babies, but for you, when you can't get to a sink for a legit hand washing, this is a great solution.

Small Top-Rack Basket for the Dishwasher

From pacifiers to sippy cup valves, lightweight, small items associated with day-to-day infant maintenance are easily sent drainward when randomly placed in the dishwasher. One of these inexpensive mesh boxes placed strategically in the corner of your dishwasher's top rack will save you unnecessary tiny-item retrieval calisthenics.

Dustbuster/Handheld Vacuum

Once crunchy solids enter the picture, crushed morsels of Cheerios, oyster crackers, Goldfish, pretzels, you name it, end up in a perpetual sandy, gritty mess under high chairs, in boosters, in car seats, smashed in the bottom of the diaper bag—in any and every tough-to-access area. Wet paper towels can only do so much. Go ahead and invest in one of these if you haven't already.

Boppy Pillows

Women who have single babies can effectively use these "C"-shaped overstuffed pillows as cozy nursing pillows. For tandem nursing twins, the Boppies are a bit too small; but did having two Boppies ever come in handy! The cradling shape of these pillows made them perfect impromptu resting places for the twins. Some of my favorite moments with our itty bitty babies were our morning naps on my bed. The three of us together formed a letter "B"; with my body as the long line, and the side-by-side Boppies, each with a baby therein, facing perpendicularly toward me. If you are bottle-feeding your twosome, the side-by-side Boppies make for a cozy dining arrangement while you hold the bottles in place and grin at them for the mealtime's duration.

EZ2 Nurse Twin Nursing Pillow or My Brest Friend Nursing Pillow

Designed with the intent of making tandem breastfeeding two infants easier and safer, these size-modified support pillows are a lifesaver for nursing twin moms.

Crib Tents

Sold as a safety measure for household with leaping cats, these baby bed toppers serve a secondary purpose. Not only are frisky felines denied access to your twins, but you can safely contain your climbing cuties. (Personal note: We discovered these too late in our household. Our daughter broke her wrist in her first attempt at crib-diving. If your twins show inclinations of evening escape, invest early.)

Harnesses (or Their Far Less Politically Correct, but Definitively Accurate, Name, Leashes)

Oh how our judgments of others justly come back to haunt us. While in my teens, I saw a mother using one of these on her child in a busy shopping mall during the holiday season. My mind was reeling in incredulous horror that this mother (who also had numerous other children with her) was employing such an animalistic restraint to keep her precious human child at a close proximity. Flash forward to when my two children are fully capable of walking, yet thoroughly incapable of self-restricted, singular direction movement in a stimulus-rich (and potentially predator thick) environment such as a mall or airport. Time to re-evaluate the use of harnesses as an effective method of keeping precious human children at a close proximity.

Although we prefer a double stroller for mobility, safety, and containment, I have profound respect and compassion for those moms who prioritize the safety of their offspring ahead of the quickly dispensed (and mommy-directed) judgments of the nonempathetic general public.

Rear-View Mirror Systems

Car seats for newborns and infants under 1 year and 20 lbs. must be rear-facing. Hmmm. If you are driving, that makes for some pretty death-defying contortions to confirm your babies are still breathing, which believe me, you'll want to confirm. God bless the genius who came up with the mirror system that can be positioned in front of your babies' faces (mounted on the back of the rear seats) so that with a mere flick of your rear-view mirror you can catch a quick glimpse of your wee cherubs. Please remember only to do the visual checks at stoplights and signs. You must concentrate on the road for the safety of your precious cargo. If you must, pull over. Or better yet, get into a parking lot to do a thorough midtrip check if necessary.

Cell Phones

Whereas this invention can be the bane of your existence, there is no substitute for the assurance of knowing you can call 911 whenever you need. With two babies in your car, a breakdown that would typically be just a whopping inconvenience becomes almost insurmountable, and potentially dangerous. If you are anti-cell phone, believe me, I can empathize. However, make the concession for your babies' sake.

The Drive-Thru Window

ATMs. Fast Food. Pharmacies. The Goodwill donation drop-off. God bless them, everyone. Now if someone could just come up with a way to do groceries at a drive thru, twin mothering would be a piece of cake. Well, maybe that's an exaggeration, but it would be nice. FYI: Krispy Kreme doughnut drive thru windows sell whole milk in pint containers. Once your babies can drink whole milk (not advisable prior to one year), the Krispy Kreme experience becomes a legitimized errand, not just an indulgence. Enjoy.

Pacifiers

Babies like to suck. Babies often cry because they want to suck. The gargantuan oversized babies you see on Maury Povich are a testimony to the fact that babies don't need to eat every time they want to suck. You put it together. Do try to wean them off the binkies by age two or earlier. According to many doctors, that's when the suck urge is no longer urgent.

Pacifier Leashes

Unless you have stock in Nuk, Avent, Mam, or whoever manufactures your babies' soother of choice, you'll want to keep the sucking device of glee inches away whenever you leave the house. If you don't have Mr. Sucky Joy somehow attached to a bib, car seat strap, or stroller belt, you'll lose him over and over. I would not however use the tethers at home, indoors. Bend over and get the exercise.

Answering Machine

If you feel guilty screening calls, get over it. Better yet, have your babies catterwalling (you and your husband can join in, too) on the greeting message. Folks will get the hint. You can call them back at some point when all babies are fed, diapered, burped, and when you've gotten some rest . . . right around when the babies turn one. Seriously, don't hesitate to put a "We really want to talk to you, but we have our hands full of twins" message on your machine. Call well-wishers back at a time of your convenience. Friends will certainly understand, so will family, God willing.

Oxi-Clean or Similar-type Laundry Supplement

Spit up. Poo. Bananas. Carrots. Blueberry buckle. Heaven forbid, the occasional blood. Your regular detergent needs support. Not that everything always comes out in the first washing, but you have a far better shot using a product like this.

Super Wal-Mart

If you can find somewhere else where you can economically get groceries, prescriptions, diapers, knock-around clothes, a hot dog, your taxes filed, and your hair cut, more power to you. Once you've got both babies cozily settled in the stroller, the ability to accomplish numerous tasks in one stop is priceless. Don't feel guilty. Take advantage of it.

Doors, Ramps, and Bathroom Stalls for Handicapped Access

Double strollers are a God-send, but they are space-consuming and sometimes unwieldy. Most shopping malls now have push-button activated automatic open doors for handicapped access. Certainly don't cut in front of someone who needs it due to disability, but make use of a convenience available to you. Even two or three stairs can be virtually impossible to navigate with a double stroller. Use ramps when possible. Never let your babies out of your sight. If you need to use a public restroom, wait for the larger, disability-equipped stall. Take your stroller into the stall with you. You'll be cozy, and the first time you do it, the babies will be very perplexed. Better safe than sorry. Truth be told, on the occasions when the stroller prevents me from closing the stall door, open it remains. Personal modesty takes a back-seat to baby safety. Resist the urge to ask a nice-seeming stranger to "keep an eye on them" while you pee. Resist the urge to accept when a nice-seeming stranger offers to "keep an eye on them." It is not worth the risk. *Do not* use handicapped parking places. You don't need them, people with disabilities do. As a matter of fact, you will often want to park far away from your destination, so you have a free parking place on either side, allowing you more room to maneuver the double stroller and your babies. Plus think of the extra exercise you will get.

Digital Ear Thermometers

Until your babies are two, the most accurate temperature readings are acquired via rectal thermometer. For those of us who are not too concerned about a tenth of a degree here and there, a digital ear thermometer is a delight. You only need one, and it may not provide the most exact reading, but is it ever a welcome alternative to its anally invasive fever-indicating counterpart. I never realized that when the babes are very young and can't fight you, a fairly accurate temperature can be taken by placing a digital thermometer in the baby's armpit. If you decide to call your pediatrician on the basis of a detected fever, be sure to alert him or her about which orifice produced the temperature reading, and what type of thermometer you were employing. (Important to note: Once a thermometer is used rectally, it should be a rectal thermometer for the rest of its existence. Each baby should have his or her own. Some things aren't meant to be shared.)

IV

At Last, the New Generation

12

A Labor Story

If you are anything like me, you probably skimmed this book to get to this point. Please make an effort to read the rest; but I agree wholeheartedly with you. Labor is where the rubber meets the road and certainly the aspect of twin pregnancy about which I was most curious. Here's my tale:

Dateline: September 4, 2001. At 36 weeks and 4 days, we were scheduled for our by then weekly check-in with my OB-GYN, Dr. Rinehardt, and an ultrasound with perinatologist (high-risk pregnancy specialist), Dr. Troyer.

Both babies (A and B) at this point had been head down for a couple of weeks. Ultrasound weight estimations between the two had always been fairly close, within a few ounces . . . until that Tuesday. On this fateful day, all skilled surveyors of the images were guesstimating approximately a 1-pound difference between Baby A/boy child and Baby B/girl child. Whereas I thought, "How sweet! He's a bulky boy and she's a delicate flower of a girl," Dr. Rinehardt was less amused. Although not too serious, a broadening weight discrepancy between twins can indicate a beginning trend toward one twin siphoning off more nutrition than is their fair share. Forty weeks is considered full term for a single birth, 37 weeks for twins. We were pretty dang close. As a matter of fact, we were told should labor begin on its own after 34 weeks, nothing would be done to stop or slow the process.

Dr. Rinehardt said, "It's time for us to start thinking about inducing these babies soon," and he left the examining room briefly for a tête-à-tête with Dr. Troyer. My husband, Scott, and I, heady with the reality of impending births, were discussing which birth date sounded better, when Dr. Rinehardt returned. Apparently "soon" is a very subjective term; he came in and chirped, "I'm on duty tonight. Go on home, get your bag, and let's bring those babies!" Holy smokes! We must have staggered out of the medical building and gotten to our car somehow, but I barely remember it. What I do remember vividly is getting home, the two of us grinning like idiots and making key calls to a few family and friends. As we walked out of the house to head back to the hospital, it hit me. The next time we crossed that threshold, we'd be a family of four. What an indescribable feeling.

We got to the hospital front desk, carrying all our insurance verifications. Sure I looked ready to pop, but I was smiling. (Note: I wasn't in labor yet!)

Now we loved our hospital, but our one negative experience came as a result of inefficiency (or lack of caring) by the individual who took our insurance information. My husband was suspicious right off the bat about how accurately our details were input into the hospital's computer system. His suspicions were justified. Believe me, the last thing you want mid-labor is for your hubby to have to leave your side to "clarify" admittance details. In a nutshell, take every card, letter, verification you have received from your insurance company to the hospital with you. We did, and we needed to show them repeatedly. Keep them in your "packed bag," or the glove compartment of the car you plan to take to the hospital. Better yet, make copies and keep a set in both locations. Bad enough if your man has to leave the room when you are in labor, Heaven forbid he need to leave the building!

Back to our story: 10 P.M. I was naturally 2 centimeters dilated, and almost fully effaced. (Side note: words like "dilated" and "effaced" become so frequently used during your pregnancy that you'll forget your nonpregnant friends and family may have no idea what they mean. Both refer to the status of your cervix, the membrane holding the babies in. Dilated is how "open" the membrane is; effaced is how "thinned" the membrane has become. For the metrically challenged, a centimeter is about the width of your fingertip.) Dr. Rinehardt was predicting we'd have our A and B before noon the next day. We were put into a Labor and Delivery Room, where monitors/sensor pads were belly-mounted to track Baby A, Baby B, and mommy—keeping an eye on everyone's blood pressure and stress levels. An IV shunt was attached to the back of my hand to be ready for any/all drugs to be administered. Except for the epidural (the anesthesia shot that desensitizes abdomen, pelvis, and gal parts), that one goes in your lower back, and much later in the game. After a short while, you feel like an octopus. Tubes seem to be coming out of you everywhere. A sensor was even attached through my vagina to the top of Baby A's head. There is a great pulse point atop babies' noggins. Even after your babies are born, you can often see their heartbeats through the top of their heads. The grandiose idea of having a "moving labor," where you can walk around and maybe even shower for comfort seemed pretty darned impossible. Shoot, even shifting slightly in the bed could be cause for readjustments of sensor pads in all their various and sundry locations around my body. The best part? The nurses didn't mind at all. Shift as you need to. You will want to do anything you can to alleviate discomfort, and if rolling to your side helps, do it.

After all our monitors and machines were attached, Baby A's water sac was broken, labor-inducing drug, Pitocin, was administered through the shunt, and the contractions began. Pitocin is not a "slow build" kind of drug. The contractions begin rapidly and magnify in strength quickly. As a first-time woman in labor, the big surprise for me was that my contractions felt like intense menstrual cramps. Of course at that point, it became obvious that I had been experiencing some mild contractions off and on the whole preceding weekend. The searing, knife-cut pains I had imagined, and that I had seen portrayed so vigorously on TV, didn't exist. However, they *do* intensify . . . and come more frequently. After all our Prepared Childbirth classes, I knew it wasn't advisable to get an epidural prior to a 4 centimeter or so dilation. So I started riding it out.

Keep in mind, with a twin pregnancy, almost every OB-GYN will heartily encourage you to have an epidural. Even if both babies are head down when labor begins, after the first baby is born, the second, who all the sudden has some room, can go breech or transverse (side to side). Baby B can also go into distress for whatever reason, and an immediate C-section may be necessary. My opinion? For your health, your comfort, and for the safety of the babies, don't be a hero. Get the epidural. As Vicki Iovine wisely illuminates in *The Girlfriend's Guide to Pregnancy*, no one is there to give out awards when the birthing process is done. You may as well be as comfortable as possible . . . and she is talking about *single* births.

Midnight. So there I was, at long last, laboring away, watching the intensity of each contraction form its individual bell curve on the bed-side ticker-tape printout. Feeling pretty uncomfortable to put it mildly. I had to stay on one side or the other throughout the bulk of my labor. As we discovered when I nearly passed out in our Non-Stress Test, the weight of the babies and uterus contents was substantial enough to cut off my circulation if I lay on my back. So on my side it was. The only real relief I could experience was my husband pushing his fist with all his force into the small of my back during contractions Bless him, he tried to remember the exact placement between contractions, but the relief spot would move. One of my clearest labor memories is of me grabbing his fist and shifting it, perhaps a wee bit violently, to coincide with the pressure point. The romantic hand massages and eye-to-eye gazes I had imagined seemed ludicrous mid-labor.

1 A.M. or so. Feeling pretty rough. The nurse offers me Stadol. She assures me it is a totally safe drug that will "take the edge off and feel like I have had a couple of cocktails." I'm game, and into the hand IV shunt it goes. A couple of cocktails? For me, it was like a bad keg party. Literally, I had bed spins. The edge of labor was off temporarily, but I was miserable. (However, don't use my experience with Stadol as your sole perspective. Most women I know were thrilled with the relief it provided; it just wasn't good for me.)

1:30 A.M. The bell curves on the printout kept getting higher and higher, and coming more and more often. Determined not to be a wimpy "Give-Me-the-Drugs-Prior-to-4-Centimeters-Mommy," I looked at the clock and was determined to hold off on being measured again until 3:00 A.M. Looking at the clock became fixation on the clock. The "focal point" framed photo of Scott and I in Vegas never made its way out of our bag. The clock had my total attention. Our nurse had departed our room for a delivery in progress and had other nurses checking in on me. No doubt you have heard it already, but labor and delivery room nurses are amazing, amazing women (and men). One of my "check-in nurses" arrived to find me weeping slightly around 2:30 P.M. or so. Plus, I was experiencing uncontrollable shivers, the teeth chattering kind; but I wasn't the least bit cold. (Unbeknownst to me pre-labor, nerves, adrenaline, drastic hormonal fluctuations, all can cause pronounced shivering/chattering. Don't be alarmed if you vi-brate mid-labor like I did. You're normal.) She went back and told our designated nurse, who had at this point wrapped up the delivery she was assisting and was cleaning up. At 3 A.M., they measured me, and I was 10 centimeters, ready to deliver! Dr. Rinehardt, rather than whisking us off to the emergency room as we had been told was protocol with twins, said, "We're going to do this here!" Bless him. In came the double fleets of neonatal intensive care unit (NICU) personnel, isolettes (incubators/baby warming boxes), and delivery paraphernalia. We pushed a few times so I could feel the muscle groups required to do the job. The anesthesiologist was roused from his slumber at no doubt the most dreaded hour of the night to perform the epidural, which he did bleary-eyed, but marvelously. Yes, the needle is daunting. Yes, you have to be immobile, often during a contraction, to receive it. With the pain you will likely be in at the time the epidural is administered, the needle will look like nothing. Plus, you know it holds relief.

Between pushes, I had to roll on my side to ease my aforementioned circulation challenges. So I would push, on my back, to a slow count of 10, and roll over onto my side until the next contraction began. Be forewarned. When you push down in your nether-regions, all the muscle groups down there are next-door neighbors. With my first push, I wee-weed a parabolic stream that my husband still giggles about. Many, if not most, women poo on the table as well. Now is not the time for modesty. Believe me, your doctor and delivery staff have probably seen far worse than you are capable of, so don't let that worry you.

Scott and I were starting to get a little giddy with excitement, thinking the 8 A.M. status calls we had promised friends and family might actually become birth announcements. No such luck. After a few rounds of pushing, Dr. Rinehardt came back in. (Note: The doctor doesn't spend all the pushing time with you. He or she will check in during the pushing and will be there for the entry into the world of your twosome.) Looking at my cervix, he said it seemed to be closing slightly, and there was no reason to make Baby A push through quite yet. Out go the fleets of NICU folk. Into the shunt goes some more Pitocin. Epidural kicked up a notch, and encouragement followed from all to "try and nap." We rested a bit; Scott claims he actually slept some. I enjoyed watching the contraction bell curves ascend to heretofore unseen heights almost pain free.

Around 9:30 A.M., started getting a bit uncomfortable again. New nurse Ginny on duty measures and checks, and we are ready to push again. Dr. Rinehardt agrees.

By 10:00 A.M., we were pushing. And pushing and pushing. My right leg seemed to have collected more than its share of the epidural juice, and was so numb it had to be lifted into the stirrup each pushing session after I rolled onto my back. I was a comical sight.

After many of the pushes, I was offered oxygen. I think it helped. Even if it didn't help physically, psychologically, the regularity of the roll to back, take deep breath, push to 10-count, exhale deep breath, roll to side, suck on oxygen seemed like a nice rhythm. The rhythm would have to do, since my idea of burning a vanilla scented candle was out of the question with oxygen tanks in the room. Who knew? Thankfully, my husband brought some of our favorite music to play.

By 11:00 A.M., I was back to fixating on that clock. Surely by 11:30 A.M., our boy would be here. Surely by 11:45 A.M. Surely by noon. Hadn't Dr. Rinehardt said noon? My stamina was diminishing. Instead of pushing to 10-counts, we began pushing in two sets of 8-counts each contraction. Surely by 12:15 P.M. I was getting pretty tuckered. All the nurses and Dr. Rinehardt kept bolstering me up with how great each push session was. If so, why wasn't he here yet? I leaned to Scott and sought a second opinion. Was our boy's head even visible? He assured me it definitely was. He saw hair, and it wasn't mine. Dr. Rinehardt said our boy was wedged in there pretty good, and if all that pushing wasn't getting him through, he needed to "guide" him out with forceps. No, it wasn't scary. At this point, he needed to greet the world. Out come these much larger than imagined, but beautifully designed Williams-Sonoma-esque tongs. In our Prepared Childbirth class, we were told that a mirror is positioned to allow the mother a visual of the birth. In multiple births, not necessarily so. At no point were we offered a mirror to watch the births, and I am confident that was a good thing in our case. I do have a hypervivid memory of a reflection in the wall-mounted TV screen when the forceps were placed in the birth canal. Scott was a trooper. Hopping between views of the birth and reassurances to me. Pretty quickly it became obvious why the tongs are called "force-ps," not "guide-rs." Dr. Rinehardt used Herculean strength, and at 12:34 P.M., our son was born. Our boy was placed on my chest briefly, Scott cut the cord (which he said felt like celery), and our A-Child was whisked away to be cleaned up and Apgar tested.[1] We started to push for our daughter, also known as B-Child. My cervix began to start closing again! Then it happened. I began dry heaving. (You don't eat or drink anything during labor but ice chips.) Dr. Rinehardt said, "Go with that!" Apparently, my push muscles had given out. The miracle of creation provided a secondary set of muscles to get our girl. Dry heaving continued, and by 12:41 P.M., our daughter was born. Both babies were out, but we still had placentas and all sorts of uterine goo to extract from my gal parts. And of course, my ever-modest cervix *really* started to close when the babes were both out. My hubby, who wasn't squeamish at all through the process, looked to see Dr. Rinehardt almost up to his elbow extracting remnants of the birthing process. That got to him a bit. Another reason I heartily endorse that epidural. After mommy's uterine cavity was cleared, the babies weighed and Apgar tested, daddy and I finally had a misty moment. Realizing the magnitude and miracle of the birthing process is overwhelming. You always hear of "death-bed" conversions of faith. You can't tell me that a "birth-bed" doesn't inspire you to an even greater degree.

Shortly, the two sweet, clean, swaddled, greasy-eyed babies were brought to us. Absolutely precious. Have your camera ready.

The Double Daddy Perspective

All birthing stories are amazing, unique, and indescribable, yet they all share one thing in common: You have absolutely no control. No matter what happens during the course of your twins' arrival, rest assured that you will be taking the most thrilling roller coaster ride of your life!

The night after our twins were born, a dear friend of ours took my husband out for a celebratory meal, and to get the real skinny on the birthing experience. His advice to her, "Stop watching 'A Baby Story'! It's more like an outtake from 'Gladiator.'" Whereas I think his assessment was a little gorier than reality, by no means is the experience as pristine and clean as TV mini-documentaries would have you believe. (Writer's Note: Let me say right now, I enjoy "A Baby Story." However, don't think for a second that you will be done and home with your babies in 30 minutes.)

Every labor story is different, single or multiple births. Aspects of my labor experience were picture-perfect. Others, obviously, not so much. Your story will have the same balance of pros and cons. Your labor story will be yours and yours alone. Share it with those who need to hear the positives. Share it with others so they'll see you made it through the negatives. The end result (and in your case, *results*) makes it all worthwhile. You will never in your life be more convinced of, and feel an active part in, the miraculous cycle of life.

So you've read the unabridged version of a twin labor/delivery and want your partner to have some preparatory insight, but doubt he'll plow through that lengthy description?

Here's the condensed, "Breeder's Digest" version.

We began with an unexpected induction, followed by the tossing away of predicted circumstances and environment, a surprising revelation of what contractions actually felt like, a determined not-to-be wimpy lady in labor, tears, bad drugs, good drugs, an ever-supportive husband, false alarm pushing, cervix closing, fourteen hours of labor (two ardently pushing), clock staring, a numb leg, laughter, oxygen, forceps, a son born, brief meeting, more pushing, dry heaving, a daughter born, brief meeting, cervix determined to close, hard-fought afterbirth retrieval, gynecological embroidery, cleaned/Apgar tested/greasy-eyed babies returned, full family hug and photo, and at last, more tears. Daddy passes two suggested names on a piece of paper to mommy. Perfect. More laughter. Lives changed forever—in 14 short hours.

Note

1. The Apgar test is administered to babies at both 1 minute and 5 minutes after their birth. The test gauges the baby's color, respiration, heart rate, muscle tone and reflexes. The 1-minute test assesses how the baby fared during the birthing process; the 5-minute test determines how the baby is coping with the outside world.

13

You, in the Hospital, Postpartum

They're out. Your body is housing only your own organs now. It's a weird feeling after the past 9 months. The delicious anticipation of your babies' arrival has likely kept you from entertaining what physical and emotional feelings you will have immediately after you deliver your twins. In retrospect, I wish I had known more about what to expect in those very early days.

Your abdominal skin and your uterus have stretched to a phenomenal degree. All of the sudden, the catalysts for that expansion have evacuated. Your skin and uterus have remarkable elasticity, but they don't retract immediately. Within a very few hours after delivery, a representative of the nursing squad will be in for your first "abdominal massage." Don't let the word "massage" fool you. It's not at all pleasurable. In fact, for me, it was quite painful; but it is necessary. It looks like they are kneading dough, and your belly flesh undulates in waves. If you have had a cesarean, my guess is the nurses are a little more merciful around your incision. If your babies came out vaginally, it's no-holds-barred.

Amazingly, your uterus takes only a few hours to return to its prepregnancy pear/fist size. Your loose tummy skin? Well, that can take longer. You will have periodic abdominal massages throughout your hospital stay, and I was heartily encouraged to do a few upon my return home.

If you deliver one or both of your babies vaginally, chances are, you will have an episiotomy (small vaginal incision to ease the babies' delivery) or you will "rip." Either way, your girl parts are uncomfortable those first few days. I will never forget a sweet nurse coming in to check on my "third degree." Had I been burned amidst all the goings-on down there? Nope. Apparently, vaginal rips are categorized by length. (FYI: A third degree equals a vagina to rectum tear. Again, hurray for the epidural.) I remember Dr. Rinehardt embroidering away in the immediate minutes after Darren and Sarah's birth. Nurses will regularly check on your stitches, however many there are. They will also share with you the joys of the peri-bottle and sitz bath to ease your discomfort and aid your healing.

A peri-bottle resembles a diner-style ketchup bottle, from which you can squirt a narrow, steady stream of water. With each urination, you are to fill that bottle with warm H_2O, and squirt it all around the perimeter of your war wounds. It is cleansing and soothing. You take your peri-bottle home as a party favor and are to continue the process throughout your early days home.

The sitz bath consists of a basin-shaped, plastic toilet seat liner and a vinyl bag resembling an enema bag. You submerge your privates in the plastic basin filled partially with warm water. You will have prefilled the vinyl bag with very hot water, elevated it above the basin. Incrementally, you release hot water into the basin, warming your parts. Personally, I was healing very rapidly, and had minimal discomfort with my stitches and swelling. The sitz bath apparatus goes home with you, and you are encouraged to continue the process numerous times a day at home. I didn't, and I lived to tell the tale. However, other moms I have spoken with swore by the sitz. Follow your doctor's advice, and do what your body tells you. If it's soothing for you, do it.

Some additional party favors from the hospital that you will likely use in your first days postpartum are hemorrhoid ointment and Tucks pads. Don't be a martyr. Use them.

Emotionally, all sorts of things are happening to you. You're tired and want to sleep desperately. You feel guilty needing to sleep, thinking you should be doing the maternal thing and hovering over your newborns 24-7. Your husband needs to go out of the room on occasion and maybe even home for a shower, and you feel deserted. If you are breastfeeding, and the babies don't take to it right away, you think they are rejecting you, or that something is wrong with your milk. You are panicky that all the visitors to the hospital are already convinced you are suffering from postpartum depression. Calm down. Chances are; you are not. You are feeling the overwhelming tag-team of major life change and hormonal seismic shift, and it can be pretty scary.

In all your Prepared Childbirth classes you are warned of the signs of postpartum depression. The syndrome is extremely real and very dangerous. Those classes, and some of your pregnancy medical books address it at length. Do be aware of the warning signs, and be vocal if you think for even a moment you may be suffering from PPD.

A standout hospital memory for me was the sudden revelation that everyone, even doctors and nurses, has strong, and often differing, opinions on how newborns should be handled.

Many nurses wanted to give our twosome formula to supplement their first few nursing sessions. One nurse wanted to give the babies glucose (sugar) water. Some nurses insisted pacifiers cause "nipple confusion." Others encouraged them. One doctor felt they were having too much difficulty regulating their body temperature. Another felt they were doing well in that department.

For me, as a first-time mommy with twins only hours old, it was somewhat distressing to discover that amongst the most learned and most experienced of baby handlers, there was no universally accepted set of "correct" answers.

In retrospect, I should have been thrilled to see the diversity of thought and practice. Surely if those who daily tend newborns in the hospital have such varied beliefs as to "best care," mommy deserves some slack in deciphering what works best for her family.

14

You, at Home, Postpartum

Upon leaving the hospital, I was sent home with a compendium of literature on how to monitor my own recovery and smoothly transition into motherhood. In the hours prior to my hospital discharge, I was visited by various representatives of the hospital staff, each delivering a highly congratulatory but clearly too-oft-repeated lecture on the first days home as a woman freshly delivered of child—or in my case, child*ren*. Each rapid-fire talk concluded with my signature on a document confirming my acknowledgment of the pivotally important information dispensed. Most of the mini-lectures' directives and warnings seemed fairly predictable.

"If you are still weepy and abnormally emotional after two weeks, touch base with us."
     (Red flag: Postpartum depression)
"If your breasts are inordinately tender or red, touch base with us."
     (Red flag: Clogged ducts or mastitis)
"If you run a fever of 101 degrees or higher, touch base with us."
     (Red flag: Infection)
"If you have pain when peeing, touch base with us."
     (Red flag: Infection)

"If your bleeding/discharge becomes foul-smelling, touch base with us."
(Red flag: Infection)

Other medically dispensed dictates regarding my maternal upkeep were thoroughly unexpected. The unanticipated morsels all seemed to start with an ignorance-confirming " . . . and of course . . . "

" . . . and of course, only two daily trips up and down stairs for the first week."

(Why? To minimize wear and tear on incisions for those moms who've had a C-section, and to reduce the likelihood of increased bleeding/strained stitches for vaginal deliverers.)

" . . . and of course, don't drive."

(Why? If you're on pain-killers, heavy machinery operation is always ill-advised. Even if not, you may be experiencing some moments of wooziness. Applying pressure with your feet to drive can cause unexpected, and in some cases extreme, abdominal discomfort.)

" . . . and of course, don't lift anything heavier than your babies for the first 2 to 3 weeks."

(Why? Over-exertion can increase vaginal bleeding or strain C-section incision.)

" . . . and of course, you can expect to bleed and have significant discharge vaginally for 4 to 6 weeks . . . just call in if any clots are bigger than golf balls."

(Why? The duration of the postpartum bleeding shouldn't seem too daunting; it almost seems penance for having dodged a period for the preceding months. But golf ball-sized clots? Call the doctor to make sure all is well.)

" . . . and of course, don't get shampoo or soap on your breasts . . . water only."

(Why? Nursing moms learn quickly that their new babies are sensitive to elements barely perceptible to us as adults. If you elect to breast-feed your twosome for more than a very few days, you'll eventually want to shampoo. Afterward, rinse your breasts to excess.)

" . . . and of course, no tub baths for 2 to 4 weeks."

(Why? Unless your tub is spic and span, [and how often could you clean it when you were superlatively pregnant?] best to avoid the prolonged exposure to dirty bath water and potential infection.)

" . . . and of course, no tampons. Maxi-pads only for the duration of your postdelivery bleeding and output."

(Why? The postpartum aftermath needs an uncluttered escape route. Biology is naturally evacuating the dual birth residue for a reason; for your health's sake, don't force it to stay in longer. The uterine expulsion is *not* the equivalent of a typical monthly cycle.)

" . . . and of course, no sex for the first 4 to 6 weeks."

(Why? You need to heal . . . abdominally and/or vaginally. With two new infants in-house, your sleep urge will likely supercede your sex urge anyway. Trust me.)

You have accepted and absorbed the directives of the medical team and are now ready to embark upon "real-world" life with twins. In your first days home as a new mom, you will vacillate from feeling besieged to blessed, challenged to cheerful, high-pressured to happy. Don't be surprised when both your physical and emotional sense of well-being cycle erratically between the positive and negative, even on a minute-to-minute basis. Physically, you may feel fantastic and simultaneously perceive yourself to be an emotional wreck. Your emotional highs may be incongruously paired with your physically depleted lows. Other times your body and mind will submerge at once and then alternately soar in tandem.

What physical occurrences can you expect to confront in your first days home after your twins' births?

Regardless of the path of entry your twins used to greet the world, their point of exit is going to be a source of discomfort for you. Don't over-exert. Care for and treat your injured areas according to your doctor's orders until you are fully healed. If you are in pain, use whatever medications your doctor has prescribed to get you over "the hump."

Whether or not you plan to breastfeed, the delivery of your twins is going to precipitate biology-predetermined changes in your breasts. To restrict or discontinue lactation, listen closely to your doctor's advice. Alert him or her to any difficulties or unexpected discomfort you may feel. If you are breastfeeding, your nipples are thrust to the front line, and are probably going to be sore for the twin-magnified duress of those earliest feedings. The soreness will decrease. For your comfort, and for the babies' ease, you may need to use nipple shields in the first days. The shields resemble shallow funnels, pushing your milk-filled breast away from the nipple, and allowing the babies access to a greater length of unobstructed nipple. As the twins suck effectively, you will experience powerful postpartum contractions combined with heavier vaginal bleeding. Another one of nature's amazingly linked processes to get your uterus back to its prepregnancy size. Postpartum contractions may happen randomly in the first days after delivering your babies, but do not be caught off-guard by the intensity of the contractions while nursing. Looking at the bright side, the more intense the contractions, the more effective the uterine shrinking. More pain, more gain.

Maybe it is hormonally based, or perhaps your priorities are focused elsewhere, but the desire to eat for many new twin moms is almost nonexistent. If you find yourself amongst the noneating, try to always have healthy nibble foods within reach. If you must, force yourself to eat, especially if you are breastfeeding, as the twins are getting a tremendous amount of nutrition via your milk bar.

Of course, the converse may be true. The babies whose growth previously kept you feeling constantly "full" have vacated your bodily premises. You are suddenly "empty," and potentially famished. If heartburn and indigestion prohibited you from eating with any sense of satisfaction during your pregnancy, your postpartum days may be a glorious reintroduction to the joys of eating. Bon appétit!

Gradually and almost imperceptibly during your twin pregnancy, you adjusted your balance to accommodate the presence of your growing (and weighty) babies in utero. Not so gradually, your balance will need to adjust after the twins' birth. Expect yourself to be clumsy and awkward while you reacclimatize to personal/independent mobility without the two babies on board. In the week following Darren and Sarah's birth, I regularly stubbed my toes on bedposts and radiators and frequently fumbled to steady myself when repeatedly overestimating the energy required to rise from bed, or even a chair. "Mystery bruises" (and some not so mysterious) were a major facet of my plural postpartum appearance. One day you will wake up and discover you're "back to normal," but it did take days—for someone like me who is somewhat deprived of natural grace, it took a couple of weeks.

The Double Daddy Perspective

Not to scare the husbands and annoy the women but fellas, you are screwed! The twin mommy you now share your home with feels as if the weight of the world is on her shoulders and nothing she can do is good enough. Her hormones are raging *and* she's exhausted. The best you can do is to be a gentle coach and remind her of the big picture, get some food down her throat and just *be there* to help or to listen or to agree or just to hug.

As part of your labor preparation, your doctors and prenatal class instructors likely advised you to practice daily Kegel exercises. Kegels are performed by repeatedly tightening and releasing the muscles at the floor of your pelvis (the exercise equates the squeezing motion to halt a stream of urine). If your twins are delivered vaginally, in the days following their arrival, you quickly understand the purpose of pretoning that specific area. With a sneeze, a cough, a case of the hiccups, or even a hearty laugh, small amounts of pee might escape. Similarly, the length of time poo could be "held" prior to releasing was diminished significantly. In those first few days at home, don't be surprised to find yourself rushing bathroom-ward often.

Even though the opportunities you have to sleep may be limited, be ready to experience "night sweats" when you do doze. The extreme hormonal downshift following your twins' births may bring on symptoms typically associated with menopause; night sweats amongst them (heightened emotions and hot flashes being others). When I awoke on our third night home totally drenched, I was momentarily fearful all urinary tract control was lost. Of course a rapid assessment of my full-body moistness (especially around the collar of my PJs) quickly eliminated pee as a source of the soaking. The prolific perspiration sessions disappeared entirely within the first month home.

New twin moms often are discouraged when their postdelivery bodies don't resume their prepregnancy shape and weight immediately following their twins' births. Give yourself time. You need to heal physically and recuperate from the trauma of delivery. If you are breast-feeding, don't even *think* about dieting until you are done nursing. As the days and weeks pass, you *will* find weight coming off. You will get more exercise than you realize in your day-to-day activity caring for twinfants. For me, the loss of leftover pregnancy weight was far less of a concern in those first days home than my fixation with returning my engagement ring and wedding band back to their rightful place on my still-swollen finger. My rings were kept on the dresser; and in the first week home, I obsessively tested them daily to see if they could be forced on. As soon as my knuckle allowed, I immediately forced my husband to put them back on. (Crazy? Perhaps. I'm the first to admit my semilunacy in the first days home. Remember your unusual hormonal situation and remember your particularly curious eccentricities will fade with your body's hormonal re-regulation.)

Oddly enough, with all the corporeal inadequacies of postpartum life, most new twin moms will experience windows of perceived physical superiority in the days after their babies' births. The magnitude of what has been accomplished bodily invokes a Rocky-esque sense of "I can do anything." Taking the heavy bags of diapers to the supercan, performing biceps curls with a baby-laden car seat carrier in each hand, extracting the double stroller from the trunk . . . all seemed paltry manifestations of my newly discovered, superhuman twinvincibility. Despite the understandable temptation, please wait until you have healed fully to don your "Supermom" cape!

Emotionally, what is in store for you as a new twin mom at home? The overwhelming sense of anticipation you felt during your pregnancy is replaced with overwhelming sense of accountability postpartum. To this point, you've been medically supervised and supported. Your twins have been in the hands of doctors and nurses who, to your perception, reflexively knew by rote the "right thing to do." Now, like heading off to college, you are entrusted with not only your own preservation but the twins' protection and management. Liberated and free, yet terrifyingly responsible for your own actions. Relax. You are ready and you are capable; they wouldn't turn you loose otherwise.

Your plural pregnancy paranoias have now evolved into nervousness with numerous newborns. When the babies cry, you are fearful something major is wrong. When they are sleeping, you are compelled to scrutinize (or in my hyperanxious case, place a hand on) their chests to confirm they are rising and falling with breath and at an appropriate rate. Any unusual physical markings, temporary afterbirth anomalies (pointy heads/crooked faces), or curious movements have you convinced an underlying long-term repercussion may result. As a twin mom, you are simultaneously blessed and cursed with the ability to *compare* infant breathing rates, severity of cries, and other "oddities" by virtue of having two in-house. To top it off, you feel guilty spending so much time superficially analyzing each baby at length, convinced you are not directing your time and efforts toward the legendary "bonding" of the first few days with your babies. Guess what? Forgive yourself. Your overwrought protectiveness and anxious attentiveness are pluperfect examples of how connected (dare I say "bonded"?) you already are to these two innocent, fully dependent-upon-you babies. No, your "bonding" at this point isn't the saccharine-sweet, soft-focus visual idealized baby formula commercials, but it is genuine, and undeniable.

Your partner or spouse and visiting family and friends are swaddling and rocking and cooing and diapering their hearts out. All your support systems are standing at the ready to help in any way they can in your first days home with the twins. Good for you! You've scheduled the assistance strategically, and now that the twins are here, you are keenly aware of how truly valuable and needed their support is. Here's the irony: You feel *awful* accepting their help. In your mind you can't shake the self-condemnation that every aspect of the babies' care is ultimately *your* responsibility. Guess what? It is—but wisely, you did your prework. Your twins *are* being cared for. You (in concert with the babies' daddy, the other consummate responsibility bearer) are the one(s) who has coordinated the twins' home-assimilation team. You *are* handling every aspect of your twins' care, whether with your own hands or alongside those who you've lovingly enlisted to serve a supportive role in your twins' early lives. Bid good riddance to ill-founded guilt.

After some introspection, you've acknowledged that you can't do it all alone. You are finally okay with that. Now, you are apprehensive about the perceptions of others. Sleep irregularities exacerbate personal paranoia. Makeup? Showers? They've likely descended a notch or two on your daily priorities hierarchy. Does a perceived "lack of caring about personal appearance" send up a flare for onlookers that you're suffering from postpartum depression? Someone is always at the house helping with the babies' care. Will visitors assume new twin mom is slacking off, or worse, incapable of dealing with the double duties of her twin infants solo? Are people who come to call calculating the time you spend with each baby, and subsequently have decided you treat your new twins inequitably, or worse, that you favor one baby over the other?

Let it all go. Your imaginings are in all likelihood without foundation. You have far more important ways to spend your time and energy than postulating on the minds of others.

You have scheduled your support team to a tee. You have learned to dismiss the questioning/hyperconcerned looks of those who are seeking a sensationalistic tidbit of gossip for the coffee shop circle. You are on top of your twin mommying game. Get ready for the curve balls. You're too tired to go and order birth announcements. You need to supplement your babies with a bottle or two of formula when your breast milk comes in slower than your pediatrician would like. Your babies are gassy and need to sleep with their heads elevated in bouncy seats instead of in their preciously bedecked crib. You can't go up and down stairs more than once or twice a day, so impromptu guests are entertained in your bedroom surrounded by double the burpie cloths, Boppy pillows, and yet-to-be-rinsed breast pump funnels. Relax. When things don't transpire as "planned," you are not a failure as a twin mommy. Embrace flexibility.

When I envisioned our "homecoming with twins," my mind's eye pictured a clear, crisp September day, complete with blue skies and puffy white clouds. Embrace flexibility. We returned home with our twins under the cover of darkness. Having been told by the hospital staff that the "first night home" is in most instances a sleepless one (even with a single child), we decided to enjoy the last vestiges of support from the medical staff during the daylight hours and handle our first night home with greater energy. And greater energy we had. Our poo journal entries are written neatly and completely; "completely" meaning that each baby's name was written out fully: "Darren Jacob" and "Sarah Jane." As the days passed, and the effects of insufficient sleep compounded, our poo log reveals our children's names were abbreviated to a mere (and scrawled) "D" and "S." Embrace flexibility.

Not only are you being discharged from the hospital with the responsibility to care for and enjoy your new twins, but you are exhorted to care for and heal yourself in those first days at home. Do not disregard the admonishments of your medical team. Naturally, you need and *want* to care for your twins tirelessly; but neglecting to care for yourself will result in a physically and emotionally impaired mom who cannot serve her new role to the best of her ability. Lackadaisical self-denial no longer affects just you, but your entire family. Maternal martyrdom is grossly selfish. Intentionally allocate time (however brief) and make a concerted effort to care for yourself; it may be the most selfless thing you can do.

15

The Days of Haze: The First Few Weeks

Fresh out of the womb, twins need feeding every 2½ to 3 hours, doctor's orders, no ifs ands or buts. Every 3 hours, 24-7. After each feeding, two babies need burping, diapering, holding, consoling, loving, stimulation, and sleep. Three hours pass quickly when you hope to grab 20 to 30 minutes of sleep every rotation. Sometimes, you don't get any sleep. You can't find a window to enjoy leisurely time with your babies, spouse, and visiting family and friends. You are scarily sleep-deprived and functioning on autopilot, yet you have never felt greater responsibility in your life. That combination makes for some difficult days. Especially when you fantasized so lovingly about the early days with your precious twins. Your situation is not at all atypical but impossible to imagine until you are living it.

Not until my twins were born did it become patently obvious why in times of war, sleep deprivation was routinely practiced as a method of torture. Throughout this book, I have sought (and will continue) to accentuate the underheralded positives and attempt to eliminate the overly publicized negatives of twin parenting. In the instance of the first weeks at home with newborn twins, remember this positive: Each day that passes, though you may not realize it while in the throes, you are gaining more experience and familiarity with your twinfants.

Subsequently, the days/weeks of utter exhaustion and round-the-clock feelings of incompetence are finite.

The idea of truthfully and universally trying to describe those first weeks home with newborn twins seems futile. Like a feeble attempt to define "love," each individual's experience is uniquely his or her own, blurred by the intoxication of monumental life-change enrobed with emotion. Add sleep deprivation and fresh physical trauma to the mix, and you have quite a potent cocktail: a concoction capable of causing memory lapses—bordering on blackouts—when trying to piece together the actual events that transpired during those giddy "under the influence" days.

Some people rightfully assert that as humans, we mentally block memories too painful to recall. If you want to view the earliest days with your twins that way, surely that's your prerogative.

When I hearken back to those daze-filled days, I prefer to liken them to similar excitement and emotion obscured memories of life's most pivotal moments: the first day of school, a baptism, a graduation, a wedding day. With personal commitment clearly at the fore, each of those events initiates us into a broader, richer, lifetime ahead. Your days of haze with your new twins are no different.

What is another common thread of those future-defining events? The surrounding, supportive presence of those you love most, who love you most . . . those same special people who will undoubtedly love your twins.

Let those same key individuals in your life offer any and all legitimate (not just holding the babies) help they can.

Fearful you won't be able to remember any of those precious irreplaceable first days with your babies? How do we remember other important occasions made fuzzy in our minds by emotion, hard work, and even chaos? Take photographs. Take notes. Take the time to stop, breathe, and savor a minute here and there. You'll be thankful you did.

When does it get easier? Honestly, each day is a leap toward easier times ahead.

One day, I woke up, and it was as if a curtain had somehow lifted. Whether the twins suddenly just "got easier," or if suddenly repetitive practice managed to ease my maternal day-to-day stress, I don't know. Either way, it got easier.

Sorry, I am not about to tell you when our day of epiphany occurred. Why? Power of suggestion is a mighty force. Perhaps it will take you less time to get in the twin mommy swing of things. Maybe it will take you more. Avoid the ever-present temptation to use someone else's (even a fellow twin mommy's) barometer to measure your personally perceived "success" as a parent. Blaze your own twin trail at a speed that works for you and your family.

V

Navigation and Coordination

16

Routine, Routine, Routine

Why is it that preparing Thanksgiving dinner for your family can be so stressful when you are trying so hard to enjoy it? If you haven't "planned ahead," dishes are completing their cooking cycles willy-nilly, relatives are grazing and "hovering"—not sure exactly when they'll be fed—TV sets in all rooms are blaring, and your house is utterly consumed by chaos. You're glaringly aware the people you love most are counting on you to pull it all together: to cook their meal and provide some conversation and entertainment and a safe, quiet, place to nap afterward. If that weren't enough on your shoulders, it's all expected to happen in a nurturing, hospitable, and ideally, calm environment. The same type of strategic timing/planning you employ to minimize your holiday strain translates well into creating a daily schedule for your twins. The light at the end of the "Days of Haze" tunnel is met far quicker when parents establish a predictable and uniform routine for the entire family.

Your babies have arrived? Start a routine and start it now. You're still in the hospital? Breastfeeding or formula, the nursing staff is already seeing to it your new arrivals are fed on a schedule. They're not just trying to make things easier; although it certainly does. The wisdom of the ages shows that everyone likes to know when to expect the important things in life. From what we observed with our twins, babies do, too.

Now I am not saying you can feed them only three times a day, or that you can expect them to sleep 8 hours a night because you have militantly (and dangerously) dictated your daily timetable as such. Far from it. Our twosome ate eight times a day and slept eight times a day (as mommy tried to do as well) for the first months of their lives . . . but it was all laid out into a regular, predictable, reassuring routine. For instance, here was how our early days went:

7 A.M.: Feed babies.

7:30 A.M.: Burp babies.

7:45 A.M.: Change diapers, and note who has peed and pooed in your poo journal.

8 A.M.: Play with/hold/stimulate babies. If very young and sleepy, let them start napping.

9 A.M.: Put down for nap if they haven't drifted off already. At this point, I would try to get some sleep, too. At the very least, lie down and try to rest.

10 A.M.: Feed babies.

10:30 A.M.: Burp babies.

10:45 A.M.: Change diapers, document pees and poos.

11 A.M.: Play with/hold/stimulate babies.

Have you seen a pattern yet? That's pretty much how our days went for the first few months. 7 A.M., 10 A.M., 1 P.M., 4 P.M., 7 P.M., 10 P.M., 1 A.M., 4 A.M., and back to 7 A.M.—Feedings started. Subsequently, we would all try to sleep at 6 A.M., 9 A.M., 12 P.M., 3 P.M., 6 P.M., 9 P.M., 12 A.M., 3 A.M., and 6 A.M. In those windows in the middle of the night, we would attempt to minimize the play/stimulate time and try to sleep as much as possible. True confessions time: We were not always "on the exact clock." What if the babies (or one of the babies) were still asleep at feed time? Our advice and our doctor's mandate? Wake them up. They need to eat regularly and often. Uh oh, they're awake earlier than feed time? We held off until at the earliest 15 minutes preceding the designated feed time before feeding them. But as you can see, you will get "off your clock." Cut yourselves some slack. Just rework your times based on the *start* time of your feeds. For example: Babies are hungry and awake at 6:30 A.M. Or better yet, one was awake and the other was sleeping. We would typically try to "hold off" until 6:45 A.M. But if it was a growth spurt, or they were beside themselves, we might consider beginning a feed "early" at 6:30 A.M.

Then, the next feed time would need to start no later than 9:30 A.M. Don't try to be too stringent in your timetable, but try to focus more on the regularity of events. Your babies will know that after eating, they'll be burped. Their diapers will be changed. They get some play/cuddle time, and then they can sleep some more. Perhaps you will find you want to feed your babies every 2½ hours, that's okay, too. Just compact activity time and adjust your projected timetable accordingly. Whatever you do, *do not* try to stretch longer than 3 hours between newborn feeds without the consent/encouragement of your pediatrician.

When your pediatrician gives the thumbs up, you can attempt the "sleep through the night" hurdle. By the way, sleeping through the night can mean anything from 6 consecutive hours in the early days, to 12-plus hours per night as they get older.

The Double Daddy Perspective

Creating a routine is probably the most important thing you can do as a parent. It provides comfort and security for both the children and the parents. Of course your biggest challenge will be sticking to it. There will be times that you will have to prod your spouse to stay on track because sometimes a short-term gain of skipping naps because the babies are in such a playful mood will end in a sleepless night for both of you!

So once you do get the okay to attempt the full-night sleep through, how can you accomplish that with two individual infants? There are many schools of thought on "sleeping through the night" and getting twins "on the same schedule." Here's what we did (with great success) to take or leave.

After you have determined your twosome's bedtime, develop a "nighty-night" ritual that will signify to your twins that this "nap" is the one intended to last longer than the daylight hours naps—ideally all evening.

For our two, we put snug-fitting warmth-retaining "sleepy time dream hats" on for the overnight "nap," giving it a different feel than the day naps. Additionally, by the time we got the okay to try the night-long sleep through, our twins were also approved for making the transition from elevated-heads in bouncy seats overnight to co-bedding side by side in their crib. Day sleep would be in Boppies on my bed, in their bouncy seats placed in various locations around the house, and if gas was a big problem, occasionally in a swing. So the crib placement gave nighty-night time a special location and feel. Before placing them in the crib, we put a waterproof pad/crib overlay under their booties in case of diaper ooze, so that the bed sheets would not need to be stripped in the middle of the night . . . just a fresh pad replaced when necessary.

Once our darlings were fed, burped, diapered, their dream hats donned, and bellies rubbed, they were reminded how much mommy and daddy loved them. We would then say their prayers, wind up their musical mobile, confirm pacifiers were well placed, and vacate the nursery. For us, putting them to bed awake worked out well. We wanted them to learn how to go to sleep in their crib, not just to be placed there once they were lulled to sleep elsewhere. Both twins tended to be calm upon being placed in the peaceful environment and were transfixed (or quieted) by the mobile music.

If either or both began to cry after the mobile tunes stopped (and they often did), we would return to the nursery, re-rub bellies, reassure them of our proximity right next to the nursery, remind them of our abundant love for them—basically a quiet, calming consolation—and again leave the nursery. If the crying restarted, we would allow them 5 minutes to try to calm themselves down. (Yes, 5 minutes does feel like an absolute eternity; but they need the time to try to self-soothe.) If they did not/could not calm down, one or both parents would repeat the nursery visit, rub the belly of the upset twin or twins (one twin would often fall asleep with a sibling bawling just inches away . . . a true, regularly occurring twin phenomenon you probably won't believe until you see it happen). We would again reiterate our love for him/her/them and our closeness to them, replace pacifiers if necessary, and leave the room. If the crying started again? We'd give the twin(s) a 10-minute attempt at self-calming. (I have never watched a clock as ardently!)

If either or both were crying after 10 minutes, we'd repeat the consolation routine. Perhaps we were more fortunate than most, but rarely did we ever find the twins unable to calm down and "require" more than the 10-minute consolation step. I can count on both hands the number of times we went to a 15-minute "controlled cry." Some parents that have employed this method needed to go to the 20-minute cry for the first night or two. Others needed never go to the 10-minute. Each family is different.

Many in our parents' generation employed the "Cry It Out" method . . . meaning the parents just let the babies cry until they realized they were fine (or exhausted) and eventually just conked out. Many in our generation believe in immediate consolation upon each and every cry. My husband and I felt after much research and just an application of our personal "logic" that giving the twins (once it was healthy to try to do so) a chance to figure out how to get to sleep without our constant intervention, but with the consistent reminder of our presence and love, would only benefit them (and us) in the long run.

By using this method, our twins were sleeping "through" the night (7 to 8 consecutive hours) in 3 days. I absolutely credit this "controlled crying with compassionate consolation" method, consistently applied.

Periodically, as our twins have experienced growth spurts, developmental surges, and changes of environment, we'll have the occasional span of needing to reapply the method to reaffirm "all is well" amidst change. Our twins respond rapidly and tend to calm down with the acknowledgment of routine familiarity. Straying from whatever sleep routine and calming method you employ will inevitably and ironically cause an intensification of the outbursts.

At least that is what we have experienced. It is as though the twins demand to know what they can expect and will compound the response-requiring behavior repeatedly to ascertain what they can count on from you. Give them a 100 percent predictable response every time, and their initiating behaviors will regulate quicker. If they know they will have a reassuring session from a parent after each window of "upset," the nightly windows of upset will shorten, and before long, diminish greatly or disappear. With double the children, double the sleeping is doubly satisfying!

Let me tell you right now, all will be happier with regularity. My advice? Whether or not you decide to try this particular method is unimportant. Do some research to discover a sleep-inducing method/routine that feels workable for you, your partner, and twins. Work diligently to get everybody on the same schedule as soon as it is feasible. You will all be better for it.

17

Breastfeeding Twins—Teats for Two

Why not? Two breasts, two babies, it can work! And for us, it absolutely did.

Let me start off by saying, do not take to heart any criticism you receive about whatever method you select to nourish your babies. That decision is yours to make. People will say you are crazy to attempt to breastfeed two. People will say you are selfish if you decide not to breastfeed. Think carefully about your family, your support system, your finances, your personal gut feelings about the process, and make a decision. Realize you also can change your mind either way at many stages, and that is also your prerogative.

Few of our mothers' generation breastfed single infants, much less, multiples. We are part of a new generation, well aware of the many benefits of breastfeeding. Undeniably, nursing is the healthiest option for your babies, for you, and most definitely, for your wallet. I will tell you here and now, although it is "nature's way," it *is* a challenge.

If you decide to breastfeed your twosome, the undertaking will require both your physical and emotional determination. Have family and friends criticized you as stubborn and obstinate? Here's when those traits will work in your favor.

Let your hospital, OB-GYN, and nursing staff all know if you intend to nurse your twins. I daresay, most nursing staff will assume you are planning to formula feed twins, so be vocal. Ideally, they will try to get those babies on your breasts in the first hour or so after they are born. If you don't tell them, don't be irritated if bottles are given to your babies in the maternity ward. Getting the babies to breast early after birth is supposed to ease them into the practice when they are at their most receptive.

Don't be shocked when hardly anything comes from your breasts. Many new mothers get fearful in the first few days and quit nursing, convinced their babies are "starving." From what I understand, babies are born with nutrition sufficient to survive 5 days with *nothing*. Now obviously, you aren't going to do that, but that tidbit should reassure you tremendously when the first few days are full of incorrect or non-existent nipple latch-ons. Most hospitals have a lactation consultant on staff, and she (maybe I am being sexist, but I have yet to hear of a male lactation consultant) will be there to help you. Use her.

The early output is called colostrum and is like liquid gold . . . full of antibodies and all sorts of goodies just right for those fresh out of the womb. Nothing synthetically produced can match it. It's just a fact. Even if you know you don't intend to breastfeed long term, consider at least getting them the early goods.

Let me dispel one of the most common apprehensions about nursing twins: No way can one woman produce enough milk to sustain two infants. In most instances, that is incorrect.

The human breast creates milk on demand. Twice the demand equals twice as much milk. Likewise, as the babies grow (through growth spurts and all) and their demand increases incrementally, your breasts should adjust and increase accordingly. If your babies aren't creating enough demand, or if your babies cannot be directly breastfed right away because of prematurity, a breast pump can simulate demand quite efficiently. The milk you pump can be fed to your babies via whatever method is feasible.

Do use care and select a slow-flow nipple whenever you need to supplement off the breast. You are probably shrieking right now, "What about nipple confusion!? Won't my babies reject my breasts in favor of the bottles?" If you don't use care in selecting a strategically nippled bottle, the babies may do just that. But believe me, the babies aren't confused; they're just lazy. Most bottles/nipples will automatically drip into the babies' mouths even if they don't suck. Those types of bottles are just easier and faster. Don't blame them for wanting the easy route, it's tough work being adored all day long. My feeling is, it's never too early to learn life rarely hands you something for nothing. Get nipples that simulate the breast, forcing the babies to truly suck hard to get the goods. As you will find out, the babies need to seriously work their suction muscles in order to extract milk from your breast. Surely my daughter will thank me in the future when she has finely chiseled cheekbones from all her diligent nursing as an infant.

Avent makes a fine booby-like nipple. We had to supplement our daughter with expressed breast milk after every feed in the early weeks. It took her an eternity to drink from those nipples.

The breast is more efficient, making it the preferable method for the babies in the long run. Even if you want to breastfeed exclusively, do express milk on occasion and let your husband (or grandparents or older siblings) enjoy feeding the babies.

Back to the first few days of nursing: I am embarrassed to say I don't remember the first time I nursed my babies. Surely it was within an hour of their birth. Needless to say, I was quite tired, and my memory is a little blurry. Okay, my memory of it is nonexistent.

What I do remember about those early in-hospital nursing sessions was how comical it must have appeared to any lookers-on. Literally, my arms were raised over my head, in a "referee indicating a successful touchdown" pose, while the lactation nurses, at least one on each side, positioned and repositioned our babies' heads on my breasts. My arms had to be directly over my head to allow the nurses physical access and a clear sight line to get the babies latched on.

Latching on. Who would have thought it was tricky? Knowing that breastfeeding is "nature's way," I always assumed babies put their mouths on the breast, and voilà. Their hunger would be sated, and the only tough part would be trying to get two babies onto the nursing pillow at the same time. If only.

Our twosome was *so* sleepy in their first days of life. We had to wake them every 3 hours for their feeding, and we had to wake them often *during* the feedings. When it was time to sleep, *that* was when they didn't necessarily care to. As mean as it sounds, we had to strip our babies to their diapers to keep them "cool" for nursing. The breast is warm as can be; your arms are, too. Go ahead and add warm milk to the equation. Sleeping pill companies wish they could create a substance as potent. So naked they were.

When the little baby necks (and bodies for that matter) have little strength/control, the idea of nursing them anywhere other than our queen-size bed (with my back to the headboard) seemed unsafe. The looming precipice off to the side of a glider or a rocker seemed way too dangerous to risk while attempting to coordinate two babies, a monstrously big pillow, and my monstrously engorged breasts. With the bed, we had soft places to "land" or place a baby should we ever have a mid-nursing challenge (excessive spit-up, explosive poo blow-out, etc.) . . . and those times did occur. Some twin moms have managed a couch; I was too hooked on lots of space and soft surface to try the sofa option.

Once our twins were in football-hold position (babies' heads positioned in front of your breasts with their bodies lengthwise tucked under your armpits) on the tandem nursing pillow, we were ready to start. By the way, the "football-hold position," as it's affectionately known, was the only effective nursing position we were able to use. When I look back now on all my "breastfeeding research" and the class I took in preparation, I get the giggles. Just about all of the "illustrations" of viable twin nursing positions were drawings, except for the football hold. There were photographs of women nursing seemingly comfortably using the football-hold position. I did see a few somewhat scary looking photographs of women employing alternate "holds," but all parties involved looked uncomfortable and somewhat smushed. If you find another position works better for you, fantastic. For me, I had enough challenges. Attempting to make the nicer-sounding "cradle hold" work would have been a waste of precious time.

In order to entice the babies, we would graze their lips with the nipple. Often a drop or two of milk would be oozing from my breasts, aiding that process. If you find that little teaser helps your babies, squeeze a drop or two from your breasts and rub it on their lips as an appetizer.

If that doesn't get 'em ready to nurse—and with sleepy Sarah and dozy Darren, it didn't always work—rubbing your thumb vertically alongside their cheeks from cheekbone to jaw will often prompt their mouths to open. When their little mouths open wide, and only when they are open very wide, literally lift the babies' heads, and thrust the babies' mouths onto your breasts. Make sure you get their mouths to encompass a wide area, including your nipple and as much areola as possible. Ideally, their lips will flare outward a bit. Sucking on nipple only is the surest way to poor feeding and horribly sore nipples.

And no, you are not going to do some perversion of synchronized swimming and move both your hands (each cradling a baby head) in one fluid motion onto your breasts. Once one baby is on and happily sucking, then you can get the other one hooked on. Don't make the mistake of lowering your breasts into their mouths. Ideally, you are going to spend hours, weeks, and months in this position. Even though it feels "easier" for you to move to them, don't. Your back will have plenty of other reasons for strain the first year; don't add nonsensical nursing contortions to your body's list of things to do.

If you are like me, you always thought once the babies were sucking, all was well for that nursing session. For us, we had a bad case of the catatonic sleepers. Frequently we needed to prod their jawbones slightly, re-rub their cheeks, even flick their feet lightly during the nursing sessions to awaken them. Often, that meant relatching.

In the hospital, we were blessed to always have the fleet of nursing experts at our beck and call. Wisely, they suggested we undertake a session or two in-hospital with no assistance. Even so, once you are home, it is a little more challenging. Each time they are both latched on and nursing, try to mentally pat yourself on the back. You won't have a free hand to literally do it, but congratulate yourself. You are truly accomplishing something special for your babies' health.

If you have idealized images of nursing your babies like an enthroned Mother Earth, you may want to let go of those fantasies now. You will not be relaxing while nursing, all doe-eyed, gazing upon your offspring as many of the breastfeeding propaganda books would have you believe, at least not in those early days. Sister, you're going to be working and juggling, but all for good reason. After a while the whole process does get much easier, and you will find it hard to remember how tricky those first sessions actually were. Try not to get too discouraged with the challenges of the early days/weeks. The babies will learn, and you will get more adept.

Our son, despite his bigger size, was dubbed "a lazy white boy" by the in-hospital lactation consultant. I would have been offended if she hadn't been right. Latching seemed like more than he was interested in. We always managed to get him on eventually, and he would eat, but he was the tricky one. In the early weeks, I was convinced he would need to be fed with pumped breast milk only.

Our daughter was like a bird in the nest, beak open, ready for mommy to fill with food. Thank God for the blessing of her desire to nurse, right from the beginning. We'd get her latched on, and could then concentrate on hooking him up. Invariably, once he was drinking, she'd be falling asleep, and we'd need to prod her. But you know what? You really do start to get used to caring for one, then the other. Breastfeeding two helped me realize early on you cannot always tend to each child immediately, a priceless lesson that continues to serve us all well to this day.

We made a decision after 2 weeks at home to hire a highly recommended lactation consultant for an in-home visit. Since it was obvious our nursing rituals would soon be well established, and our son was still a bit inconsistent in his latch ability, we felt it would be well worth the investment. Was it ever!

Our appointment was scheduled for our 1 P.M. nursing session so she could watch us in action. She brought a scale with her and weighed each baby pre-feed and post-feed. I now had a basic idea of their actual consumption. Not knowing is very disconcerting, especially when your babies are smaller, as twins often are. She had great suggestions on how to position Darren so he'd chow down with greater ease.

She brought a nursing pillow much more suitable for breastfeeding twins than the one we were using. It even had a mini-back support pillow for me. She brought nursing bras and fitted me in the comfort of my own bedroom.

If these are your first babies, don't let the challenges of the early days of breastfeeding make you feel inadequate and incompetent. It took us about a month and the help of the at-home lactation consult, before I truly felt breastfeeding was working well each and every feed. Your body is doing something it could not practice for. Cut yourself some slack, and congratulate yourself for attempting, and hopefully succeeding, at a very daunting goal.

If these aren't the first you have nursed, and you are committed to tandem breastfeeding the twins, don't throw in the towel at frustration's first blush. It *is* going to be more challenging to coordinate, but there are advantages. For one thing, you don't need to switch breasts halfway between the feed. The maternal weight loss as a result of breastfeeding twins, I daresay in my nonmedical opinion, occurs extremely rapidly. Don't even think about dieting at all. (Even with a singleton, I am told you should never "diet" while breastfeeding.)

Each baby can stay on his or her own breast for the feed and have the other breast the following session. Do keep track of which baby is on which breast at which feed session and try to make sure they flip flop with each nursing. I have heard some women have allocated a specific breast for each baby. If both babies seemingly consume equal volume per feeding, no problem should arise with the concept of assigned teats. But, since your breasts create supply for demand, it would follow that if you have one ardent feeder, and one grazer, at certain times of the day, you would teeter, and as we say in the south "look right funny," with the unbalanced breast weight.

There is no way I could have ever made nursing work the first few weeks without an incredibly supportive husband. Logistically, with two infants who have minimal body control, the more hands that can help with support and positioning, the more comfortable you and your babies will feel. Emotionally and physically, breastfeeding is literally draining. You will need encouragement and support. If you don't feel your husband is the one for that role, enlist your mom, a treasured friend, *someone*. Breastfeeding, for however long you undertake it, will require a level of commitment from the entire family.

Likewise, the entire family will benefit from its success. From my perspective, it seems much easier to give your midnight feeds without the hassle of having to mix formula, warm it, fill bottles, feed babies, burp them, diaper them, then wash bottles and put babies then yourselves back to bed. You can get a few precious extra minutes of rest, whip out your breasts equipped with prewarmed milk, feed, burp, diaper, and then ideally, all go back to bed. No fuss, no muss. Well, except for the diapers.

Financially, breastfeeding is a God-send. Formula, even the generic, is expensive. Many babies exhibit allergic symptoms to one or more ingredients in a particular formula, requiring even pricier varieties. Nothing can match free; breastfeeding rocks the budget.

As a family, we decided to tandem feed our twosome at each feed, and feed on a fairly strict schedule for the first year. Simultaneity saved us time. Regular routine provided predictable opportunities for much-needed rest, as well as the accomplishment of necessary twin and non-twin related household maintenance. For us, priorities of primacy. Some twin breastfeeding mommies have fed individually and on-demand. Others have pumped breast milk and fed through bottles due to prematurity or other feeding hurdles.

Try to find a helpmate who has accomplished twin breastfeeding in the manner you are trying, even if it is only online. Throughout the nursing period, questions will inevitably arise. Reassurance from someone who has been through the same course is priceless. Select that support individual carefully, making sure their perspective on nursing is congruent or compatible with your own. From the moment of discovering my twin pregnancy, I was fully committed to breastfeeding as the healthiest way to nourish my babies. Subsequently, I needed a helpmate/consultant who didn't view nursing as a religious experience, but rather someone who could offer genuine encouragement and experienced advice. There are individuals (in and out of organizations) who strongly feel breastfeeding is an imperative instead of an option and are quick to vocalize their condemnation of any feeding choice other than 100 percent breast milk from the breast only, for as long as possible. If you believe similarly and respond positively to that type of coaching support; by all means, maximize the ardent mammary missionaries! Do what you can to make it work. For me, as committed as I was to "making it work," the last thing I wanted was guilt and pressure. Reassurance and support was what I wanted and found through an independent lactation consultant. Find the support that works for you, and make no apologies.

Do be forewarned. Challenges in breastfeeding don't vanish after it becomes well established. For instance, at around 5 months, every time I would latch my daughter on, she would quickly start screaming and turn her head away. That was pretty jarring considering breast milk was her only nutrition at that point. Common culprits for sudden breast rejection after nursing are well established? Spicy food intake on mommy's part, baby teething, baby nasal congestion, mommy's soap or deodorant residue/scent . . . a surprising myriad of reasons may explain the sudden refusal to feed. Our final answer? Crazy garden-hose-like milk streams from my breast shooting at the back of her throat. Supply increases with demand, and apparently, production was overwhelming her. The solution? Tip the baby-laden nursing pillow upward toward my breasts slightly while nursing so that the milk streams wouldn't be hitting the back of her throat. Side benefit was that I got to lean back and relax a bit while feeding the twins instead of sitting upright as I had been the first months.

Perhaps a portion of that particular stage provided one of the best nuggets of nursing wisdom: lean back and relax a bit while feeding the twins. Whether you are anxiety-ridden in first attempts that seem to be thoroughly unsuccessful, or have spans of difficulty with one or both twins months into the breastfeeding process, remember that each nursing session is essentially just a "meal." Each feeding is its own entity and consequently, each feeding provides another opportunity for a better experience the next mealtime. So both physically and mentally, try to "lean back and relax a bit while feeding the twins."

18

Breastfeeding Surprises
or Tit-Bits No One Talks About

My preconceived image of the human breast during lactation consisted of a single stream of milk emerging from a single, centrally located hole in the nipple. Imagine my surprise when during a breast pumping session, I saw multiple hair's breadth streams squirting from all around the nipple and areola. All is well if you see the same. You haven't overloaded your breasts to the point of popping, it is totally normal. In addition to dodging sore nipples, that is a major reason for having the babies latch on to a wide diameter of your areola.

Two days after giving birth to our babies, the in-hospital lactation consultant came into my room, thumped the rope-like bulging veins on the top of my chest like a raw melon, and declared, "Oh, your milk will be in soon, Honey." What?!? It felt like some bizarre medieval divination process, but, she was right. Despite all of the amazing advances in medical technology, the cycle of life essentially remains the same. Often, the advice given seems extraordinarily old school, too. Milk-flow issues? Drink a beer a day, it'll increase your flow. Doctors and nurses nationwide have dispensed that advice. (Please check with your own doctor and pediatrician prior to adding any alcoholic beverage to your diet while nursing.) Plugged duct or the beginnings of mastitis? Put a cabbage leaf in your bra, it will potentially remedy the problem if caught early enough. Sore nipples? Slather on 100 percent pure lanolin (a sheep derivative); the babies can nurse through it safely, and it provides uncanny relief. With these types of advice being doled out liberally in the first days of my motherhood, I was starting to be optimistic that there was also some closely guarded secret to halt babies' crying . . . something like spinning around in the backyard wearing a purple hat at midnight. There wasn't, but there genuinely are many helpful and healthy tips from ages gone by on how to ease the challenges of breastfeeding.

The Double Daddy Perspective

My only bit of insight on breastfeeding came from a rock star that I was interviewing for a local paper. We were walking along, engaged in some small talk, and I told him that my wife and I were expecting twins. He stopped, looked me square in the eyes and said with conviction, "Get a lactation consultant. You'd think breastfeeding would be the most natural thing in the world but it's not. Find one now. I mean it."

One of the best tips to keep you and your breasts a'flowing is to intake gallons of water. As much as you can drink. Try to always drink some prior to nursing. Coffee and caffeinated beverages should be dodged or consumed in *very* small quantities. I drank a lot of milk, and our babies both seemed okay. Other mommies have had bad experiences with dairy and their babies' digestion. Be careful of juices, too. The acid can be too much on your babies' systems, and you'll hear about it later. Drink juice in moderation until you know how your twins will react. Ours reacted badly, and I did eliminate juice entirely.

Which brings up a whole other breastfeeding issue . . . the belief that if the babies cry after nursing, surely it is something mommy ate, disturbing their otherwise happy existence. Do not let yourself freak out about this! Foods can and are passed through breast milk, but just because your babies are crying in the afternoon does not mean your morning Cheerios need to be cut immediately from your diet. Look for repeated similar reaction after you have consumed the same item, and then consider cutting back or eliminating the violator altogether. Our babies were extremely gassy. After one visit to the pediatric office, I was given an extensive list of foods that are sometimes culprits: dairy, peanuts, spicy foods, juice, beans, wheat, soy, citrus, bran, cabbage—virtually anything with any fiber content, the list went on and on.

Amidst being told to consume an additional 1,600 calories a day, it was being suggested that I seriously consider not having any cereal or vegetables. Sugar seemed the only clearly safe item, and as much as I would have loved to eat nothing but sweets, I couldn't believe that was a healthy option either. You need to eat, and you need a variety of foods. Unless your babies develop allergic reactions to your milk (and you'll know a real reaction when you see it), use your best judgment. Crying after feeding doesn't necessarily mean they didn't like last night's roast beef sandwich with horseradish. If you feel better about it, keep a running diary of your food intake in your babies' poo journal. If you sense strong reaction after a nursing session, see what you ate in the preceding 8 hours or so. Highlight the potential causes, and the next time you consume that item, see if the babies react the same way. If they do, it may be due to the element in your diet. It might not be. Our babies were diagnosed with a slight case of reflux. Diet changes or no diet changes, they were going to have gas. I could minimize it by not having 100 percent All Bran and a big glass of juice, but they were still destined for some digestive discomfort. It is hard to watch your babies cry, but do not feel you have total control of their happiness by manipulating your food intake. Again, use your best judgment. They are your babies, and your judgment is best.

Another aspect seldom addressed with the reality of tandem breastfeeding twins is logistics. Moms of single babies can be out shopping, visiting a museum, flying on an airplane, and breastfeed their children easily and discreetly. Not so with twins. You need space. You need both hands. You need support from a nursing pillow or arrangement of pillows. It is far more demanding space- and support-wise than feeding a single infant. By all means, you can go out shopping, you can visit museums, you can even fly on planes; we did all of those things. We just worked our nursing schedule around those activities. If you are on a tight nursing schedule as we were (every 3 hours in the early months), you may need to sacrifice some social engagements out of the home at the beginning. Better yet, if you are highly motivated and getting some rest, have folks come see you on your home turf. You'll be able to break away to nurse as needed, and you can show off your babies as well. (By the way, the tandem nursing of twins is an amazing source of curiosity for many women. If you are comfortable with the process, and someone asks to observe, consider allowing her to. You have undertaken a major commitment for you and your babies' health. Your example of dedication may prove an inspiration for others to nurse their offspring in the future.)

Prior to having our babies, I was under the impression that if my husband gave a bottle of expressed breast milk or formula, I could get some rest during what would be a nursing session. Wrong. Your body miraculously prepares to feed your babies on your determined schedule. If you normally nurse every 3 hours, and you give bottles instead of nursing your twins, you will need to pump your breasts instead to ease the pressure of the accumulated milk. Pump for at least 10 minutes, or longer if the pressure is not relieved. With twins, you are producing twice the milk. The likelihood of blocked ducts is increased with the increased production. Do not "short cut" out of nursings or pumpings. You may pay the price later with another oft-ignored breastfeeding topic, mastitis.

The dreaded "m" word, mastitis. Do whatever you can to avoid contracting mastitis. It may be unavoidable, and you will certainly live through it; but it is incredibly unpleasant, and makes nursing while ill that much more challenging. What is it exactly? For me, the first time I contracted it, the onset was almost immediate. I went from feeling tired one minute (which is totally normal in the days after giving birth) to feverish and nauseated with uncontrollable chills the next. There was also a rock-hard "lump" the size of a golf ball in my right breast. Antibiotics safe for a nursing mom were prescribed, and I was advised to continue nursing and to press hard on the painful planetary orb while doing so. Ideally, opposing pressure from both sides would "pop" the plugged duct. Hot compresses and warm showers are also advised in this situation. My first case was too far gone, and outpatient surgery was required to "lance" the befouled duct by syringing out the backed up milk. At the time of the lancing, the golf ball had blossomed to a racquetball size. Round two of mastitis: Same deal. Suck out the obstructed duct with a plumbing snake in outpatient surgery. Chances are, my second case followed so closely on the heels of the first, the duct was never fully cleared. Round three: What?! You can contract it again 7 months into nursing? Apparently so. But this time, I knew it was coming. The antibiotics combined with nipple-directed pressure on the duct while nursing knocked it out.

In my breastfeeding preparedness class, we were told only 5 to 10 percent of breastfeeding moms ever contract it. In my own social circles, including nursing moms of singletons and twins, that number runs closer to 60 percent-plus. However, do not let the "fear" of mastitis be a deterrent to breastfeeding. My feeling is that the reality number wouldn't be anywhere near so high if new moms knew what symptoms to be looking for and could respond more quickly after detecting warning signs. So here, my friends, are key symptoms of pending/potential mastitis. Call your OB-GYN the second you feel you're at risk, or have contracted the wicked breast beast. The earlier the diagnosis is made, the greater the likelihood of an easier, less-painful remedy.

Warning sign #1: Bleeding nipples. My nipples bled before I even left the hospital. Singleton mommies can give a sore nipple a "rest." It's trickier with two hungry babies. Bacteria can be contracted through the wounded teat, often resulting in mastitis. Had I known that, I would have contacted my OB-GYN immediately for advice. At least then, I would have had the baby-safe antibiotics on hand, ready to ingest when I saw warning sign #2.

Warning sign #2: Red, splotchy breast(s). Having never nursed an infant, much less two, I thought the pigment irregularity was due to inordinate wear and tear. Wrong.

Warning sign #3: Breast(s) is hot to the touch. Naively, I just thought the milk was "warming" for the babies. Infection was setting in. My breast was running a fever.

Warning sign #4: Swelling and/or hardness in your breast. Okay, at this point, I was starting to wonder, but then . . .

Warning sign #5: Flu-like symptoms. Aches, exhaustion, nausea, and violent chills.

Please learn from my mistake(s). Nip it in the bud around warning sign #2. Two of my three cases of the boob-fliction resulted in outpatient surgery to drain the abscessed fluid from the breast. I repeat, nip it in the bud. The good news is, even if you contract mastitis, you will make it through. Not only can you nurse throughout the illness, it's encouraged for healing. We didn't miss a feed.

While registering for gifts, I saw a very reasonably priced, hand-powered breast pump. It looked easy to work and was unobtrusively sized. Onto the list it went. Thank God no one purchased it. With your mammaries kicking into overdrive to feed two mouths, you need an industrial strength, electric, double breast pump. Rent one from the hospital while you are establishing that breastfeeding is going to work for you. It will take about a month to feel confident. Conveniently, most hospitals rent the pumps by the month. Then, spring for one of your own. It is worth the investment. Your breasts will thank you. Hospitals and pharmacies cannot sell used breast pumps, as some of the apparatus comes into contact with bodily fluids. You will have your own set of booby funnels and tubing from the rental. Ask the advice of your doctor, and perhaps check out e-bay, moms of multiples club yard sales, and the newspaper classifieds. Not realizing that used ones were out there, we bought a brand new one. Either way, new or used (with the okay of your doctor), get one.

You might also consider investing in the bra-style hands-free accessory. Spending as much time as I did pumping, it would have been nice to read, eat, or do something other than hold funnels in place.

If you decide to nurse for a few months or more, you will be periodically surprised by new responses, movements, and adjustments your babies will invariably make while feeding. For instance some months into the process, Darren began open-handed "slapping" of my breast mid-nursing. Well, maybe not slapping so much as flat-handed kneading. A good friend shared the fact that nursing kittens do the same. Go figure. Sarah never did anything of the sort. However, Sarah, without warning, did bite down on my nipple at one nursing session. Note how I said *one*. The possibility of nipple munching had crossed my mind when her first tooth broke gum at around 7 months. I had certainly entertained the thought prior to deciding to breastfeed our twins. Strangely enough, I was unprepared for how I would respond when the clamp-down actually happened. Without thinking, I involuntarily yelped, "Ouch!" She pulled off, gave me a surprised, but not frightened, look. It never happened again. Darren never bit at all. Granted, he had no teeth until he was 14 months, but a vice-grip of those tooth-bud pressured gums would have hurt. Some babies do bite. Plenty don't. Don't let the fear of it deter you from attempting nursing.

There is a lot of written support out there for women starting to nurse. Books line the shelves at Barnes & Noble. The funny part is, there is hardly any information out there on how to *stop* nursing. After the first 12 months, most of the babies' nutrition begins to come from their solid food intake. I knew we were going to wean the babies at a year, but I realized I had no idea of how to go about it. By 11 months, we were already down to three short nursing sessions a day that occurred along with their breakfast, lunch, and dinner. After consulting with our pediatric office's nurse practitioner, a breastfeeding support queen, she advised the following: Figure out a date when you intend to be done breastfeeding. (For us, it was to be their first birthday.) Then, on the basis of how many nursing sessions a day you have, back up the date by that many weeks. Thus, ours were 11 months and 1 week when we started the weaning process. Our pediatrician okayed cow's milk at that age. If you elect to wean earlier, you can substitute a sippy cup or bottle of formula. Check with your pediatrician. For the first week of your weaning process, figure out which session they/you are least "attached" to. (For us, it was the midday feed.) Then, for the second week, substitute a sippy cup of cow's milk or formula for that particular feed, continuing to nurse for the other feeds. If your breasts are uncomfortable or engorged when skipping the nursing session, pump a bit to take the edge off. *Do not* pump to empty your breasts. If you do, your body will continue to produce milk for a demand you are attempting to eliminate. Then, the following week, discontinue an additional nursing session and replace it with a sippy. For us, we decided to cut the dinner nursing. However, many families are most attached to that last nursing before bed. Do what is wisest for your family. The final week, work on eliminating that last feed. Chances are, you may be fully weaned before your deadline, especially if you nurse up to that first birthday. With increasing amounts of solid food filling their bellies, their "drain" on you diminishes accordingly. Your body creates supply for demand, and if their demand decreases, your body produces less in response. Many babies "wean themselves" prior to that first birthday, by just "sipping at" or even refusing the breast. My personal advice is never force an older, healthy, solid food-eating baby to nurse. They know what they are doing. Nature works the way it is supposed to. You may be nostalgic for the days when your babies relied solely upon you for their nutrition, but you have done your job. A primary role of parenthood is to raise children who can live self-sufficiently. They have accomplished their first step toward that goal once weaned. The American Academy of Pediatrics encourages breastfeeding infants at least to their first birthday. By age one, your babies will have acquired a marvelous quantity of valuable antibody protection and nutritional advantages provided by breast milk. Other groups (including the World Health Organization) advocate extending nursing to age two and beyond. You (in concert with your twins) will determine the appropriate time for the conclusion of breastfeeding in your household. Wean 'em earlier if you want, later if you want. The one-year mark worked out well for all of us.

What is one of the most underdiscussed "tit-bits" few twin moms feel comfortable talking about? Surprise: Breastfeeding may not always be the wisest feeding option for every twin family.

For a spectrum of legitimate reasons, many twin moms do not (and sometimes cannot) nurse their twosomes. Not every twin mom tries or even wants to breastfeed, and that is *her* (and her family's) decision to make. Well-intended, but often crusade-like, pressure to breastfeed twins is often a tremendously guilt-inducing, stress-magnifying, joy-robbing aspect of a new twin mom's earliest days with her infants.

Common medical knowledge indicates correctly that nutritionally and from an antibody-providing perspective, milk from the "breast is best." However, plenty of viable, healthful, nutritional, and ever-improving formula feeding alternatives are available.

If the "drain" of nursing two is too much, but mom wishes (and is able) to nurse, a "bottle-plus-breast" combination method is a great option. Twin A nurses and Twin B is bottle-fed (formula or expressed breast milk) at Feed #1; for Feed #2, B is breastfed and A is bottle-fed. Alternating back and forth keeps both twins on a level playing field.

Often, one twin is a "good nurser" (latches well and nurses actively) and the other isn't/doesn't/can't. Prematurity plays a definite role in feeding ease and ability. There is nothing wrong with nursing one twin and bottle-feeding the other!

Yes, bonding with a child is wonderful via the nursing process; but I can speak from experience that some of our most intimate bonding moments occurred when cuddling close while playing, while changing diapers, and through lengthy adoring gazes.

Surely bottle-feeding provides the same opportunity for closeness.

For you moms who do not or cannot nurse your twins, whatever the reason, *do not feel you are depriving your babies (or yourself) of a singular bonding experience!* If you envisioned implementing one feeding method and are forced to rethink your plan, *it is okay!* Keep your flexibility at a maximum and your self-flagellation to a minimum.

Whether your twins' meals are mammary-manufactured or pharmaceutically formulated, whether transmitted to your babies via a breast or a bottle, your twins will be supplementally nourished with your engaging eye contact, your physical cradling touch, your loving voice, and of course, with nutritional sustenance.

Make, and prepare to modify, a feeding decision that seems healthiest for your unique family. Offer no excuses, make no apologies, stand on no soapboxes, and never judge another mother for the feeding choice she has made for her family. People should always supersede process.

Bottle, breast, or both—feed your twosome in a way that feels "right" for your situation; after all, it is *your* situation.

19

The Poo Log

Call it your "defecation documentation" if you desire a more dignified title. Regardless, in the early months, you need to keep track of the most basic bodily functions. When you are running on limited sleep, it is very easy to forget who has pooed/peed/spit up/had needed medicines, etc.

Our journal was highly informal. You can acquire or create pre-printed sheets for each day, and fill in the blanks as necessary. We used a spiral notebook. Here's how a typical day looked (Of course, ours is handwritten in the dazed scrawl of the poorly rested. It makes me nostalgic to look at it now!):

10/15/2001—Sarah   Darren
        poo: IIII   poo: II
        pee: VI   pee: VII

9:30 A.M.   15 minutes feed time
             Sarah = L (left breast)   Offered supplement, refused it
             Darren = R (right breast)   1 ounce expressed milk supplement

             *Sarah had some spit up.
             Breast pump: 3 ounces (1.5 each breast)

12:30 P.M.	15 minutes feed time
	Sarah = R Took 1 ounce supplement
	Darren = L Took 1 ounce supplement

*S—Little fussy. Went down easy. Some spit up.
*D—Fussy. Some spit up. Took another .5 ounce of expressed milk
@ 2:15 P.M.
Breast pump: 3 ounces (1.5 each)

3:30 P.M.   15 minutes feed time
               Sarah = L   Took 1 ounce supplement
               Darren = R   Took 1 ounce supplement
* Both screamy. Small amount of spit up each. Once down,
zonked.
Breast pump: 2 ounces (10 minutes)

6:30 P.M.   15 minutes feed time
               Sarah = R   Took 1 ounce supplement
               Darren = L   Took 1 ounce supplement
*Both screamy. S—Lil' spit up, very fussy. Hiccups.
D—3 shooting spit ups. Paci soothed. Fussy. Hiccups.
Breast pump: 3 ounces (1.5 each)

9:30 P.M.   15 minutes feed time
               Sarah = L   Took 1 ounce supplement
               Darren = R   Took 1 ounce supplement
                                  (and later another .5 ounces)
*S—Lots of spit up, but not upset. Totally calm. Hiccups.
First dose of Zantac for reflux
*D—Screamy. Took another .5 ounces of expressed milk. No
burps.
Breast pump: Didn't pump

1:30 A.M.   Gave formula in bottles (30 minutes+)
               Sarah = 2 ounces
               Darren = 2 ounces
*Both a bit fussy, hungry after feed?
S—Some spit up
D—No burps or spit up
Breast pump: 5 ounces

5:30 A.M.   Gave breast milk in bottles (30 minutes+)
               Sarah = 3 ounces
               Darren = 2.5 ounces
*S—Lots of spit up/slightly fussy. Down easy. Zantac dose.
*D—Fussy. Some spit up. Down easy. Then screamy.
Breast pump: 5.25 ounces (3.25 L; 2 R)

10/16/2001—Sarah   Darren
       poo: II   poo: IIII
       pee: VIIII   pee: VI

8:30 A.M.   15 minutes feed time
          Sarah = R   No supplement
          Darren = L   No supplement
          *S—Little fussy, then down
          *D—Zonked!
          Breast pump: Didn't pump

       . . . and so it goes . . .

Okay, I can hear you now, with the "Good grief! Did you really need to document all of that detail?" In retrospect, maybe not. Especially the detailed description of the fussiness and spit up. However, we were experiencing a bit of GER (reflux) with Sarah. All her spit ups were making our pediatrician apprehensive, hence the prescription for Zantac. In the coming weeks, Darren was put on it, too, as a preventative measure. Elsewhere in the book, I know I have discussed our strict "every 3 hours" feeding/nursing schedule. Lo and behold, the day excerpted here from the poo log is a day/night in which we "stretched" to a 4-hour span between middle of the night feedings. A feat achieved by giving a formula bottle at 1:30 A.M. The theory behind the extension is that formula takes longer for babies to digest. A kindhearted nurse suggested trying a single night feed of formula to allow me a longer sleep window between night feeds. As long as our babies got eight feeds within a 24-hour day, that was sufficient. Her intentions were good. Sadly, it didn't take long to realize that between the preparation and warming of the formula, the lengthier time it took the babies to drink from the bottles, and then the breast pumping afterward to drain the prepped-to-feed-two-babies mammaries, we were taking more time in the middle of the night than in the middle of the day. Curious as to why the bottle feeding took longer? If you are breastfeeding, the babies have to work hard to extract the milk from your breasts. Most, if not all, lactation consultants will recommend a nipple that is also challenging to the suck, in an attempt to simulate the breast. (Avent was our system of choice.) If the nipple is a constant drip without any suck necessary, as many are, you can well imagine how a baby will opt for the easier process and may begin to prefer the bottle over the breast.

You may have also noted that nursing sessions were capped at 15 minutes. If you elect to breastfeed your babies, here is perhaps the best piece of advice I was given: Nurse each baby for a maximum of 20 minutes per feeding. In my first few weeks, I was naively nursing them for as long as they were sucking. Some feedings lasted upwards of 45 minutes-plus. Can you say "human pacifier"? That is essentially what I was. Although it is lovely to be a physical soother for your children, *you need rest*. Not only for your sanity, but to keep your milk supply and breast health at its apex. If you are feeding them on a tight 3-hour schedule, they will do the majority of their actual intake in the first 15 minutes (if you have concerns about appropriate quantities of consumed foremilk/hindmilk, talk to your pediatrician or lactation consultant. We were assured this timing would be sufficient and learned way too late that it indeed was!). After 15 minutes, hello leisurely sipping. It is important, however, to keep potentially sleepy babies awake at the breast and actively sucking if you are limiting their mealtime duration. Jossle those jaws and rub those cheeks. I also made notations of which infant was manning which breast at each feed. Your doctor will recommend that you switch stations at each feed. At any given stage, one may provide a bigger suck demand than the other. If they have permanent breast assignments, you can picture how a visual disparity might develop. Singleton mommies are advised to switch breasts midway through the feeding to keep their bosoms evenly supplied and sized. At least yours don't need to change restaurants midmeal!

If you formula feed your babies, I can imagine that your feed times may go even quicker, depending upon the bottle system you select. Some nurses I have spoken with suggest that when formula feeding, wisdom still dictates the selection of a "tough suck" nipple. Get those facial muscles working. A key way to save time is to have two folks feeding the babies simultaneously. Your opportunities for sleep/rest are dramatically increased. Never fear, you can tandem bottle feed a twosome, even if only one person is administering the meal. For more on that, check out the chapter on maneuvering multiples.

Speaking of maneuvers, the hash marks at the top of each day tallied our bowel maneuvers/poos and pees per baby. When you are changing between 16 to 24 diapers a day, you can easily forget who has done which deed and how recently. In order to confirm that your babies are getting enough nutrition (especially if you are breastfeeding and can't accurately determine the amount "going in"), the daily diaper count is a pediatrician-dictated imperative. Eight wet ones a day, and you're in the clear. Don't hyperexamine each poo diaper trying to verify if the presence of pee is also there. Chances are, it is.

The Double Daddy Perspective

I remember being shocked when other fathers I would talk to could not recall their children's early feeding habits and health issues until I had my own. I realize now that no one remembers because we were all exhausted! So I must say that for as much as I teased Cheryl about her obsessive excremental journaling, the Poo Log has been a valuable resource for us as well as our new-parent friends. It will help your pediatrician's questions and it will make you look like the most attentive parent on the playground.

Don't be alarmed by the texture and color of the early poos. The very first poos (called meconium, for you trivia buffs) are dark greenish-black and have a tar-like consistency. For Heaven's sake, use petroleum jelly liberally, or you will be chafing your babies' bottoms in attempts to pry the stuff off. Shortly thereafter, the poo becomes far more yellow, and somewhat seedy . . . very similar in appearance to a gourmet honey mustard. A happy surprise we discovered was that the early poo had virtually no scent whatsoever. We made use of an actual diaper "pail," and let our olfactory-preserving Diaper Genie sit dormant until solid foods entered the mix. Believe me, exit aromas change quickly when chewing begins the digestive process. Rumor has it that formula feeds do result in stinky poo at an earlier age, so if you aren't breastfeeding, don't freak out if the poo comes out in a scented form. Make use of the Genie when needed. Certainly once solid foods enter the picture, you'll want to have some scent-sealing system in place.

20

Mommy Is Outnumbered!

In the early days and weeks home with your twins, you likely will have lots of help. If you haven't already planned for who's on deck in the early days/weeks, please do so. You will not only want help, you will *need* help.

My husband (whose boss has triplets) had 3 full weeks of paid paternity leave. What a God-send! My in-laws overlapped the latter part of his time off, and stayed a few days beyond. My mom tagged in after that. However, I knew at some point, I would be flying solo with Darren and Sarah. As a matter of fact, I knew that I'd be flying solo at exactly 5 weeks. Fortunately, by about 4 weeks I was feeling pretty good about the rhythm we were getting into. Breastfeeding was well established. A schedule was in place. Our seemingly every-other-day weight checks at the pediatrician had dropped off. The babies' poo journal was revealing what was going in was coming out regularly. I had memorized the phone numbers for the pediatrician's office, the lactation consultant, and the hospital nursery. (The nurses there encouraged us to call with any/all questions until the babies were 2 months old. The staff is there 24-7. See if your hospital offers the same service. It came in handy.) I was as ready as I would ever be.

Preparedness or no, the ratio was still inevitably two babies to one mommy. Most moms of twins I have spoken with indicated the single biggest challenge in dealing with twin newborns is the impossibility of handling each baby's individual needs immediately. The sooner you acknowledge the reality of that fact, the less-stressed you will become. As with all aspects of twin-raising, you will need to become comfortable in assessing priorities . . . to some extent, a twin triage. For instance, burping preceded diapering in our house. If one had a dirty diaper, knowing our babies' extreme gas discomfort, a dirty diaper would wait while one was de-gassed. Trimming the fingernails of one and smell a sinister stench emanating from the other's britches? I'd contain the partially manicured and re-trouser the soiled. Granted, those are seemingly easy decisions. Both crying? I would try to determine if one was discomfort-based over general agitation. Both screaming as if in pain? Do a quick visual check of both. No obvious cause of suffering? Here is the nugget of wisdom it took me way too long to discover: *just pick one*. Try and pick the other one first the next time. I apologize if that sounds somewhat cavalier, but the truth is, you *cannot* single-handedly handle all needs for both simultaneously. The sooner you come to grips with that fact, the better you will feel about your mothering skills. Even as your babies progress to toddler-dom, you will still have to use your rock-paper-scissors-like methods of attending to their unique needs. It's inescapable.

Here's a remarkable twin trait: your babies may uncannily (and developmentally inexplicably) realize that there is only one of you and will often "scale-back" their outbursts. Maybe I am giving them more credit than their due, but I could swear that early on Darren could see Sarah was in a "worse way" and would cease crying (or at least would reduce the decibel level and intensity) until she was okay. She would do the same. Now don't come after me when this doesn't happen every time. Believe me, I had, and continue to have, my share of dueling banshees. However, when it happens, it's a beautiful kinship/twinship to observe. Keep your eyes open for it.

21

Maneuvering Multiples: Logical Logistics

As the old saying goes, necessity is the mother of invention. As a mother of twins, you will become quite inventive due to frequent necessity. With practice, you will discover ways to maneuver your multiples that work best for you and your family.

Here are some leaping points for attempting needed navigations with numerous newborns.

Picking Up Both Babies at the Same Time

The token "twin chapter" in one of my pregnancy books indicated that I would need to figure out a way to pick up both babies, by myself. At the time, that didn't sound odd at all. However, once Darren and Sarah arrived, with heads way too heavy for their wee necks, it became obvious there was absolutely no way to safely achieve that task. In reality, there was no need to, either. In those first few months, there's no rolling over, no scooting, no traveling whatsoever. When you need to move them, pick up one and carry to destination. Then the other in sequence. Keep them in safe locations. No danger . . . no problem. Once they can sit on their own (around 6 to 7 months) then perhaps you will find the need/desire to move them around at the same time solo.

The easiest way I found to accomplish this feat was to have them sitting up with their backs to me. I would wrap my arm under one twin's arms, and scootch him or her up to my hip using my corresponding thigh if necessary for leverage. Then scoop up the other baby the same way. We could weasel ourselves into a fairly comfortable carrying position without the aid of anyone else. Finding a method that works well for you comes in very handy around this time. Once babies mobilize even slightly, it is no longer safe to "leave" one even momentarily while you tend the other. You may be playing together in one area, and need to get to the changing table, get to a high chair, get to the other room for whatever reason. From that hold described, I could then lower one down onto the floor or into a crib or playpen while I got the other baby changed or whatever was needed.

Once you've got "crawlers," it's a whole new ball game. If you haven't lost your pregnancy weight by this point, you will put a good dent in it now. Containment and baby-proofing are of the essence at this and future stages. Get some baby gates. Get outlet covers. Get doorknob covers. As the Boy Scouts so wisely advise: Be prepared. Determine which room(s) is going to be entirely safe. For us, it was our den/sunroom. Even so, with the presence of any furniture that can be fallen from, under, or into, there is no substitute for supervision. Keep the square footage of your safe haven limited, and stay nearby.

Tandem Nursing or Bottle Feeding

Unless you have acquired, or are blessed with, a second full-time caregiver for your twins, there will be occasions when you single-handedly need to (or at the very least, *wish* to) feed both twins simultaneously.

For nursing moms, the challenge is getting all parties safely positioned, latched-on to your breasts and feeding comfortably at the same time. Practice makes all the difference. Use the in-hospital lactation staff if your newborns are developmentally/physically able, and start getting the "feel" of what works for the three of you. Once you are all home, give serious consideration to a house call visit from a lactation consultant. Before hiring one for a session (they can be expensive, but worth every penny), confirm their experience in assisting moms of multiples who wish to tandem nurse.

What did we do? We nursed tandem every single feeding, and always on a spacious bed, with my legs either extended straight or cross-legged, and my back to the headboard. Prior to Darren and Sarah's birth, I had researched and mentally noted some various positions suggested for easily and effectively tandem nursing twins. When it came right down to actually *doing it*, the only position we found to be both nurser and nursee-friendly for us was the football hold (each baby facing mom on their own breast, with their bodies each tucked under a maternal arm, allowing me to cradle heads with my hands, and the inner part of my arms to "hug" them inward) on an appropriately and intentionally designed twin nursing pillow. Getting to that position required some orchestration . . . but again, the orchestration became easier with repetition.

Since you are rendered semi-immobile during a tandem nursing session, make sure you have a glass of water, lots of burpie/spit-up cloths, a pair of pacifiers for post-feed if you use them, and the TV remote if desired within reach.

Immediately preceding each nursing session, each twin would be placed in a Boppy pillow toward the middle of our bed. Since the three of us often napped together in that position, many of our daytime feedings started that far ahead of the game. Once they were situated, I'd assume my position right alongside them, allowing plenty of soft bed space along either side of me in case one accidentally "dismounted." Next, I'd get the nursing pillow into place around my waist, and its little support pillow behind my back. As a matter of personal preference, I tended to latch whichever twin's turn it was at my left breast, then I'd gingerly reach (yes, with both hands . . . another important reason for investing in a broad/wide/twin accommodating nursing pillow) across the nursing twin to get the other into position on my right breast. It is also possible to sit with your legs extended betwixt baby-laden Boppies, and then lean forward to get each baby to their respective breast. Oddly enough, the reach-over worked better for us. Try different positionings to see if something feels better for you.

If one twin unlatched mid-feed, I'd release my caress on the other in order to use both hands to get the loosed baby back "on." After 15 to 20 minutes, first twin on the pillow would then be the first off.

Having a clock on the wall straight ahead helped for maintaining awareness of nursing session durations. Likewise, I've never been so grateful for the TV in our bedroom . . . despite all the marital maintenance propaganda condemning them. Sure, I spent much of my breastfeeding time gazing irresistibly at the twins, but during bleary middle of the night feedings, turning the television on with volume down low and catching some news or other visual stimuli was very helpful.

How do you/can you bottle feed two babies simultaneously? Just as with nursing, you have a spectrum of potential positions to consider and will likely discover your favorite(s) early on.

Consider placing the babies in Boppy pillows side by side, with mommy facing the twins wielding a bottle in each hand. Mommy is tired? Place a baby-loaded Boppy pillow one on each side of a seated or semirecumbent dual bottle-administering mommy. Concerned the babies' heads are not elevated enough while taking their bottles? Bouncy seats can be arranged in the same positions and the bottles fed accordingly. Same positioning works with the car seat carriers if preferred. Many high chairs currently available have reclining positions, safety straps, and removable trays. You might decide to invest in a set earlier—as opposed to later when solid foods enter the dietary plan.

If you are combination breast and bottle feeding, you can set a bouncy, Boppy, or car seat nearby for the bottle recipient and nurse the other baby for half a session; then rotate positions between babies for the remainder of the feed (if both are nursers). If you have a single breastfeeding twin, and a bottle-only twin, you can likewise position eating-seating right alongside you so you can maintain close to equidistant proximity to both babies.

Whether you nurse, bottle feed, or a combination, both babies need burping following their meal. I've yet to find a soul who claims they can safely simul-burp two newborn infants who have minimal-to-no neck control/head support. Sequential burping is a must. Fairness would ideally dictate you take turns as to which twin burps first, but if you discover one twin is particularly gassy, you may elect to burp him or her first every time in the interest of avoiding discomfort.

Whichever baby is awaiting his or her turn at burp bat can return to the on-deck circle of a Boppy, a car seat, a bouncy seat, a still swing . . . any place where his or her head is elevated to aid the gas escape and lessen the chances for excessive postmeal spit-ups. If your babies enjoy, and you have decided as a family to utilize pacifiers, the sucking action may keep him or her contented until it is either one's turn to release gas. After burping one twin, trade the two. We liked to do the feeding and burping session with all three of us on the bed. It was a great opportunity for talking to the twins and singing little songs.

Even if you are ambidextrous, realizing that diapering even a single baby is a two-handed job, the task of twin diaper changing must be a sequential process . . . a task that needs to happen after each and every feed. Before our twins arrived, no one warned us that as the babies are "taking food in" they are invariably "pushing something out." As unsavory and unappetizing as it seems, don't interrupt an unfinished feed in order to change the filling diaper(s). Infant digestive tracts are so mobile; the incoming will continue to provoke the outgoing for the duration of the feed for weeks. Once the feed and burp aspects are done, the diaper will have collected the bulk of what can be expected for that particular feeding. Don't forget to note on your poo log journal which twin output what following each feeding session.

Infant/Child-Centric
Activity Outings with Your Twins

Mommy/Baby yoga classes. The Barnes & Noble or local library's story time. Mommy and Me at the local mall. Gymboree music classes. When the mom to child ratio is a congruent one-to-one, the only obstacle those maternal fantasy-inspiring excursions raise is the possibility of an ill-tempered infant . . . whom you can easily remove when the going gets tough, or disruptive. When you are one mommy to two babies, you will need to rethink the logistics (and sometimes the wisdom) undertaking each particular outing. By all means, you can and should get out and about often with your twins, but spend a bit of preexcursion time anticipating what may or may not need to be confronted midtrip. Preparedness with supplies and a predetermined course of action when those instances arise keep your maternal stress at a manageable level. When "trouble" arises, you simply implement the predicated Plan A, B, or C. Even very early on, before they could talk, I found it helpful (even if only for me) to verbalize our plans in the car en route to wherever we were heading. Pep talks went somewhat like this: "We're going to go have fun at story time! Now other kids may be running around, but we are going to stay in the stroller, since we're *one* mommy and *two* kids. You'll be able to see really well from your seats. I'll sit on the floor right beside you and listen, too. We'll need to be very polite and quiet so other kids and their moms and dads can hear the stories, too. I know you can both behave, but if one of you can't, we'll have to leave. That would be sad, and certainly not fair to the other two of us who are behaving and trying to have fun. So let's all hold it together!" (FYI: a mommy-inflected, sing-songy "Hold it together!" was one of the first phrases our twosome uttered. Not at all a surprise.)

You may not feel comfortable with the luxury of "letting your twins walk" just because they can. I know I didn't, and depending upon the situation, still don't. Bear in mind that a single-child outburst/clothing-contaminating diaper explosion/spontaneous illness will result in the necessary removal of *two* children from a fun activity . . . often to the dismay of not only the instigating twin, but particularly to the innocent bystander twin. Be ready for the vocal (and maybe physical) opposing party response to the forced halt of fun. As they get bigger and stronger, single-handedly removing two thrashers from a social context without the benefit of a stroller is not only stressful but physically challenging.

Befriend your stroller. Passers-by our stroller-parading twosome often will say, "Oh, you just wait until they can walk!" In the interest of twinforming the general public, I'll often respond, "They've both been able to walk for many months. They are just really smart kids who realize mommy only has two hands and legs; and they have four hands and legs between them. The stroller facilitates our daily outings with a greater element of courtesy and safety."

Now, before you think my children ever-shackled and restrained, there are occasions when extraction from the stroller is feasible. Typically those destination environments are less populous and more geographically removed from dangers like busy streets. The twins' attitude and disposition preadventure greatly impact the likelihood not only of "out of stroller" experiences, but whether or not we will leave the house at all.

Getting to/from/in and out of the Car

When your babies are newborns, and for some months afterward, you will be able to maximize the handled car seat carriers in traversing to and from the car; one in each hand. Of course, if you need to tote (and you certainly should be toting) a diaper bag, purse, or any other accoutrements for your out of house adventure, you would be wise to run those items to the car prior to the double baby haul out.

When our twins were very young (before they could sit on their own), I'd get them cozy and safe in their car seat carriers by the front door, then quickly run out the diaper bag, party gifts, pot luck contribution, whatever nonbaby peripherals were part of our trip.

Once they were a bit older, I would let our twins play in their exersaucers or in their playpen prior to loading them into their car seats, while I loaded the car. Pretty quickly I learned that although I *could* have the diaper bag slung over my shoulder while snapping and securing a car seat into its base, the contortions of leaning in the vehicle often caused the bag to drop bruisingly to my inner elbow or precipitously swing around the head of the car-seated twin at my feet who was patiently awaiting his or her turn for car seat connection. More preliminary mommy trips to the car equaled less stress for the twins starting our trip.

If you have a driveway or garage, the task of snapping the baby-laden car seats into their respective bases should be a fairly easy (and it gets even easier with practice) process. For those of you, like us, who have on-street parking, and own cars as opposed to a bigger vehicle (with vans and SUVs, an adult can actually enter the vehicle to snap in car seats. The twin load-in is still awkward but less problematic); take a deep breath . . . it is navigable.

Situate your car seat bases in such a way that they are side by side (no space in the middle, as you need to allow an accessible space for an adult to sit by the twins in the early days anyway) on the back seat passenger side. In their very youngest days, you will experience some moderate back strain as you load the one car seat over the base of the other. You will get stronger and more used to the range of motion. As they get bigger/heavier/older and you won't need an adult space available alongside your twins, move the previously positioned "middle" car seat base to the position closest to the driver's side back door . . . leaving an "empty" space between the two car seat bases. You'll no longer need to lean spine-wrenchingly while lifting and maneuvering a weightier twin into their base. But eeek! You won't want to set the babies in their car seats down on the street while you open the back door to get them in!

You don't have to. Always load in the nonstreet side baby first while the other is at your feet right beside you. Once Baby A is in and cozy with the back passenger door shut behind them, trot behind your car until the coast is fully clear traffic-wise (. . . and you would howl with laughter if you could have seen the nonrisks I was unwilling to take in those very first days), then open the driver's side back door with the non-twin-toting hand, swing and secure Baby B into place with the other, and off you go.

The decision is yours to make, but we elected to keep our double stroller in the car at all times. Hauling it to and from the house seemed to add an unnecessary layer of labor to our twin mobility playbook.

We had acquired a "travel system" for which the car seats not only functioned within their in-car bases, but snapped securely onto a companionate double in-line stroller as well. Priceless.

When we registered for the double stroller, the travel system "came" with a single car seat; seemingly designed for families expecting a new baby who had a toddler already in the house. In a twin-arrival scenario, with two babies requiring car seats, we simply needed to purchase a second car seat compatible with the stroller.

So once you get where you are going, then what? We almost always made a point to park a distance away from the entrance to wherever we were headed. Why? The further out we parked, the more likely we were to be able to maintain available parking spaces on either side of our car. Personally, I liked having the room to wheel the double stroller (and it is bigger than its single-seater counterparts) alongside the car on both sides, as I'd load in the twins.

Here was my routine: Upon parking, I'd retrieve the stroller from the trunk and open it for use. The diaper bag (within which I'd always stash my wallet and any personal effects—dodging the need for a purse) would be pulled from the front passenger seat, and its fully extended shoulder strap would be looped over the stroller handle, with the zippered front-pocket holding my wallet facing outward for easy access. (FYI: My husband hated doing it that way, and felt the bulky bag projected out too far and limited his range for walking. He tended to put the diaper bag in the basket underneath.) I preferred to leave the basket vacant for whatever might be acquired during the trip. I also liked the immediacy of being able to retrieve wipes, a spare pacifier, burpie cloths, etc. without unwedging the bag from under the stroller seats. You will discover what works best for you. Some moms swear by the backpack as diaper bag for twin outings.

Of course, all the while, I'd be chattering away to the kids . . . talking about what we'd be doing, going, seeing. Whichever baby was the first *in* the car, that baby would be the first *out* of the car. Once that dumpling was snapped into place onto the stroller, we'd promenade to the opposite side of the car to collect the other. Protective new mother instincts being what they are, taking your eyes off stroller-bound Baby A while you unlatch Baby B can cause a sense of panic. I know it did for me. In addition to applying both stroller wheel brakes (which I assumed would slow any nasty baby snatcher while I was momentarily focused on Baby B), I virtually threaded my awkwardly outthrust ankle around the stroller wheel closest to me while unhooking the second twin. You have no idea what you are physically capable of until your babies' safety comes into question . . . you are twinvincible!

Getting the Double Stroller into a Store/Mall Single-Handedly

Many, many stores and malls now have automatic doors. Never did I truly realize or appreciate the magnitude of that invention until it became glaringly obvious which locations did *not* have automatic doors. In the first days with our twins, if I was in a hurry or already overstrained (neither of which is necessarily a good time to go out with your twins, by the way), I would often select a grocery store or destination not by virtue of their bargain sales or convenient location but because they had automatic doors. Of course clearly, we would be forever limited in our choice of destinations if we allowed the obstacle of door navigation to thwart us.

So fear not, twin travelers! Assuming you are using an appropriate-width (read: narrow or in-line) double stroller, you can and will develop door opening dances allowing you and your twosome access to bookstores, museums, drug stores, churches, pet shops, restaurants, the pediatrician's office, coffee shops . . . virtually all those locations that are woefully unblessed with electronic door technology.

Here are some of the choreographies we found effective,

For Double "Pull" Doors, Handles Centrally Located (Barnes & Noble/Museums)

Push the stroller toward the entrance, lining the left-side line of your stroller up with the left side of the door on the right. Leaving the stroller a few feet back, allowing space to actually swing open the door, stand alongside the right front of the stroller, open the door with your right hand, while you have your left hand free, able to touch the stroller. As the door is fully opened, prop it with your right foot, and pull the stroller using your left hand on the front tray, push the back of the front seat through, pull the back tray on through, the seat back of the back seat if needed, and then grasp the stroller handle to push the stroller all the way in and allow the door to close. If the door is a double door (and you'll be surprised to discover how many are), once you've "cleared" the first door, back the stroller up a bit so you can perform the same dance progression on the second door.

For Doors with Door-width "Push" Bars That Open from the Left (Churches/Hospital Interior Doors)

Approach the same way as the "pull" doors, but push the door open with your right hand, while pulling the stroller with your left hand by the front tray. Once the door is fully open, use your back to hold it open and pull/push the stroller through—first with your left hand pulling on the front tray, moving your hand to push the back of the front seat, then pull the tray of the back seat, push the seat back of the back seat, then grasp and push the handle on through. For doors that push open from the right, just reverse the process (e.g., line up the right side of the stroller to the right of the door, push the door open with your left hand, and use your right hand to navigate the stroller through).

For Doors that Swing/Push Inward (Dairy Queen/Starbucks/Pediatrician's Office)

With the stroller facing outward, 180 degrees *opposite* of the direction you truly want to go, keep your hands on the handle of the stroller. Back into the door pushing it open, and once it is fully open, keep it open with your back/booty, keeping your feet fairly stationary. Pull the still "backward"-facing stroller through, moving from the handle, to the seats, eventually pushing the front tray all the way in. Allow the door you've been holding open with your backside to close, then re-grasping the handle, pirouette spin the stroller around, and you're on your way. The kids *love* the spin.

Despite how convoluted the descriptions of door management sound, you will find yourself getting so adept with repeated practice, you won't linger an extra moment waiting for an offered hand of help. While vocalizing effusive gratitude, I frequently decline offers from folks willing to go out of their way to assist with what appear to be unwieldy/unmanageable doors. Other times, I've graciously accepted the offer of assistance if the individual seems compelled to reach their quota of good deeds for the day. After all, your twins should see as many examples of voluntary kindness as possible.

Getting Groceries/Running Errands

In your first days/weeks home with your twins, consider some outings sheerly for outings' sake.

Get a good idea of the time onlookers/complimenters spend adoring your twins. Bear that extra time in mind when you venture out with some objectives/goals to accomplish. Always better to underestimate what you can "get done" when you are out solo with infant twins (or older) than to overestimate. Err on the side of making numerous trips in a relaxed fashion rather than attempting one expectation-rich foray out. Your stress is *so* easily perceived by young twins, and keeping your goals easily achievable will aid in keeping you calm. Plus, you'll find yourself far more pleasant when strangers come to fawn over your twins. Experienced twin moms will universally testify that attempts to dodge curious strangers only add to your strain. Pad your time allotment appropriately. Allow your twins to get the attention and smiles who wish them (and you) nothing but well . . . despite the occasionally inopportune timing. Your twins will also see a great example of friendly social interaction from you and the twin-fascinated general public.

Shopping and errands, like so many other activities requiring skillful twin management, working out your own family method is pivotal. Many configurations may need to be attempted prior to discovering how you and your twins can best accomplish day-to-day errands with the least stress, and with practice, enjoyment!

Of all the necessary "errands," grocery shopping seems the most daunting, as it requires not only the most time but the most space to accommodate two babies and groceries.

To this day, I elect to make numerous abbreviated trips to the grocery store, using only the storage space basket under our in-line stroller. Depending on the ability of our twosome to "hold it together" for lengthier periods of time (and for us, that can change from day to day), you may be setting all three of you up for too perilous a journey by attempting a full-week's shopping spree. Plus, it is nice to have the impetus to get up and out daily.

Now I am not implying that the task of shopping for the full week (or more) is impossible . . . it isn't. We have done full pantry and refrigerator stocking sessions numerous times.

The method most likely to work for the endeavor with small twins in tow is the "push the double stroller in front of you with one hand, while pulling the grocery cart behind you (using the back end, not the handle end) with the other." To turn corners takes some switching of hands and alternating of pushing and pulling, but with practice, it *is* doable.

In honesty, I was *way* overconfident the first time I tried this maneuver and was so rattled when we got home, I was close to tears (the kids by contrast did *great*; it was my lack of dexterity that disturbed me). With repeated attempts, it *does* get easier. However, if you think you get abundant attention pushing a double stroller with twins, just wait until you become a 9-foot long train of grocery acquisition! Give it a try if you're game, but you may decide it's easier to get the big grocery trips taken care of when someone else can watch the kids and you can go solo.

As the twins get bigger, double-seater grocery carts are a more viable option. More and more stores nationwide are investing in them. Grocery stores have clearly seen the need and have gone above and beyond the call. Many have "race car"-style two-seater carts, including steering wheels for two!

Although they are becoming more commonplace, the stores that do have the two-seater carts have them in limited supply. When pulling into the store parking lot, drive by all the cart-corrals seeking a two-seater. When we find one, we ideally park right alongside the corral so there is no stressful attempt to convey two unfettered wee ones some great distance (typically to the store entrance), only to discover the desired cart is somehow in disrepair . . . or that they are all taken. Parking by the corrals is genius all-around. After leaving the store, you can unload your kids and the groceries into your car then return the cart to its adjacent rightful place without leaving your twosome unattended.

Realizing the extensive use those particularly popular carts get, I make a point to use an antibacterial wipe on the handle, the perimeter of the seats, any area on the cart within the reach of the twins before I put them in. Believe me, their reach always surpasses your estimation! For some reason, the diameter of the cart handles inspires tiny twins to wrap their mouths around it like two puppies sharing the same bone.

Sure it's cute, but it may as well be an engraved invitation to the pediatrician's office. Wipe that sucker down!

Whenever you do grocery shop with your twosome, whether using a double stroller or a two-seater cart, here are a few of tips:

- Always bring along lightweight books and toys in significant quantities. Entertained and occupied twins are well-behaved twins. Before long, they will even learn to "trade" between themselves, extending the time frame before you as mom will need to step in and replace fresh amusements for both. You may even consider allowing older twins to handle some lightweight (and fairly indestructible) objects you plan to purchase.
- Learn where the store in which you are shopping keeps their restock baskets. If you need to leave quickly for any reason (not the least of which is behavioral), you can scurry there and either empty your stroller bin, abandon the pulled-behind cart, or worst case scenario, extract your kids from the two-seater cart and high-tail it out as politely as possible. In those unfortunate instances, don't reattempt a trip in the same day. Call your husband and have him (or a friend) pick up any emergency items; or plan on getting a solo trip out yourself later.
- When you've gotten to the check-out, position yourself in a place where you can unload your items without allowing your twins access to the brightly wrapped candy/magazine/impulse buys racks. (Be sure to enjoy the twinfancy nonreaching days!) Four arms in-and-out are virtually impossible for two-armed mom to restrict simultaneously. Dodge the stress. If you're using your stroller, spin the twins around backward without pulling them into the grab temptation zone, so you can unload the under-stroller basket onto the belt. The folks in line behind you will love getting to "face" your twosome and often unwittingly provide great diversion/entertainment. Once you've depleted the basket of all desired purchases, and the person in front of you has left entirely, rapidly pull the stroller all the way through to the end, spin it around 180 degrees, and then back your way (holding the stroller handle) back into the check signing/pay area. If you are using a cart, position yourself in front of it (alongside the back, nonhandled end) unload your purchases, and when the person in front of you has departed, pull your kids (still in the cart) all the way through quickly so

the groceries can now be loaded in without your twins being in a position to pull items down and add to your take-home load.

- If you are using a stroller as your purchases are being bagged, kindly let your bagger know (or if you are self-bagging) to place only a few items in each bag so you can re-wedge them below the kids for transport to your car. Whereas it may be their regular protocol to coalesce all three cereal boxes into a single bag, that severely inhibits your ability to rework your stuff down below. Invariably, I do end up holding some bags around my wrists for the postshopping stroller push to the car . . . it's not too traumatic.

What about those "in and out" errands you are used to accomplishing? Bank trips, convenience store coffee/soda purchases, prescription pick-ups . . . brief errands in which the accomplishment of the task itself typically takes less time than the process of loading two babies in and out of the car?

You have a couple of options. We maximize drive-thrus whenever we can. Banks, pharmacies, pay-at-the-pumps, Krispy Kreme. Other times, we just decide we'd like an outing. We'll do a speedy Target pharmacy pick-up and then just stroll the store at our leisure. Again, your diaper bag of diversions is an imperative. You'll be surprised how things we as adults don't even notice provide uncanny entertainment for fresh eyes. The decorative neon slashes adorning Target's varied departments are a case in point.

What about errands like mom's doctor and dental appointments? Haircuts? The choice is yours to make. We've gotten so accustomed to (and fond of) the stroller on a daily basis, that for obligations requiring 30 minutes or less, with an ample supply of books and small toys, our twins will sit alongside me in the stroller and will usually entertain themselves. Before the excursion, I'll usually give a little pep talk to the twins explaining that like them, I need to go to the doctor's/get my haircut, and that I know they can wait patiently—just as I do during their appointments. A dangled carrot of a mall-playground visit or a trip to the swimming pool for exemplary behavior provides additional motivation when I think it's merited. Now if you are having a medical procedure, or highlights put in, I'd think twice before expecting your twins to remain contained longer than the duration you as their mom feel is appropriate.

Bath Time

Even with two parents supervising the baby-bathing process, we always bathed our newborns one at a time. The baby who was waiting for his/her turn in the tub would be placed in a bouncy seat, reclining high chair or car seat carrier facing us while we suds-ed up his or her sibling. Using a baby bath tub on our kitchen counter kept parental back strain to a minimal, which was helpful since the process of washing two babies back-to-back was a fun, but lengthy one. We always had warm hooded towels awaiting the baby exiting the bath. The cozily wrapped, freshly washed infant could then fill the seat his or her twin had used while waiting a turn in the tub.

You probably received a plethora of adorable bath-time accessories as gifts. Don't be disappointed to learn in your earliest double bubble-fests that the teddy bear washcloth puppet may be more cumbersome than useful, that the use of aromatic bath bubbles[1] does *not* guarantee peaceful sleep will follow, and perhaps saddest of all, that rubber duckies hold limited to no allure for your newborn twins. Give them all time and additional auditions in future bath times . . . they'll all prove fun, and photo-inspiring, eventually.

Professional Photos

Best time to get a two-shot of your twins taken by a professional photographer? Any time before they can crawl! Once mobility comes into play, the chances of catching a moment with two infants/toddlers in the same picture frame (much less smiling or looking in the same direction) diminish significantly.

As the twins get bigger, of course you will still want to have their photos taken. Search out studios that make use of semirestrictive "props" that can keep young children in place and amused. You might consider bringing along some items that your twins particularly enjoy to guarantee some smiles.

You will receive photography coupons en masse once your twins are born. Read the small print carefully, and take advantage only of those offers that waive the per-person sitting fees.

Reading Aloud/Storytime

A two-word suggestion: Captive audience. The complaint you hear often from multiple moms is that their twins "won't sit still" for a story to be read. If you anticipate being able to plop both twins in your lap and expect them to both remain immobile while you lovingly read aloud, you are setting yourself up for disappointment. Forced abandonment of those idyllic preconceived notions makes the situation doubly frustrating. Don't assume your twins "don't like books," have no intellectual interest, or are likely to manifest attention deficit disorders based on their lap exodus, quite the opposite is true! The twins are actively moving and absorbing their surroundings; their method of learning just isn't coinciding with your idea at the time. Don't give up on reading aloud, just rethink your staging.

Quite mistakenly, we discovered the best way for our twosome to enjoy books read aloud was to exploit those opportunities when their attention was more likely to be fully focused. In our twins' very first days and weeks, when we were exploring various ways to "stimulate" them, we'd often read books librarian-style (holding the book aside and letting them see the pictures as we read) to the twins perched in their bouncy seats or Boppies. As they got older, we realized we were all "used" to that mimicked story-hour positioning. Before, during, and after mealtimes we read book after book while the twins sit in their high chairs. (A big tip in keeping their "attention" book-focused is to eliminate peripheral distractions like a television droning away in the background.)

Do think creatively. When using the stroller, you have a captive audience. Take along books. If you have a long grocery store line to endure, or a park bench looks inviting while on your afternoon walk, extract a book and have an impromptu story time.

Mommy's Personal Hygiene
and Household Management

Two fully dependent infants in the home curtail the time available not only for leisurely activity but for many of the activities heretofore regarded as mandatory . . . things like meal preparation, laundry, sleep, even a daily shower for mom.

Take the time to re-evaluate and re-prioritize your daily itinerary. Certain elements are absolutely must-happens: for instance, sleep and meal preparation are nonnegotiables. What is negotiable is how you work those mandatory aspects into your twin-blessed household schedule. Sleep when the babies do. Reduce your meal prep time by employing a crock pot, re-heating a frozen meal, or ordering take-out/delivery.

Showering? Filth-be-admitted, my daily shower was one of the first things to go onto a "secondary level" of necessity. When I did take a shower, it was during nap times or when another adult was available to watch the babies.

Domestic tasks such as vacuuming, dusting, bathroom cleaning, mopping, and laundry all needed to be reprioritized. Laundry and dishwasher emptying would need to happen with greater frequency than prior to the twins' arrival. Vacuuming, dusting, and mopping? Low on my list of priorities prebabies, and lower yet on my list with double babies present.

So how do you accomplish any non-baby-revolving task with two infants in the home, especially in those early days when you should be sleeping whenever the babies are?

Containment and entertainment. When the twins are very little and unable to crawl or walk, if you have kitchen activities to accomplish, pull the bouncy seats or a Pack 'n Play into the kitchen so the babies can see you (and you can see them), and proceed to peel potatoes, load up the crock pot, purge the refrigerator, whatever chore you have deemed imperative.

Pulling the bouncies into a bathroom is not unheard of . . . consider a bath (maybe even indulgently shave your legs!) while the babies look on.

In moments of sheer maternal exhaustion, you may just need a few minutes to take some deep breaths, read a magazine or book, have a moment of prayer or meditation, some quiet mommy time. Do not feel guilty about placing the babies in a playpen, in bouncies, exersaucers, or even their crib(s) for a short time to allow you to regroup as an individual. The occasional short-term mom-instigated time of safe twin containment is wise investment in mom's (and subsequently the twins') long-term well-being. Ten to 15 minutes of rejuvenating "peace" amazingly can enliven and reactivate an overextended mommy. Everyone, including the twins, will benefit.

Whatever twin-based feeding arrangements, day-to-day outing, or domestic modifications you face, follow a course of action that feels comfortable and most importantly, *safe*, for you as a family maneuvering your multiples. If something feels risky; then for your family, it is.

Ask for help when you need it. Seek the suggestions of other multiple moms, and temper their input (including mine) with your own logic and capabilities.

Note

1. Vapor bath bubbles do smell wonderful, and some parents swear by them. We used them regularly, but set our expectations low on their sleep-inducing impact.

22

Destination: Double Duty Diaper Bag

Sure, as the name implies, the diaper bag needs to contain all the necessary paraphernalia for changing the dirty diapers you are bound to discover within mere minutes after leaving home. What you may not realize, is that the strategically stocked diaper bag can also be your secret weapon in preparedness for any and every tricky away-from-home challenge you may encounter while out with your twosome. Stoke it up with an array of diversionary tools, and your babies will appear to all onlookers as peaceful and content as a couple of cloud-sitting angels. You'll be able to accomplish so much more, and for such a greater duration of time by just investing a bit of mind-power into your bag of tricks.

How tempting it is for me to itemize each and every component held within our nappie-sack, and promise that if you stowed the same you'd be equipped for any and every out of house challenge. Sadly, such a "guarantee" would resemble a campaign promise; well intentioned, but unlikely kept.

Each set of twins is made up of two individual children. Each mommy is different, too. You will likely elect to store your mommy maintenance tools in the diaper bag, rather than carry a purse. Select a baby bag with an easy access zipper-pocket, and stow away your wallet, lipstick, keys . . . whatever you consider your "mommy must-haves."

Twin maintenance "must-have" objects needed for out-of-house adventures are fairly universal. Here is a good foundational diaper bag twinventory:

* 4 to 5 diapers (for outings lasting 4 to 5 hours—you may not use any diapers, you may use all)
* Travel box of baby wipes (Keep that well supplied and check it before every outing. One diaper dirtied can require the use of 4 to 5 wipes. Stock generously.)
* Changing pad
* Diaper rash cream and/or petroleum jelly (in a tube)
* 3 to 4 spit-up cloths (cloth diapers are ideal)
* Small plastic dirty diaper (and wipes) disposal bags
* Infant Tylenol (or generic)
* Infant gas drops
* Pacifiers (and a set of spares) if your twosome use them
* Bottles for small infants/finger food snacks for older babies
* Cellular phone and your pediatrician's office phone number
* Spare set of clothes that either twin can wear (for when diapers leak inconveniently)
* A large zip-close freezer bag (or you can use your diaper disposal bags, just don't confuse them) for storing diaper explosion sullied clothes
* Infant nail clippers (you would be amazed how often a snagged fingernail appears . . . usually manifested by a bloody facial scratch while shopping)
* Travel pack of tissues
* Trial-size/travel bottle of antibacterial no-water-needed soap (for your hands following the emergency diaper changes that occur miles away from a sink-outfitted bathroom)

However, the real and more frequently retrieved treasures in your diaper bag trove will be the strategically stashed objects that compel your babies to scrutinize and explore for a lengthy periods of time.

Suggestions?
* Small handheld toys/rattles (quiet ones!) for the very young
* Chunky board books
* Tiny inexpensive plush toys

* Teethers
* 4 to 8 thin single-story paperback books for older twins

You can also be creative with objects you allow your twins to handle and explore, based on their age, and the location of your outing. For example, the strip cards with paint color samples have proven endlessly fascinating to our twins. Plastic spoons (young twins) or paper-wrapped straws (slightly older twins) from food courts? Equally enjoyable. Tongue depressors or cotton balls (not if your twins still put everything in their mouths) at the doctor's office? You can't top 'em. Almost every locale you visit will have some free or very inexpensive novelty item that will keep your twins curious and entertained while you attend to the tasks at hand.

Best of all, when one twin's attention span with a particular object has expired, voilà. You can trade objects betwixt the babes and literally double your distraction time. Thus doubling your contented/well-behaved time while getting groceries, meeting a friend for coffee, having your hair cut (styled/highlighted might be pushing things), and the like. If you do your preparation well and store (or acquire on the fly) numerous pairings of entertaining items, you'll be amazed at the duration of stroller-happy time you can facilitate.

Warning: don't get overconfident once you have packed your bag efficiently and have had a flawless day of good behavior with two terrific tots. Maintaining an ever-changing cache of diversions and entertainments in your double-duty diaper bag will require military-style observation, constant vigilance, and regular rotation. Your twins will do their half of the job if you do yours.

Diaper bags: They're not just for diapers anymore. For sensible moms, I doubt they ever were.

23

Financial Finagling

L ike the dual residents in utero, the flood of emotions experienced on hearing the "It's twins!" diagnosis often has a distinct duality. Intellectually and spiritually, the gift of twins is undeniable. Physically, emotionally, and perhaps most tangibly, financially, the gift of twins is daunting.

Learning not one but *two* infants are on the way forces parents to re-examine their projections and ideas on what life will be like as a rapidly expanding family. Revising budgetary plans is no exception.

Yes, the initial monetary outlay will be greater with twins than with a singly born child; but in the long run, you may find you *save* money over having two children in sequence.

How do you start preparing yourselves for the redirection and re-allocation of your current income? How do you develop a fiscal plan for scaling back to one income if one parent is making the career change to stay-at-home parent?

Estimate

When you discovered you were pregnant, and perhaps even before, you likely began some early guesswork on the additional expenses that would become part of your household responsibilities with a new baby.

Be not dismayed, your efforts will not be wasted now that you know two are en route; you will just need to re-calibrate your projected financial plan.

Diapers, formula, pediatrician's office co-pays, clothing, car seats, crib, nursery regalia, toys, college savings, daycare/nanny care . . . each family has specific predictable needs. With twins, some of those expenses will double and others will not.

When it comes to wise preparedness, best to add cushion to your anticipated budget. You may plan to breastfeed your twins, but add formula costs into your estimated budget. You may plan to use non-brand name diapers and baby toiletries. Allow those savings to manifest in your real-world spending, but guesstimate generously when creating your spending projections. Acknowledge that unpredictable expenses will surface in those early days of full-family financial fluctuation.

When anticipating your high-dollar investments, don't immediately jump to the "we've got to get a minivan" and "we need a bigger house" conclusion.

If the twins are your first children, a minivan is far from an imperative. A four-door high-safety-rating car will do just fine. If you have other booster/car seat requiring children, you may indeed be thrust into a situation where a bigger vehicle is necessary in order to accommodate two additional car seats. When it comes to a bigger house, consider the possibility of reworking, re-assigning, and doubling up room spaces before defaulting to the "we have no other choice" call to the realtor.

If you plan to hire a nanny, au pair, sitter, housekeeper, or plan to make use of a daycare facility, the costs for those services are higher for the care of two infants than for one. Some child-care establishments do offer a twin discount, so do ask if a reduced rate is applicable when you are calling for rates to include in your estimated expenses.

The Double Daddy Perspective

Someone once told me that if you wait for the right time to have kids, you never will because you'll never have enough time or enough money or a big enough house or a big enough car. And that person was right! Because on paper it never adds up and yet in most instances it does work out because the moment your children are born, your entire universe shifts and puts your babies in the center. Suddenly, recreational shopping is no longer as captivating, fine dining doesn't taste as good, two hours are better spent on the floor with your babies than at the movies and all those things that you thought you had to have and had to do seem a little less important. And I think it's because of this that the lights in your home stay on, the tank in your car has gas, and the table in your kitchen has food placed upon it.

Evaluate

Look at your current spending patterns. Pull out those stashed checkbook registers. Look at your tax receipts. Many credit card companies provide year-end statements pie-graphed to reveal what percentage of your charged pie goes for which category of your lifestyle (e.g., groceries, dining/entertainment, medical, clothing, charitable donations).

What are the "constants" of your current budget? Mortgage/rent, utilities, phone expenses, cable/dish TV, insurance, car payments, college loan repayments, credit cards . . . some of those will need to remain unchanged. Others may be more malleable than you currently believe.

When you review your pre-twins spending, seek out the areas where a seemingly elective "glut" of your money goes. Also realize which areas will need more financial investment once the twins arrive (e.g., groceries and clothing).

By determining your predicted expense "constants," your current spending "gluts," and your twintensified future financial needs, you are ready to embark on the next step of your strategic spending strategy.

Eliminate and Designate

We had decided before I became pregnant that I would leave my job to care for a child (which suddenly became child*ren*); so jarringly, the first thing eliminated from our budget was a second income—which at the time constituted half of our annual finances. While that might seem very scary for those of you considering the same option, you may well find your decision fiscally sound after deciphering the actual *cost* of both parents working full time with two newborns.

Beyond the fact that we would not need to finance daycare arrangements for two infants, expenses affiliated with my day-to-day workplace experience would evaporate. The annual investment made in refreshing my work-appropriate wardrobe, the daily lunches, the frequent after-work get-togethers, even the cost of keeping gas in the car for the daily commute, all of those rarely tallied but collectively costly expenses would disappear.

Whatever decision you make regarding parental work roles, numerous expenses will vanish from your budget once your twins arrive. In our DINK (Dual Income, No Kids) household, an amazing proportion of our annual spending went toward out-of-house social adventures.

Weekly dinners out, impromptu movies, and an annual anniversary vacation carved out a gluttonous slice of our financial pie. As a TWINC (Two Wee Infants Needing Care) household, we knew that those frequent outings would be replaced with more home-based, less-expensive entertainments.

Do a survey of your expenditures that may be regarded as luxurious. Depending on your personal scale of priorities, you will be able to readily determine the easily sacrificed as well as the mandatory to maintain.

For us, we knew we'd actually get more benefit from our expanded cable TV once the babies were born; but we knew that the voluminous numbers of periodicals to which we subscribed would rarely be read. Twelve magazine subscriptions were pared to four—quick and easy decision.

Other decisions may not be so simply made. Maybe you have an affinity for your weekly manicure/pedicure. Maybe your partner is dedicated to his weekly golf game. Consider a temporary moratorium on the indulgences that you may find yourselves too sleep-deprived to enjoy fully in the first weeks with twins.

Potentially harder decisions may need to be made. Is your mortgage/rent crippling you financially? Even though you may be multiplying in number, your family may be better served by scaling back (rather than the reflexive scaling up of) your residence. If reducing the monetary outlay for your shelter allows you the financial flexibility to handle unpredictable twin-related expenses, moving may be the most courageous and appropriate decision you can make.

Investigate, Then Incorporate

Thankfully, since the expenses involved in having and raising a single child are fairly well publicized, there are many, many organizations that seek to ease your twinflicted financial drain.

Who are these kindhearted folk, and how can you as a twin-expectant family take advantage of the savings opportunities afforded by your pending twin-family status?

Baby Product Manufacturers

Get thee to a computer and use any search engine. Input variations on "freebies," "discounts," "offers," "multiples," and "twins." Find out the requirements to access coupons and special offers that diaper, formula, baby bath products, and toy manufacturers make available to expectant twin/multiples families.

Many baby-centric corporations have mailing lists to which they send regular product samples and coupons. Get your name on those lists early!

While on the computer, visit some of the numerous twin support sites. Many of them keep fairly current listings of which special offers are available for new and expecting twin parents.

Baby Product Vendors

Never be afraid to ask what offers and discounts are available to you as a family with twins. Many stores have "unpublicized" but long-standing reduced rates for twin/multiple families applicable merely for the asking. Early on, I learned to keep a photocopy of our twosome's birth certificates standing by for twin verification when needed. Many baby clothing stores, baby furnishing stores, daycare centers, baby exercise/music/swimming class providers, and even a grocery store or two endeavor to ease your financial burden. Let them!

Your Pediatrician's Office

Clearly, you have two children, so two insurance co-pays or sets of billable services apply. However, pediatricians' offices are beset with pharmaceutical company representatives, who in generous efforts to familiarize families with their brand offerings, leave abundant product samples for distribution to the office's patients. As a twin family, you will often be the recipient of whatever samples you ask for . . . and many you don't even need to ask for! After our first weight check, a kind nurse asked if we were breast or formula feeding. Even though we were in the fledgling stages of nursing our twosome, she wisely stated that "you never know," and sent us home with *eight* full-size cans of formula. After each and every set of immunizations, we were asked if we had plenty of infant acetaminophen on hand. On the rare occasion we responded, "Not really," we were sent home with handfuls of sample-size bottles.

Moms of Multiples Club Yard Sales

Who better to realize the need for inexpensive twin-needs acquisition than twin moms themselves? Most multiple moms clubs have two annual yard sales, one in the spring and one in the fall. The savings experienced in those twice-yearly yard sales alone make the nominal club registration fees worthwhile. Additionally, communication with a local corps of fellow multiple moms gives you access to other women actively seeking local sales and twin savings opportunities.

Kiddie Consignment Stores

Not only can you reasonably purchase "gently used" clothing and baby accoutrements at stores such as these, but you can also sell your gently used and outgrown items. Money saving and making simultaneously . . . these stores are a true boon for twin parents.

What other methods and opportunities should parents consider in attempts to finesse their twin family financial strategy?

Coupons

Not only for products you know you will be using but for those you *might* use or need. Case in point: anytime I see a coupon for a $10 gift-card or free groceries with a new or transferred prescription, I cut the coupon out and put it in my wallet. With two infants, you may have a prescription-requiring ailment at a moment's notice. Be ready and save some money.

Be sure to check your grocery store receipt coupons. Often, the receipt companion coupons bear thematic resemblance to the products you have just purchased. So for those trips when you have bought diapers and baby food en masse, you probably have a cash register provided coupon for your next purchase of the same. Use 'em!

(Caveat emptor: The companies that produce the most coupons are also typically the companies that manufacture the most expensive products. If you elect to use the more expensive brand name, definitely use coupons. If you are more of a "whatever is most affordable or on sale" shopper, be sure to compare the price of an off-brand product against the brand name with the coupon. On many occasions, even with a coupon doubled by the grocery store, the off-brand is still cheaper.)

Photography studios strategically send coupons to households with new babies. With twins, be sure to read the small print carefully. Many coupons offer free photos and great savings but often require a sitting fee for each individual who participates in the photo shoot. Keep your eyes open for, and make use of, the coupons that waive sitting fees.

Tax Write-Off

Double dependents . . . enjoy!

Credit Cards That Offer Cash-Back or Airline Miles

If you are the kind of person who is tempted to charge beyond your means, then don't heed this tip. However, if you can keep your spending within budget, and use a credit card to do so, credit cards that offer goodies proportionate to your usage are a great payment option.

Telecommuting or Home-Based Businesses

If one parent will be staying home with the children, once a regular sleep pattern is established for the household (and only then), explore the possibilities of money-making efforts from home. In an Internet-connected world, many parents have been able to retain a modified role with their pre-children employer, while others have embarked on entirely new ventures that allow for frequent interruption and flexible work schedules.

Savings Accounts

Most banks allow you to establish a fee-free/no-minimum balance savings account in the name of a minor. Most hospitals provide the paperwork to start the process to acquire Social Security numbers for your twins. Once you have received the numbers for your children, go ahead and start up an account in each baby's name.

Re-negotiate

You may discover after your babies are a few months old that your budgetary plans have provided you with more "left-over" cash than expected. Fantastic! You have a few options.

Stay the course with your financial course of action and build up a monetary safety net for emergencies, increase the amount deposited into (or start up) college savings accounts, or sock it away for a future trip to Disney World.

If you have scaled back your lifestyle so stringently, relax the purse strings a bit in the areas where you feel you have "deprived" yourselves.

Your decisions aren't working out the way you had hoped? You are finding yourselves financially strapped?

Closely examine your postpartum spending and see if there are areas that can be tightened.

Maybe you've splurged on more "irresistible" baby gear than truly necessary. In well-intentioned efforts to have some needed "couple time," the two-infant babysitter rate combined with your dinner and movie out may not be the wisest fiscal decision. Maybe you purchased a new vehicle and the payments are paralyzing.

Sit down with your partner and put to the true test your current spending practices. Put everything under the monetary microscope. Even a daily cup of coffee adds up.

As a couple, you may have declared your savings accounts as "off-limits," to be used only in an emergency. If you have *truly* honed every spending option, the first few months with twins may be your "emergency."

If you have no savings, you may consider a low-rate loan to get you over the hump . . . but only if you have *genuinely* winnowed out all unnecessary spending. You don't need to be paying interest on a loan to facilitate your daily latte.

When it comes to your budget, think creatively and collectively and communicate openly and often with your spouse. You may, as we did, be surprised at how naturally the twin-family finances shake into place.

24

Air Travel with Twinfants

If you are anything like my husband and me (pre-children, of course), you bravely attempted to mask your dismay and apprehension when you saw parents boarding your flight with an infant in arms. Now, if you are anything like my husband and me, with the forces of the universe karmically in play, you have occasion to board a plane with not just one but two infants in arms. Fortunately, with a fistful of air travel awareness and some skillful/strategic planning, air travel with twins can be undertaken with minimal stress to you, your spouse, your twins, and your fellow flyers. However, if you skimp on your preparation even a fraction, your probability of traumatic twin travel time is increased exponentially. Thankfully, the corollary is also true; if you go above and beyond in your preparedness, your likelihood of trouble-free (dare I say, terrific?) twin-travel time is similarly increased.

To lend the following suggestions credibility, we have flown with our twosome a total of three times: at 3 months, 15 months, and most recently, at 27 months. Each trip presented its own unique challenges; all were surmountable, and at worst, certainly endurable. According to our fellow passengers, our twins' behavior was even commendable. No doubt, with some forethought and effort on your part, your twins will be fine, too. You might even have fun!

So without further ado . . .

Air Travel Awareness

Many, if not most, airlines permit a parent to carry a child under age two in lap for the duration of a flight. Assuming you are traveling with one adult per child (and I wouldn't suggest it any other way, although it can be done), two seats are all you need to purchase for four travelers . . . a financial twin benefit. But here is where you need to be careful: when booking your tickets, let your booker know you are traveling with infant twins, one per adult.

Unbeknownst to us when we embarked on our first full-family trip, air safety regulations prohibit two infants under two from flying in the same airplane row. My understanding is that it has something to do with the emergency air masks, but regardless of the reason, you can't do it. Flight attendants and courteous copassengers shuffled to get us near each other; but that little morsel would have been helpful to know prior to arrival at the gate.

Be polite, but assertively vocal with your ticket-seller. Ideally, you and your spouse should be seated directly in front and back of each other. That way, you can share access to not only the diaper bag (your treasure trove of travel tricks) but more important, each other. Let the airline (or your travel agent) know that the chances of inconveniencing other passengers will be significantly minimized if you all can be in close proximity to one another.

You have concerns about lap-safety? You are concerned about "fidgety" twins who are older and can walk? You want to simulate car travel for your twosome? You may elect to go ahead and purchase four seats. Be sure to ask your airline; they may offer a discounted seat rate for your twins. Bring your twins' car seats, and be sure to take advantage of the "preboarding" option. That way, you can get seats and infants safely strapped in before mass boarding occurs. Plus, since you will already have your car seats, you won't need to rent them at your vacation destination. (If you aren't traveling with car seats and plan on renting a car on arrival, make your reservation not only for the car but for two appropriately sized car seats as well. Car seats are easily forgotten in the planning stages, but oh-so-mandatory. Many car rental companies have a limited number of car seats available, so don't wait until you pick up your car to ask for them . . . especially since you need two. You don't need that stress to start off your holiday!)

When buying your plane tickets, don't be shy to your own detriment. Ask questions! Is the plane equipped with a changing table?

(Many are not. Those that do have changing tables are cozy at best. You may decide to preemptively change diapers prior to boarding. Alleviate oversaturation potential . . . after all, they're on your laps.) Is there a way for flight attendants to warm formula or breast milk if needed mid-flight? Is there an outlet in the plane lavatory that you can use for your breast pump if needed? (Nursing moms: Speaking as a mom who nursed our twins the first year, I would not attempt to nurse one or both twins midflight. There is enough awkwardness and stress in a cramped plane seat without trying to orchestrate an effective nursing position. Don't use this opportunity as a bully pulpit to extol the virtues of nursing. Consider your neighbors comfort, and most important, your babies'.)

Guess what? When boarding, you can wheel your double stroller all the way to the end of the jetway, collapse the stroller, cozy up to a baby each, and board the plane. With a gate-bestowed tag, your stroller will await you at the plane door upon reentering your destination's jetway. Very, very helpful.

When you feel you have grilled your airline/ticket booker to your satisfaction, then ask them a final question: What can WE do to ensure we are good passengers with children in tow? They may have some suggestions, and many will involve your . . .

Strategic/Skillful Preparation

Be aware of your twins' feeding schedule when booking your flight. At three months, our twins were relying exclusively on breast milk for their nutrition, every 3 hours. And as a twin-nursing mommy, if I went much longer than 3 hours without relieving breast pressure/milk accumulation, my breasts would have encroached and/or exploded on neighboring seatmates. The idea of a previously enviable "direct" flight became out of the question. And by necessity, my dairy-strength electric breast pump was declared carry-on number one. (Side note: Airline security staff was highly curious as to what exactly the stylish, yet suspiciously mechanical, black bag contained. Once we revealed its nonsinister nature, it was rapidly returned to my care. Especially when I described that the "liquids" [evident through x-ray] were bottles of breast milk, so that when we hit our layover, hubby could tandem bottle-feed them in the double stroller while I pumped out the supply for the next feed. With twins, sometimes revealing a bit too much information can work to your advantage!)

Believe it or not, you may well want a substantial layover. Why, you ask? Whether you are bottle-feeding, attempting to nurse in the airport (if so, you're a braver woman than I), or solid food feeding your twins, you will want to prepare and feed them their meal without the stress of having to rush to a connecting flight. The meal, however administered, can and should provide your twins with a midtrip reassurance that all is still "on or close to schedule." Count on at least 30 minutes for eating.

If you are a breastfeeding mom and typically tandem nurse your twins for 20 minutes, any breast pump session lasting less than that time frame may not empty your breasts enough for the twins' next feed. You'll still feel engorged and uncomfortable. In order to keep our layover somewhat sensible in length, hubby bottle-fed our twosome simultaneously in the double stroller while I pumped. If you each decide to each feed a baby individually, you'll need to pump after the feeding. In that instance, count on 20 more minutes for pumping. (Side note: I was surprised to discover that airport restrooms rarely have discreet install outlets. As a first-time-twin-traveling nursing neophyte, I wore a comfy pullover. In order to double pump my breasts, I had to pull the front of my sweater over my head and behind my neck so that my hands were free to hold the noisy, churning, sucking funnels in place while I nonchalantly gazed at a paper towel dispenser. The spectrum of reactions was hysterical. Ranging from the sympathetic reassurances of those who had been in my shoes [or funnels], to the squeamish moms who shielded their young son's eyes, to the loudly articulated biology lecture my conspicuous presence inspired, that 20 minutes was without doubt my most memorable pumping session. Short story long: Wear a front closure shirt.)

You will probably need to change your twins' diapers before, and quite possibly after, they've had their meal. Most airport restrooms have a single changing table. It's a popular destination. You may have to wait in line. Potentially four times. (Don't even think about hauling both babies into the restroom simultaneously. Let hubby keep one entertained in the stroller while you change the other, then flip flop.) Add 20 more minutes to your layover.

You may want to rinse the bottles from the twins' meals. You may want to mix formula and/or fill them with freshly pumped breast milk, so they're ready in case you're stuck on the plane for any reason. Add 5 more minutes.

What? You think you and your husband may want to eat or pee during the layover? And you don't want to sprint to your next gate? Add whatever time you think you and hubby may need for your own well-being.

Have I proven my point? Please trust me. Book a generous layover. Yes, it's a hassle to deboard and reboard but far less hassle than the alternative of coordinating twin maintenance comfortably midflight.

In the weeks before your trip, try to look at your day-to-day activity with fresh eyes. Note key items that might be useful in making your vacation time more relaxing and safe for your twins (e.g., things like nightlights, portable CD players with familiar night music, your nursing pillow, special "cozies," are easily overlooked but can be very helpful in reducing your twins' away from home stress). Plan on purchasing diapers, food, sunscreen, and the like upon arrival at your destination. You'll have enough to haul without adding the weighty and space-occupying sundries that are easily acquired anywhere to your packed bags.

Determine if laundry facilities are available at your vacation destination. If so, pack lightly, knowing you'll do a wash. Even if your twins are boy/girl (as ours are), pack plenty of outfits both can wear.

Think about what you have implemented in your home for safety. Will you want to take along some outlet covers, toddler-proof doorknob covers, a Pack 'n Play for "containment" and safe play? We typically rent cribs, but at 27 months, we had a bad case of the climbers. We packed our crib tents in daddy's golf bag.

What will you want within reach during your flight? Those items form the foundation of your in-flight diaper bag. You may decide to upsize your regular at-home diaper bag to an as-big-as-airline-will-approve carry-on.

What was in our diaper bag for our 3-month-old twins air adventure?

1. Diapers/wipes/Vaseline. (More than we thought we'd need of all three. Air delays happen.) A changing pad rounded out our diapering supplies.
2. Burp cloths and bibs. (To mop burp cheese, vomit, and basically absorb any/all bodily output.)
3. Gas drops and infant Tylenol. Adult Advil.
4. Pacifiers and spares. (Altitude fluctuations impact infant ears dramatically. Sucking not only provides comfort in a new and

unusual situation but relieves that ear discomfort. Suck 'em if you got 'em. If your wee ones are non-binky babies, have a bottle standing nearby for the take-off and landing or encourage them to suck on your finger.)

5. A spare set of clothes (for each 3 hours of travel time) per baby. We packed unisex outfits even though our twosome is boy/girl. That way, if one culprit had two diaper malfunctions, he or she wouldn't be forced to crossdress as a consequence.

6. Lots of toys and small books. (We read aloud throughout the flight, and traded toys and books back and forth between each other. Entertained babies are courteous babies)

7. Antibacterial wipes. (For cleaning our hands, the babies' hands, and public changing tables prior to use.)

8. Our wallets, cell phone, emergency phone number list, sunglasses, nutrition bars, and breath mints. (True confession: I stashed a lipstick in there, too. The last thing I wanted to do was add a purse to the mix. Vaseline doubles as a wonderful lip gloss . . . I snitched a swipe of the babies' booty protectant.)

9. Our tickets, itinerary, and photo IDs were easily accessible in front pocket.

Last, but far from least, we had stoked our secondary carry-on (the breast pump storage bag) with bottles of milk . . . again enough for one feed more than anticipated, in case of delays.

Surprisingly enough, the contents of our diaper bag changed little when we traveled again at 15 and 27 months. The breast pump was no longer a necessity, but more books and solid foods/snacks were. You will be able determine the imperative contents for your family's diaper bag based on your twins' age and unique needs . . . the above should just serve as a leaping point.

So you're all packed? Think about how you are going to handle your trip to the airport. Will mommy, twins in stroller, and bags all be dropped off curbside, while daddy parks the car in satellite parking and removes car seats if needed? That's what worked for us, but you may have an alternate plan. The specifics aren't too important, but to have a prediscussed plan is.

Anything you can do to keep your parental stress at a low level will help in keeping your twins stress-free. Which in essence is truly the key to pleasurable air travel with twins. You can prepare as best you can. You can be ready for the situations you can anticipate, but there will be those you can't. Try not to lose your cool when the unexpected happens. Traveling with twins, much like planning and executing a wedding, is fraught with unpredictable, unforeseeable surprises. Despite all best intentions, flights are delayed, even canceled. Children "hit the wall," or get sick at inopportune times. Try to relax, and do your best to roll with the punches. Babies/toddlers can sense your calm (or stress) and will mirror your attitude. If you sense your twins starting to "wig out," step back and see if you are starting to "wig out." Breathe deeply. Speak slowly, softly, and soothingly. You may diffuse the pending dual-detonation by modeling the behavior you desire from your twins.

Whatever you do, don't let the fear of twin-induced turbulence deter you from air travel. Chances are, armed with your carry-on of airline awareness and your suitcase of skillful preparation, your friendly skies will prove smooth sailing indeed. Bon voyage!

25

Full Family Flu and Other Sagas in Sickness

How can you manage when one or both infant twins are sick . . . especially when they cannot actually tell you what ails them? Perhaps the best advice is to stay calm, and realize what you can and cannot control. Certainly, you can control your powers of acute observation.

Make sure before the twins arrive that you have a reliable, pediatrician-recommended infant/childcare medical reference text. My husband used to get very amused upon arriving home from work to a coffee table (or bed) full of texts opened to chapters on whatever affliction I feared the twins might be suffering from. Sure, it looks silly to those who haven't spent the day with two babies, one of whom seems out-of-sorts/lethargic, the other who seems to be breathing too rapidly, but the reassurance of knowing what to look for when early symptoms begin to surface helps greatly when an eventual call to the pediatrician may be necessary. (Plenty of times, it wasn't.)

Before you think the medical books just foster hypochondriacal alarmism, let me tell you, reassurance galore was provided when the tomes revealed our symptoms were incomplete for a life-threatening diagnosis. Equally reassuring was acquiring the knowledge of what we should be keeping an eye out for . . . an elevated fever or excessive grogginess . . . whatever might help the doctor in deciphering what ailed our little ones.

You can and should document in writing which baby experiences, which atypical symptom, and when. You may feel as though you can remember each and every unique aspect of their dual existence, and perhaps you can. But when you are exhausted, emotionally invested, and maybe even ill yourself, err on the side of safety. We made a point to keep our snot spectrum status/temperature tally/medications menu written down by the phone, so that if the pediatrician call was necessary, we had the up-to-date information on each baby ready for dispensing. My husband also would benefit from check-in calls home, and I could accurately relay how everyone was faring.

Even when the medical books declare the twins are not in danger, you often will (and should) call or visit the pediatrician just to see what, if anything, you can do to ease your babies' discomfort, as well as confirm there is not an undiagnosed problem. On occasion, you may just have a gut feeling that "something isn't right." Respond accordingly.

Early in our twins' lives, many well-wishers declared: "You will know when something is seriously wrong; it's mother's intuition." Another oft-repeated prediction was: "You will be able to tell sight-unseen what each cry means." Imagine my disheartenment when I did *not* sense any "intuitive" instincts regarding my newborns' health. Feelings of gross inadequacy compounded when not only could I not discern what a specific cry "meant" but frequently I could not determine which baby was even crying!

Please don't allow yourself to feel incompetent if you experience the same "lack" of maternal mystique. As time passed, my experience, *not intuition*, increased. My familiarity with what was "normal" and what was out of the ordinary solidified and allowed me to act with greater expedition and confidence than in those first trying days. Time-earned experience has helped me respond with more "maternal" wisdom than any miraculous birth canal enabled bestowment of magical mommy powers.

Your twins may manifest symptoms of the same virus/illness differently. For instance in our house, when strep has reared its ugly head, Darren runs a fever and loses appetite. Sarah shows no symptoms until it is well rooted, then she typically wakes, asks for water, and vomits it up.

As much as you dislike your children being ill, with repeated illnesses of the same ilk, you *do* familiarize with how your twins individually respond and can anticipate the course of action you need to take for each. Practice and experience, as unpleasant as they are to acquire, alleviate the extreme anxiety parents feel with repeated occurrences of sickness.

Treat the forays to the pediatrician's office as you would a trip to the grocery store. Bring along diversionary books and toys, as well as bottles or sippies for keeping your twosome hydrated. Pack extra spitty/burpie cloths if someone is throwing up, and plastic bags to store any that are put to use.

Whether your twins' pediatric diagnoses are made via phone or by office visit, you will have a parentally led home-based course of TLC for a window of time ahead.

What can ease the strain and duress of the recuperative period?

Reassuring Attitude and Extra Affection

Parents notoriously adopt nonthreatening monikers for some of the more intimidating aspects of biology (wee-wee, poo-poo, booty, pee-nie, and girl parts are a few we've used in our house). Perhaps no occasion merits the softening of words quite as much as a household bout of illness. Physical energies and spirits are depleted, and everyone's nerves are on edge.

Lightening the mood with softened terminology like "Beep-Beep" (the ear thermometer), "Purple juice" (grape-flavored Pedialyte, or its generic), "Boogy sucker" (the nasal syringe), and "Spitting the Ickky" (vomiting) has had a mentally coddling effect not only for our twins but for us as parents. Verbally reinforcing that the sickness is a temporary state, and we'll all feel better soon helps.

Although you undoubtedly proclaim your adoration of your children frequently, during times of illness, a little extra lovin' goes a long way. Stabilize their sense of dis-ease by reminding them often of your constant love . . . with words, kisses, and hugs.

Dry Erase Board

You will need to keep track of which twin receives what medicine and when; which twin has a temperature and when; which twin has eaten what and when; and which twin has vomited and when. Your pediatrician will have numerous factors you will need to track. Even if only a single child is ill, the dry erase board comes in very handy for noting specifics regarding the ill baby's status and progress.

When our twosome has been tummy sick at the same time, the dry erase board proved very helpful in keeping track of when the specifically timed incremental spoonfuls of water had been given as well as how long saltines had "stayed down" for each child.

Appropriate Means of Medicine Dispensing

Age and development play a role in how best to administer medications to your twins.

Measuring accurate doses that correspond to such a small amount of fluid mandates a dispensary more reliable than the flatware teaspoons our parents used.

Over-the-counter infant drugs and vitamin supplements often come with a conveniently calibrated squeeze dropper included in the cap. As the babies get a bit older, or when prescription medications are added to the mix, an oral syringe works well. We found it helpful to pour a half-shot of the medicine into the shallow cup that comes atop many bottles of nonprescription drugs, and then from that cup, syringe up the amount needed—as opposed to awkwardly submerging the syringe into the neck of the medicine bottle and attempting to siphon from there. Regardless of whether you are using a dropper or oral syringe, when giving the meds to your babies, aim the outflow toward their inner cheek. They will more likely (and calmly) swallow the bulk of the dose. If you aim for the back of their throats in order to "force" the swallow, you'll likely be met with an anxious and fighting patient when it comes time for the next dosage.

As the twins get older, medicine time gets easier . . . well except for when only one twin is sick. With children's medications being so delectable (barring a persistent few that we can certainly remember from our own childhoods), the challenge is to explain to the healthy twin that they *don't* get the amoxicillin ambrosia.

Do seek out the unusual minor tasks that bring smiles amidst the chaos. Deftly pouring the exact amount of liquid medication into a pharmacy-given dispenser spoon with the well-practiced precision of a Manhattan bartender always proved a joy bringer for me.

High Chairs and Videos

If your twins are old enough to sit up, and God-willing you won't have a tummy bug before that time, high chairs can be a tremendous aid in establishing your in-home twinfirmary. Excessive TV and/or videos are rarely advisable for young children. However when our twins were sick, our limits were loosened. I found it helpful to place the high chairs in our living room, and set up a mini-entertainment (or more accurately, distraction) area. We would get an appropriate new video or two and some new books. When the twins were in the high chairs, their mobility was restricted . . . forcing rest, quelling the temptation of overexertion in moments of sudden energy, and containing not only their bodies but any unsavory bodily output as well. Dispensing medicines, a sometimes messy process, was easily accomplished in the high chairs. Likewise, the doling out of saltines, dry toast, and other crumb-prolific bland solids for recuperating babies is more easily contained with the high chairs.

Vinyl Mattress Covers

Your twins' mattresses should always have these under their adorably patterned sheets, but when rotavirus or some other dreaded stomach destabilizing illness is in-house, to ease your intensified workload, strip the fitted sheets and have the babies sleep on the washable/wipe-friendly cover. Cozy them up with soft receiving blankets that can easily be thrown in the laundry when soiled, and reduce your voluminous quantity of wash by a fraction.

Antibacterial Cleaners, Wipes, Sprays

The mattress covers, exersaucers, small toys, high-chair trays, the nursery, the playroom, the changing table, the baby bath tub . . . when you have had a major bout of a contagious illness in your home, you become keenly aware of locales where germs can multiply and be spread. Put Lysol, Purell, and their cleanliness-loving cousins to use when sickness visits your home. Pediatricians stay remarkably healthy in the sickest of seasons with relentless exposure to communicable diseases. How? Repeated hand washings between patients. With two little patients, you essentially have a mini-pediatrician's office in your own home. Employ the same methodology they do to make every effort to stay well.

Sometimes, despite all your best efforts, you will find yourself simultaneously sick alongside your twins. Remember the ad campaign with the tag line, "I haven't got time for the pain"? Never will that line ring truer than when you are caregiver for two (or more) utterly dependent and ill children. Twin-mommyhood imbues you with motivation you've likely not experienced before. You will be amazed at how you can continue to accomplish maternal feats . . . especially when prior to the twins' arrival (if you are like me) you would have resigned yourself to bed and wallowed in sick misery. However, just like so many other instances in twin-parenting, if you need help, *ask for it*!

Medically, a parent (unless a parent is a doctor) can only do a limited amount to help. Take comfort in the knowledge that there are pediatric specialists for just about every scrape, illness, and condition your twosome can develop. Before age two, we had visited (not from curiosity, but by necessity) a pediatric orthopedist (Sarah broke her wrist not once but twice before her second birthday. Be sure to note the crib tents in "Maximizing Modern Mommy Marvels"), a pediatric ophthalmologist (Darren had a tear duct blockage and a subsequently diagnosed disparity in eye strength), a pediatric allergist (Darren exhibited extreme shortness of breath when given amoxycillins and cepholosporins), a pediatric endocrinologist (Sarah was diagnosed with diabetes after a bizarre episode of post-tummy bug dehydration and blood sugar fluctuation), and last but not least, a pediatric urologist (Darren's foreskin "reattached" a few months after his circumcision.)

For those of you who have just had or are about to have your twins and whom I have now frightened into a flustered phone book "Pediatrics" scanning dither, calm down. Let me give you the "conclusions" of all those appointments.

Sarah's bones in her wrist healed marvelously. All that remains of the experience are her cast-encumbered two-year-old portraits and an abiding affection for Dr. Sharps and Nurse Tina who let her select the colors of her casts.

Darren's duct blockage procedure went famously, and only one operation was needed. The follow-up appointments to check his variation in eye strength revealed that his eyes were equalizing on their own.

Allergy testing revealed that Darren's reactions to the two families of drugs were not allergies but rather dramatic responses to the illnesses he had exacerbated by the prescriptions given. No drugs are off-limits.

Thankfully, Sarah's diabetes diagnosis was retracted after overnight in pediatric intensive care, her body regulated blood sugars on its own. We have monitored her blood sugars periodically and with the passage of time, it seems indeed she may have just outgrown her bizarre stress-induced hyperglycemia.

Darren's peenie is fine and has required no further foreskin intervention.

Whenever your household experiences a doubled wave of health problems, treat it as you would any other obstacle. Remember to maximize your resources. Err on the side of caution by taking no unnecessary risks. Perhaps most important, when the situation seems almost insurmountable, focus on the transience of your challenge. Never forget Scarlett O'Hara's mantra, "Tomorrow is another day."

VI

Maturation

26

Adventures in Solid Foods

Your pediatrician will have the best advice on when to have solid foods enter the menu for your twosome. With tiny babies, as twins often are, be ready for family, friends, elderly mall walkers, and the like to suggest you "get some solids" into those babies.

Medically, it seems the suggested start time for solid foods has moved in somewhat of a cyclical fashion. My mother was told to put my brother on cereal at 5 days. He was 9 pounds-plus at birth, so the implication was that he "needed" more sustenance. We were given the go-ahead at 5 months. Many doctors suggest waiting until 6 months. In the United Kingdom, many doctors suggest starting at 4 months. Like so many other aspects of baby-raising, the appropriate age for solid food introduction is yet another subject with widely varying feedback. Be ready to use your own judgment to some degree.

Undoubtedly, the most disconcerting aspect of the first solid food feedings is the fact that the food seems far from solid. When you dilute the rice cereal with the liquid measure advised, it appears no different than the liquid you started with. Be ready. Your babies will know the difference. Have a camera ready. The faces are priceless.

Slowly, you will be introducing various vegetables and fruits into their daily diet. Your pediatrician will have recommendations about what to try and when. Ours suggested starting with "light" vegetables and fruits (e.g., bananas, squash) and work your way toward the "dark" (e.g., spinach, blueberries). Also avoid "mixed" combinations such as "carrots and peas" until you have tried each of them singly. In case of an allergic reaction, you would like to be able to accurately pinpoint the culprit. As a matter of fact, when we began trying new solids, it was advised to try only one new item for a 3-to-5-day span. For instance, if you introduce bananas on Sunday, do not try any new items until at the earliest Wednesday. Some allergic reactions take a while to manifest physically. While we were very fortunate and had no reactions to speak of (other than Sarah's uncomfortable booty rash after apricots), many children do have allergies. Take your time trying new foods. The temptation for parents to "rush" new tastes is great. Avoid that temptation. They have a lifetime to try new foods. Do check with your pediatrician regarding items to dodge. For instance, strawberries, peanut butter, honey, yogurt, all can cause potentially serious negative responses and should be tried only after your pediatrician approves. We knew our babies had problems with gas. Fibrous vegetables were delayed a bit in order to avoid worsening their discomfort. Your babies may need for you to alter their diets as well.

One of my early goals was to make all our baby food. Surely it would be healthier for the babies, and certainly we would save an enormous amount of money. Have you priced a butternut squash lately? Out-of-season sweet potatoes aren't exactly cheap either. Decide what your true motivation is for making your baby food. There are many, many good reasons to do so, and there are fantastic resources to support you in your venture if you decide to go that route. However, do not be deluded into thinking that homemade baby food is always cheaper than jarred. We ended up "home-making" bananas regularly as well as in-season fruits and veggies. Plentiful coupons, manufacturers' special offers for families with multiples, and frequent store sales kept us purchasing the bulk of our baby food prepackaged.

The babies' actual consumption process took more time to develop than I ever would have imagined. Sarah inevitably put her thumb directly into her mouth after each and every spoonful. Our only explanation for this ritual was that the "sucking" process enabled her to swallow the contents in her mouth. Of course the oddest part is that she was never a thumb sucker. If a pacifier had been handy on the high chair tray, she would have clutched at that after every mouthful. So don't be too shocked if your babies incorporate their own methodology on how to down the alien foods shoved into their unsuspecting mouths.

Darren never put his thumb in following a bite. He had his own unique solid food consumption idiosyncrasies. If some food was smeared around the perimeter of his mouth after taking in a spoonful, scraping his outer mouth with the soft rubberized spoon to then funnel in the portion that initially "missed" was not well received. Eventually, he did get used to the gentle spoon-directed re-aiming of food, but it took some time. Darren was also the king of the open-mouth-and-let-food-roll-out routine. You would think this practice would have stopped entirely as solids became de rigueur, but no. When faced with a new tooth, strep throat, or just plain completely stuffed-ness, the food came rolling out without warning. Once table food entered the picture (around one year), I was often deceived into believing a mouthful was heading to his digestive tract only to see a fully to partially chewed wad drool out. Mmmmm, delicious. It's particularly fetching in public places. No doubt many local mall visitors can attest to the appetizing expulsion of a glob of Jr. Cheeseburger chewed just beyond recognition. Here's the extra gross part. Maybe it is my "waste not, want not" mentality, but I often catch myself grabbing the rejected morsel and popping it into my own mouth. Expectant moms, I hope that didn't generate a wave of nausea. New moms, mark my words, the reflex is there. Sometimes I feel one gorilla-esque step away from plucking bugs from my children's hair and consuming them.

One of the great benefits of having twins is that they don't always like or dislike the same foods. We're talking far less potential waste than with a single infant. Frequently, in our case, one would spit out or refuse a new offering, only to have the other lap it up voraciously. (And no, I don't feed the spat-out food to the other infant. I have dibs.) A word of warning: if both babies enjoy an item on Monday, don't be surprised if they hate it on Wednesday. Often, we would be so excited with a new favorite item, we'd rush out and purchase enough to stock a bomb shelter. Invariably, on the next exposure, the previously adored "Country Garden Vegetables" couldn't get within an inch of either face. The good news is you can always re-try an item after a few days. In all likelihood, it will eventually get eaten. Similarly, do not assume because "Tender, Sweet Peas" were drooled out, followed by the gag reflex, that your children will never like them. Chances are, they will. We gave up on the idea of keeping a list of which baby liked this and hated that. The list had too many mark-outs and arrows over to the other baby's column. Just try to stay flexible.

Liquids are a whole other story. Cow's milk is not to be given to infants under the age of one without a doctor's okay. We began introducing it to the babies when we started the weaning process at 11 months. If you are nursing and wean earlier than 11 to 12 months, your doctor will likely advise a formula replacement for the breast milk. If you are formula feeding, remain on formula until 11 to 12 months, or until your doctor advises otherwise. Not all dairy is verboten, however. Our pediatrician recommended full-fat yogurt for ours at around 9 months. They loved it. Hard to find and expensive, but the additional calcium in those first two years is tremendously important for bone and brain development. Go ahead and splurge.

If there is one word I can hear infants in shopping malls, grocery stores, church hallways, hollering in my mind's ear, that word is "Juice!" Our family philosophy, and the philosophy of our pediatrician, is little or no juice for infants or toddlers. The sugary nature of most juice, along with its very limited nutritional value, makes it a poor substitute for milk, solid fruits, or just good ole water. It's like baby crack. Don't even get me started on Kool-Aid or soda. As mentioned in other areas of this book, babies have a fairly strong suck urge until age two. If you have already eliminated the pacifier as an option, a juice-filled, ever-in-hand sippy cup is a pediatric dentist's nightmare . . . or dream, financially.

Believe me, I cannot take the moral high road and claim that every morsel I have placed in my babies' mouths has been thoroughly and completely healthful. Far from it. But, if you can make an easy decision for their dental and general well-being, why not this one? Once introduced, it's hard to take away from what I understand. If you do want your babies to have some beverage variety, and cannot bear to dodge juice, at least consider diluting it 25 percent juice to 75 percent water, or at least 50–50. It may sound gross to adults, but still a yummy, and more healthful, option for babies.

Which brings up another challenge for families embarking on "big people" foods . . . discovering well-received (meaning the twins will actually swallow), healthful options, especially for snacks, in those earliest of solids days.

If you have been to a wedding, church service, or public performance with tiny children in attendance, surely you have memories of ill-at-ease parents hastily retrieving Ziploc baggies of Cheerios, Goldfish, and raisins to assuage the fidgety/fussy wee ones. With two babies to appease, you have decisions and deciphering ahead. Either you unilaterally avoid those situations in which your twins' dual detonation might disrupt the experience of others (and there are certainly occasions where you can and should make that sacrifice), or you carefully winnow the opportunities your family can enjoy with some peace of mind. Skillful snack stashing will help you breeze through many a challenging situation. (Word of warning: don't pack snacks so enticing that less-than-charming behavior subsequently results in the guarantee of a treat!)

What about outings that you know will incorporate a regular mealtime? How can you minimize the stress of preparing the meal, the twins and the environment? As with just about every aspect of twin parenting, dedicating a bit of time to anticipatory forethought will save you parental perspiration and torrents of twin tears.

Here are some questions to ask yourself before packing up and heading out. Where will the meal actually need to occur? Will sinks be nearby so I can wash all hands, or should we pack antibacterial wipes? Are high chairs available? Should we consider our double stroller as dining seating? Are we going to be in a private home or church? Should we bring a "splat mat"? Is there a way to heat the twins' food, or should foodstuffs servable at room temperature be on our menu? Will child-friendly utensils be available for mom/dad to use, or should we pack a disposable spoon?

For our planned menu, are disposable bibs a viable option, or would a set of regular bibs serve our purposes better? (Can the twins remove Velcro-closure bibs? Pack the old-school tie-on types. You don't need twice the airborne bibs when eating out of house!)

Putting a little bit of thought into your pending dining environment will allow the dining out process to transpire with minimal discomfort and potential pleasure!

At a restaurant or in the home, eating has become such a well-practiced, mundane event in our adult lives that watching a tiny two-person team explore every new aspect of dining provides unexpected surprises and entertainment galore.

So for the dessert course, here are a few fun twin-feeding facts and finds: Do not feel as though you need to prepare two separate bowls of rice cereal and use two individual spoons for your first solid food feedings. Most experienced moms of multiples will attest that they made a practice of shared table service for their babies. However, if your twins have allergies, and you feed the non-allergic twin the allergens for the other, for safety's sake, you are a two-bowl, two-spoon family.

Once your twins can eat table food, check with your pediatrician about do's and don'ts. Then consider introducing your twins to some approved, but out-of-the-ordinary, food items. Our Sarah was on the smallish side, so we were seeking healthful, yet fatty, foodstuffs. Avocados and black olives were surprising favorites. Her brother demonstrated an unexpected penchant for salsa . . . using restaurant chips as a vehicle to scoop it into his mouth. On a whim, we offered our 18-month-old twins a taste of our baked haddock, having prepared the twins a more "child-appropriate" meal. They both ate it voraciously.

Be careful describing your twins' eating tendencies in their presence. The stages and phases of your developing dual diners are transient. Don't inadvertently provide expectations you don't want the twins to meet. "She is such a picky eater!," "You sure aren't a vegetable eater," "Sweets are all we can get him to eat" are all off-the-cuff assessments that can casually escape a frustrated feeding parent's lips. Instead, concentrate on verbally reinforcing the eating habits you want repeated for the long haul.

If one of your twins has a severe food allergy, do not feel guilty about "depriving" the nonallergic twin by not serving the dangerous catalyst. We don't miss what we have never had. You may decide you don't even want the potentially life-threatening substance in the house. Sippies change hands. Food items get dropped on the floor and eaten hours later. Understandably, you may feel better safe than sorry.

Once your twins are in high chairs and have increased manual dexterity, prepare for the "toss the bottle/sippy" over the edge of the tray game, times two. Decide if you want to play along for a while or if you won't tolerate it at all. Either way, when the beverage is thrown overboard, you have three choices:

1. You can leave it there. (The twins learn about gravity and consequence.)
2. You can pick it up and return once, and warn the high chair quarterback(s) the next time the drink is tossed, it stays where it lands. (The twins learn about gravity and a compounded consequence.)
3. You can laugh and return the drink(s) every time, sending both babies into a frenzy of throwing everything off their trays, every meal. (The twins learn mommy likes bending over and over and over and over . . .)

If your high chairs are being used over a nice hardwood floor, or atop an expensive carpet, consider investing in "splat mats" . . . washable plastic overlays to place under the high chairs limiting the damage done by projectile food or beverage.

Family mealtime can and should be fun (whether grown-ups feel comfortable eating while feeding the twins or not, table-centered time is valuable). Just be ready for food-based mimicry of all kinds. Try to restrain your parental laughter when you don't want to encourage a particular behavior. Laughter is as happy and desirable a response as a kiss or smile. One twin gets a laugh? Not only will that twin repeat the act but the other twin will join in the fun. Dinnertime parental laughter and smile reinforcement work to your advantage when the twins precariously work their own spoons into their mouths . . . not so much so when they simultaneously "cookie monster" saltines into their mouths.

You may bemoan the fact that your twins eat the same breakfast (or other meal) everyday and declare you are in a menu rut. Your choices are simple. Either stop offering that meal (if it is an unhealthy meal, your choice should be a simple one), and prepare for a few vocal feedback sessions; or continue feeding the twins that same meal, and stop projecting the adult desire for variety onto the babies. If they are eating healthily, repetition may actually be better than incorporating less-desirable food options just for something "different."

Try to limit your maternal anxiety when your twins have phases of food disinterest. An occasional meal or two with minimal consumption is no true cause for parental alarm. Of course always keep your eyes out for emerging teeth, symptoms of colds/coughs/sore throats that inhibit appetite, or make eating uncomfortable. If the twins are otherwise healthy and don't eat what you deem a full meal at one sitting, relax. The next meal will probably resemble an all-you-can-eat baby buffet.

Twins tend to be small, so instinctively we as twin parents want to make sure they eat. A mistake often made is to offer option after option just trying to make sure something "gets in them." Precedents for future mealtimes can be set very early. Obviously, use your best judgment and bear in mind your twins' specific needs, but stay aware of what and how you are feeding your twins.

Meals and snacks can be made even more fun by implementing child-directed dining accessories. Melamine child-size (nonbreakable) plates and bowls, character bibs, even multicolored sprinkles are inexpensive (often available as "dollar items") ways to enliven table time.

Just because an item is designed for use by newly solid consuming babies does not mean it is mandatory, or is even advisable, for your family. When we introduced utensils to our twins, we learned quickly that just because miniature forks and spoons are "designed with kids in mind," there is no guarantee that every child appreciates that "design." We tried numerous types of plastic kids' utensils of varied prices only to discover that both of our twins found sets from the Dollar Tree the most user-friendly.

Inventions like the infant bowls and plates undergirded with powerful suction cups to adhere to the high-chair tray seem brilliant . . . especially considering the "tray toss" games addressed earlier. However, depending upon your twins' individual natures, incorporating the attachable tableware into your double dining repertoire may not be so genius. One of our twins, surely a physicist in the making, empirically observes, pokes, prods, and worse pulls at any new object in sightline. Exert enough pull power against the suction, and the bowls release and propel into the air . . . with their contents in tow. Gauge your twins' natural inclinations and make your decision on investing in these bowls accordingly.

Meal-focused outings with your young twins can be great fun. However, don't set your sights too loftily on how much you as mom will be able to personally ingest while feeding and supervising your babies. As the children get older and more capable of independent self-feeding, your ability to eat alongside them increases dramatically. In the transitional time, it may be wiser for you to get a beverage and small nosh as opposed to purchasing a full meal that will get cold or remain uneaten.

Enjoy the fun days of food exploration with your twins. You'll have twice the photo opportunities, twice the entertainment, and twice the pleasure observing your children develop and mature in tandem.

27

Avoiding Assessments

So which is the active one?" "He must be the outgoing one."
"Which is the cuddlebug?" "Is one the lover and one the
fighter?" "Which is more high maintenance?" For whatever reason,
people love to categorize everything. With twins, comparisons seem to
be inevitable. As a new twin parent, you will be besieged with questions from friends, family, and strangers who are ever-curious about the
nature of twins.

Whether born as a single or as multiples, human nature wants to
project lifelong physical characteristics, talents, and temperaments onto
newborn infants. In retrospect, I remember myself doing it repeatedly
to friends' babies. The intent is most-often complimentary, "He'll be a
heartbreaker!" "Look at those long legs; she'll be a supermodel!"

With one infant, it's typically harmless. Unfortunately, with two,
almost automatically a contrasting comparison is made. If one twin is
"the dominant one," the implication follows that the other is "the sub-
missive one." There is an ill-conceived, reflexive mental process that as-
sumes twins are yin and yang. While never conveyed with intentional
malice, it's important that your twosome not feel "obligated" to con-
form to complementary or supplementary roles. The reality is you can
have two outgoing twins. They may both be cautious around strangers.
They may "flip-flop" qualities regularly.

Don't get offended and lambaste everyone who makes "judgments" on your babies' natures. Give strangers the benefit of the doubt, and realize they are probably just excited to see twins. Try to be polite and use it as an educational opportunity. If the individual who just declared your daughter a "beauty" and your son a "beast" is going to be alongside you for a window of time (e.g., in a grocery line), bring your kids actively into the conversation. Smilingly rub your twins' heads and broaden her comments, "I don't know about that, Ma'am . . . Sarah can be pretty strong; and if I had Darren's eyelashes, I sure wouldn't have to buy mascara!" Or you can always frame her comments within a window of time, "Every day they are both growing and changing before my eyes." No matter the age of your twins, best to get in the habit of speaking in unlimited terms and growth potential . . . whether you think they can comprehend your words or not.

Sometimes the twin-directed comments are far more difficult to understand. Occasionally it seems as if the individual feels they are viewing a science experiment and are being graded on their ability to empirically determine which child is superior. Looking straight at a single twin a stranger may say, "Aren't you just the friendly one! Your sister doesn't seem to like me very much." While you bite your tongue trying to keep from declaring you don't like them very much either, remember the conversation initiator *is* attempting to be very kind to your "friendly" child . . . albeit at the expense of your less-gregarious-at-the-moment twin. You can diffuse the tension quickly with a "You are right, Darren is a very friendly boy; and I am certain Sarah doesn't dislike you. She is a bit quiet today." You don't have to diminish the compliment given to one child by automatically applying the same kind words and quality assignations to your other child. Just subtly enlighten the dispenser of judgment that context and timing play a factor in his or her first impression of your twosome.

When strangers, even extended family, proclaim your twins as opposites in temperament and appearance, as the parents, you can remedy it fairly easily. When it comes to daddy and mommy making assessments however, your words are high-impact and life-altering. You need to be very careful.

"If you can't say anything nice, say nothing at all." You cannot count on strangers to follow the wisdom of years gone by, but as parents, you must.

Self-fulfilling prophecy is a powerful psychological tool. You've certainly seen commercials alerting parents to the fact that our words have

Twinspiration

tremendous power. Calling children negative names and describing them with ugly adjectives is deleterious to their self-image. Sadly, and logically, they resign themselves to meeting the low bar that is set for them.

Thank God the corollary is also true. Set your parental expectations high, and the twins' behaviors will usually raise to the loftily-set goal. (Within reason, of course. Remember developmental timing and context.)

Your twins are individuals. They possess skills, physical characteristics, and personality traits all their own. Clearly, many of those special unique qualities will evidence themselves early on, and they will continue to emerge, in your children's lives. Don't feel your twins must possess every positive quality in equal measure . . . or feel compelled to equalize your twosome regarding each compliment given. Each twin can and should be reinforced positively about the similar and differing aspects of their personalities.

In your twins' presence, "If you can't say anything nice, say nothing at all." Once the twins are in bed, you and your partner without inhibition can discuss Baby A's sudden hypersensitivity, or Baby B's aggression; and your thoughts about how best to handle the tricky traits that in all probability are fleeting phases.

If you throw discretion to the wind and use words (and the inflection and tone that accompany them) like overemotional, whiny, and clingy to describe Baby A in his or her presence, those adjectives will be part of what they assimilate into their wee developing vocabulary of self-description. Same applies to casually remarking within Baby B's earshot, "He or she does have a violent streak." Don't permit your unedited speech to unwittingly aid them in deciphering unique (and sometimes undesirable) aspects that differentiate them from one another. Don't take unnecessary risks with what they do and do not understand. Err on the side of safety.

Of course, reinforce the positive attributes each display vociferously. Compliment them often to their faces and to your partner when they are in hearing range. When one parent is away from home, make a point to describe with pride the accomplishments and good behaviors of the day by phone with the twins in the room.

The reciprocal twin and phase-spurred assessments attributed to your twins individually aren't the only twin-based assessments you will confront as twin parents.

The lore, mystique, and even mythology about the special relationship twins share causes many twin parents to negatively assess their twins' bond in comparison to other "more connected" twins . . . genuine or exaggerated. Likewise, many expectant and excited twin parents have researched so thoroughly and are so attuned to the legendary twin-bond manifestations that the specific behaviors are often projected onto the newborn twosome . . . a "seeing what you want (or expect) to see" scenario.

You may be crestfallen if your twins do not speak their own language. On the flip side, you may be thoroughly convinced yours do. Your twins may not make eye contact with each other. You may be certain your twosome can read each other's minds. You will likely find that half the time, you feel twins are mystically bonded. The other half of the time they behave as if they are not even of the same species.

Fear not: your twins are normal, and so are you. Every parent's unspoken penchant is to differentiate their children from the masses. So when one twin falls and the other twin across the room cries, we as twin parents quickly isolate a specific instance that substantiates the twin-connectedness phenomena. Rest assured—twin parents, as any others, don't broadcast (and sometimes don't even notice) the times when their children not only seem disconnected but disenchanted with each other. Avoid assessing your twins' relationship as inferior, based on comparison to the extraordinary, and often embellished, tales of telepathic twin unity.

Some twin assessment is best left to the experts. Babies born prematurely, as twins often are, sometimes experience "lags" in their milestone achievements based on their chronological (actual date of birth) vs. gestational (40-week pregnancy due date) age.

Just as expectant twin moms get used to adjusting their due date to allow for the likelihood of earlier delivery, so too new twin parents get used to giving their twins' actual birth date juxtaposed with their gestational due date at most of the early pediatrician's office visits.

In weight, height, and developmental curves, you can almost always expect young twins to "catch up" with the bulk of their singleton peers. Within the family, one twin may accelerate in size and skill before the other. Avoid alarmist assessments and panic. Allow your doctors to provide the reassurance and care you and your new twins need.

28

From Foreplay to Floor Play:
Your Evolving Relationship with Your Spouse

Unless your double blessings were foretold by an archangel's annunciation, you have an earthly companion in your twin acquisition. Ideally, intimacy (beyond the sheer act of the twins' conception) exists between the two of you that will need to be maintained amidst a cavalcade of new emotions and adjustments.

So what can you expect as a couple in the early days with newborn twins? How can your relationship not only survive but thrive? What can you do to keep love alive?

Most predictably, both partners should anticipate joint exhaustion. When you are sleep-deprived, the loving kindness typical of day-to-day interactions between husband and wife is often the first unintentional sacrifice made. Lengthy, relaxed, even romantic conversations pre-twins can easily mutate into truncated, militant, curtly barked commands when sleep time is at a premium. Ironically, sleep deprivation also contributes to heightened sensitivity. So not only are you more likely to be abrupt to your spouse, you are more likely to have your feelings hurt by an equally abrupt and overtired spouse.

Make a conscious effort to keep your partner's feelings in mind before rapidly snapping. When you are on the receiving end of the less-than-affectionate exchange, take a moment to remember that you both are under transitional strain. If the moment is a suitable one, with compassion and understanding, remind your partner you are working as a team, and to please treat your exhausted emotions with kid gloves. Ask him to call you to task when you're less than loving in your discourse.

What moments are "unsuitable" ones for addressing your issues as a couple? Any time you are in front of your babies. Before they arrived, virtually any time was the right time to discuss your differences as a husband and wife. You have a perpetual audience now. Of course they don't understand the intricacies of marital relations; but they can and do perceive anxiety, stress, and tone. Why else do we coo in their wee faces? Babies learn through absorption of their environment. Keep the surroundings peaceful and calm. In the twin's presence, demonstrate through your voices and physical interactions the reassurance that mom and dad are in control and have a special union all their own.

Avoid the temptation to talk "around" each other . . . talk *to* each other. If you have a grievance with your partner, find the time to address it with him or her directly. Using visiting relatives, or worse, the infants, as a conduit for the information you should direct to each other privately is a bad precedent to start.

For instance, looking at your twins and baby-talking manipulatively (intentionally within your husband's earshot), "Daddy doesn't understand how tough it is taking care of you both all day, does he?" is a reprehensible way of insulating yourself against the rebuttal your husband deserves to provide. Compounding the horror, the twins are being told *to their faces* that you are resentful of the responsibilities (through no choice of their own) they've added to your daily docket. You may believe such contorted and contemptible communication is rarely practiced, but listen to families around you at the mall or grocery store. Assuming infants have limited understanding and thereby subjugating them to the status of unwitting puppets/ventriloquists dummies is unfortunately far from unusual. Be aware of the temptation, and avoid it.

Don't introduce the concept of parental or marital inadequacies (legitimate or merely perceived in a time of minimal rest) to anyone outside your coupled union . . . and *never* to your young twins. If disagreements escalate betwixt you to a checkmated impasse, then by all means seek the intervention of a professional therapist, an objective, skilled negotiator who can help you work toward compromise. I am not suggesting that you cannot confide in, and vent to, your friends. You should, and that is healthy . . . but only *after* you have discussed the subject matters with your partner. You may learn that when you talk to your spouse prior to airing your issues to friends, you don't need to "complain" about your husband to them at all. Resolutions made between you and your man often negate the urge to kvetch to gal pals.

Once the twins arrive, expect prolific advice on how to coddle your marriage, from girlfriends and elsewhere. "Mandatory date nights," "appointments for sex," "child-free weekend getaways," are phrases that have permeated our pre-procreation mindset.

Magazine psychology and talk-show fodder aside, it is important to discuss how you both approach maintaining your special husband and wife relationship after the twins are born. Scott and I felt liberated when we talked about the oft-extolled concept of "mandatory date nights" and realized for us, the idea was ludicrous. Yet, other couples may find it an integral piece of their parental pie. Get all ideas on the table. In our case, we did commit that if we ever felt we were due for, or just wanted, some non-twins-in-attendance man and woman time, we would address it and arrange it.

Of course, calendar dictated occasions like Valentine's Day provide the romantic cattle prod some of us need to orchestrate a night out. Can you guess what we spent the bulk of the evening giggling about over our first Valentine's Day Thai meal as plural parents? You guessed it: the twins' antics and developments. Don't be misled into believing that if you spend time talking about your twins, that you are neglecting yourselves as a couple. For us, and I daresay for many couples, conversation revolves around common interests, goals, and loves. As new twin parents, you will now have two splendidly conversation-inspiring loves to explore. Don't feel badly about your shifting topics of collective interest. Maturation is just that way. My guess is that in retirement communities, there is a great deal of talk on retirement, health issues, and grandchildren.

As a couple, think about what common threads have drawn you together and what you enjoy most about each other. Work your "couple time" around those factors. Some of our most romantic, bond-intensifying moments have been shared with our twins. Prior to the birth of our twosome, a good friend said to me, "If you thought you loved your husband before, wait until you see him hold and love your child(ren)." She could not have spoken truer words.

Shortly after your twins are born, find a moment with your partner to readdress (and revise as necessary) all those prenatal agreements you made before the twins' birth. Just like studying in college for a career path, your time in acquiring knowledge and in defining your goals as a twin-expectant couple is well spent. But, when you get to the "real-world" application stages once your twosome arrives, unanticipated variables may present themselves. Your predicted and mutually decided upon course of action may need some modification. Don't jeopardize your spousal relationship by not sitting down and airing how you both feel your pre-twins'-birth-formulated "plans" are going.

You may both have a joint pat on the back if you have discovered all those early decisions were well made, and you are hip-to-hip, congruent about the direction for the future.

You may find yourselves back at the negotiation table if you collectively realize your prelaid courses of action are not proving successful or were not as developed as they needed to be. Pat yourselves on the back anyway; you are a team, and can work to get a new responsibility and practice flowchart implemented quickly so all can move ahead as a unified, resolved family.

Or, the third alternative: One of you is convinced all is going splendidly according to well-laid plans, and the other is confounded by the muddled mess he or she perceives your "twin-blessed" situation to be. Sit yourselves down at the discussion table, and pat yourselves on the back. As parents, you are two distinct individuals, often with two distinct viewpoints. You have created an opportunity to develop a compromised plan by readdressing the key issues of difference between you. Do so. Your twins will thank you, and your relationship will be better for the discussion.

The temptation to make this a one-word chapter was intense: for the love of your twins, for the love of each other, *TALK*.

Holding grudges, harboring feelings of resentment or inequity in how twin-household responsibilities are being addressed, will do nothing but fester if unaired.

As much as I dislike the liberal dispensation of negative statistics in reference to twin parenting, this one merits a "scare you straight" mention: ". . . higher stress among families raising twins (or higher order multiples) has led to a divorce rate two to three times higher than the national divorce rate" (www.twinstuff.com). Now by all means, don't interpret that citation as unavoidable relationship death knoll. Like all other statistics, use it as a provocateur to endeavor full-heartedly to remain on the corresponding side of the stat . . . a surviving (and ideally thriving) twin-blessed couple.

What course of action gives you optimum chances of marriage maintenance? Our one word chapter: *TALK.*

Sometimes when you give voice to some of your concerns, you may laugh realizing how silly they sound. Don't let that stop you! Laughter is an unmatched tension-reliever.

On the opposite end of the spectrum, sometimes tears will start flowing when you only anticipated a simple revelation of a "small" issue. Tears are equally healing. Let them roll and get it out.

Once the twins are born, evaluate the communications/negotiations practices you and your partner currently employ, and make sure they are appropriate for perpetuation once you have twin newborns in-house.

For instance, many couples, in sincere efforts to keep the distribution of responsibility and individual time at an equitable balance, exercise a "quid pro quo"-style of marriage management. Man takes trash; woman does laundry. Woman goes to book club; man has golf Saturdays. If you attempt to tally which partner accomplishes each and every aspect of twin upkeep, and who has had more "time away" you both will be totally bogged down and resentful of one another before you know it. Learn to gauge your individual needs and let your partner know when you need some relief. Be open to your partner's requests for the same.

You and your partner may be used to sublimating your personal feelings with the intention of "keeping the peace" . . . confronting them only when volatility reaches an apex. Letting anger build to that level is no longer an option. Your household peace will be best kept with fluid, open borders.

Similarly, if you have been tight with words of compliment or appreciation, release those flood gates. Keep your eyes open to notice those things that too often go unnoticed and underrewarded. Allow your twins to hear the mutual affection and respect mommy and daddy share.

Watching your partner swaddle a baby, create giggle-provoking tandem belly poke games, rinse the breast pump funnels, empty the diaper pail while singing "Old McDonald Had a Farm" . . . a whole new collection of attractive qualities will emerge in your spouse with the arrival of your twins. Even if you are too tired to act upon it, you will be amazed at what becomes "arousing"!

What about "arousal" after twin-arrival? How soon and how often will we have sex after the twins are here? What is the "norm"?

First and foremost, wait for your doctor's okay to rejoin the world of the sexually active. Most OB-GYNs schedule a 6-week postpartum examination for new mommies, and in that appointment, typically an "approval" is given. No doubt you have heard tales of women (and men) who were chomping at the bit to resume physically intimate relations following the birth of their children. Guess what? Plenty of new parents, especially those with newborn multiples, *do not* feel the urge to (and consequently do not) rush back into sex right away . . . but do you think those people proudly and publicly proclaim that fact? No way!

Remember the bravado and lurid embellishment of those high school "locker room" talks? What you are hearing now is the full-grown adult parental version.

Just as in high school, some of the vocal folks are genuinely libidinous and may even be good-heartedly trying to encourage (or peerpressure) you to get in the game. Just like in high school, as a new twin mom, I listened in utter fascination to those who were willing to share their erotic exploits, but was thoroughly unwilling to participate personally. A sociological study should be done on those locker room lecturers to determine if they are the same new parents who jump the gun (and each other) before the OB-GYN blesses the act. So for those of you around the perimeter of the locker room who laboriously folded your gym clothes, while the few, the proud, the libertines shared stories suitable for soft-core porn; you are not alone. Raise your head, and be honest about your feelings with your partner. You may just be of the same mind. Fortunately in our house, we were. But it took a bit of courage mustering before I could even address the topic of resuming physical intimacy.

In addition to being completely exhausted physically, I had posttwin-delivery concerns about the grisly gynecological goings-on to which my husband had been witness. Plus, even though they were an impressive 40-D (up from my prepregnancy 36-barely B); my breasts had become totally utilitarian. My primary "lovey" zones had a new, and seemingly unsexy, history. Weeks (note: *weeks*, not minutes, hours, or days) after Dr. Rinehardt gave me the all-systems-go sexual permission slip, and after viewing a Dr. Phil episode about "sexless marriages," I apprehensively asked Scott, "Do you think we should be having sex?" He responded, "Have you felt like it? I really haven't." Further discussion revealed that thankfully, he was not repulsed by the reproductive reality to which he'd been privy. Despite my lack of initiated sex, I shared that glimpses of him as a father were providing me abundant fresh reasons to find him attractive. Together, we agreed that our energies with two young babies in-house had mandated a redirection (on the basis of emotional and physical overload) of our collective energies . . . for the time being. Never fear, we are back amongst the sexually active. Please don't despair or feel alone if you aren't perusing the lingerie at Victoria's Secret for months after your twins are born.

Months? What is the "norm" for returning to the marital bed after the birth of multiples? *You* decide the norm for you. Respondents to surveys regarding sexual habits are notoriously more concerned with how they think they *should* respond vs. the actual truth, and answer questions about their sex lives accordingly. Shun the skewed surveys, and make your own decision as a couple. When you both are ready, resume.

The Double Daddy Perspective

On a recent business trip, I sat around a hotel bar with two other fathers of two and one single guy. By the time we were done comparing notes and laughing hysterically about the romantic habits of parents, we found ourselves apologizing to the bachelor and attempting to explain the unexplainable: That everything is the same but completely different and that you can't imagine a life without your kids.

What about the couples in which one partner is ready and randy, and the other is lethargic and lustless? The dilemma presents a particularly tough situation, especially since many twin-expectant couples abandon prenatal sex for a plethora of reasons. Add to those months the sex-prohibited weeks immediately following the twins' birth, and you have a potentially very lengthy window of time sans sex.

So what is the best course of action? The partner who would like to be physically intimate denies their own desire? The partner who is uninterested in sex acquiesces to appease the long-denied partner? At the risk of redundancy, a reiteration of our one word chapter: *TALK.*

A compromise needs to be reached, and both partners will likely need to meet each other halfway. Exhibit empathy for each other's positions, and realize your intimacy-stealing exhaustion will last only for a finite period of time . . . assuming you get that twin-household routine in place as soon as healthily feasible. Until, and even after, that routine is in place, *TALK.*

29

Everyone Makes Mistakes, Oh Yes They Do . . .

Big Bird said it best, "Everyone makes mistakes, oh yes they do. Your sister and your brother and your dad and mother, too."[1] When I was pregnant, and in my early days of twin motherhood, everyone shared their personal maternal successes and tips to make those challenging early days "easier." In retrospect, I desperately wish more moms had told me about the most idiotic mistakes they had made. That way, when I made my glaring errors, I'd feel less like an awful mommy and more like I was adding to a well-established history of mommyhood unintentionally, but occasionally, gone awry.

So, for your enjoyment, edification, and potential future rationalization, here are some of my greatest Mom bombs. Read them knowing you are not alone. Despite every best intention, "if everyone in the whole wide world makes mistakes, then why can't you?"

Dateline: September 8, 2001 (Babies' ages: 3 days)

All four of us load into the car to go home for the first time. Our car seat bases had been safely installed by the local fire department. Our babies had passed their "Car Seat Stress Tests" administered by the hospital with flying colors. We strapped each baby into their seat, tightened their belts as the manufacturers dictated, and popped the seats into their rear-facing bases. Mommy hopped into passenger seat; daddy into driver seat, and homeward bound we were. After a short, 3-mile trek, we were home at last.

I leapt out of my seat to retrieve Darren and shrieked upon seeing his big baby head slumped onto his chest. The cushiony head-surround did it's job in keeping his head from angling uncomfortably to either side, but there was no means of keeping his head from flopping forward on his weakly muscled baby neck. He was absolutely fine. I was the one in distress. From that point on, we knew an adult would need to ride with the babies in the back seat until neck muscles were more developed (right around 4 months). Have your car-seat bases installed into your back seat accordingly, allowing an adult access to a seat and access to both babies. For us, that meant rearranging ours from our first placement (closest to each back door) to a wiser side-by-side arrangement (one in the "middle" of the back seat, one right next to it, right beside passenger back door). Later, we placed the bases right next to each door, so that there would be minimal back strain in snapping heavy baby-laden seats into their bases. Musical chairs was played far earlier in our four-person family life than expected. With twins in the car, in the house, in your lives, be ready to discard, or at the very least *adjust*, your "old way of doing things." Even if it's something as menial as your seating assignments in the car, be ready to redefine your modus operandi. Embrace the excitement of a family in flux.

Dateline: September 9, 2001 (Babies' ages: 4 days)

Dear friends want to bring us breakfast our first morning home. My husband, Scott, realizes our son's fingernails, wee though they be, are sharp as little razors. Bravely, he attempts our first baby manicure before our friends arrive. Miniature clippers and miniature fingers make for a quite a challenge with Scott's big, manly hands. The teensy thumb gets cut, and as my husband so delicately declared, "bled like a scene out of 'Apocalypse Now.'"

First parentally caused bloodshed. Suppose it had to happen eventually. Am convinced to this day that daddy was far more upset than Darren.

Dateline: September 11, 2001 (Babies' ages: 6 days)

America experienced one of the most horrific tragedies of her history. As a new mother, and as a citizen of the world, I was in a state of complete disbelief. Addled by raging hormones, this event took on a magnitude I found overwhelmingly upsetting. Although I have no regrets about the time I spent remembering, honoring, and praying for all those directly affected by that awful day, in retrospect, I wish I had spent less time watching the nightmarish footage over and over for the days and weeks that followed. Hopefully, none of you will have such a dramatic, heinous act of terror or disaster in your first days with your twins. However, it is not uncommon for new mothers to obsess over the horrors of the contemporary world shortly after the arrival of their children. If this happens to you, try to redirect your focus from the negatives of the present day onto the most positive things this world has to offer: the conquering love of family and the innumerable possibilities of new life. Squeeze the pudding out of your babies, and tell them you love them.

Dateline: October 8, 2001 (Babies' ages: 1 month)

It was bound to happen. We were on a strict 3-hour feeding schedule around the clock. Needless to say, alarm clock setting was necessary to assure all parties would wake up for the all-important middle of the night feeds. Amazingly enough, on this evening, I woke up naturally just in time for our scheduled 4 A.M. feeding. The mistake? We all slept through what should have been our 1 A.M. feeding! In my sleep-deprived haze, I had mistakenly set the alarm for 1 P.M. as opposed to 1 A.M. No doubt, I awoke because of the engorged monstrosities my breasts had become after skipping a feed. Horrified at my lapse in responsible motherhood, I roused my sleepy wee ones, and we resumed our schedule . . . right on time. The babies were fine. I was a guilt-ridden wreck. My darling husband's response? "Wow. All three of you must have really needed the sleep." Never underestimate the strength of biological urge. For a growing set of twins, biology demands food and sleep, and typically, in that order. A singular reversal of the two was not damaging but jarred me enough to keep my alarm-setting en pointe for the remaining 3 months of our tight feeding schedule.

Dateline: January 2002 (Babies' ages: 4 months)

During our first plane trip, I made the mistake of not thoroughly wiping down the changing table in the Detroit airport before making use of it. Now by no means am I claiming the Detroit airport changing tables are any worse than any other public changing tables. My point is, any surface upon which multiple babies are placed should be cleaned well if you intend to avoid communicable diseases. Sarah mysteriously contracted prolific diarrhea within days after our return home. Pediatrician dictated "poo-culture tests" are quite the undertaking when there is little solid material to be culled. Happily, and as predicted by the doctor, all tests came back negative for dangerous parasites, and the diarrhea subsided after 4 weeks. Yes, you read that right, 4 weeks. Intestinal bugs often take an inordinately long time to fully evacuate. Sarah was fine, and no medicine was prescribed. It is highly possible that the diarrhea was not even contracted in the airport, but I learned my lesson. Be a wiper before you diaper.

Dateline: June 2002 (Babies' ages: 9 months)

Okay, breaking Cheerios into fourths for fear of choking is a bit extreme. However, I still defend my right to be choke-conscious, especially since Darren had no teeth.

Dateline: July 2002 (Babies' ages: 10 months)

A nostalgic moment every parent anticipates: our first call to the poison control board. Because our babies were still fairly tiny at this point,

I was still able to get them to and from the car using the infant car seat carriers, one in each hand. Just because their size was small, their reach was not. Traveling toward the car, we walked as we always do, between the two fairly scrawny bushes that flank our walkway. As I placed Sarah's carrier on the ground to snap Darren into his car seat base, lo and behold, she had managed to pluck leafy branches from the bushes, and had juniper leaves sticking out of her mouth. My fingers coursed through her mouth extracting debris so quickly, I am confident she never knew what hit her. We trotted back inside for the call to poison control. The amazing fact was that I even knew the type of bushes they were. After assurance from the cool-headed individual manning the PCB phones that juniper leaves wouldn't harm Sarah, we headed back out. Be aware of your surrounding plant life. Be aware of your child's reach. Be aware of the poison control board's phone number.

Dateline: October 2002 (Babies' ages: 13 months)

Coordination and speed have increased so significantly by 13 months, that fingers can get into spaces quicker than you can imagine. Sarah gets her fingers smashed in a closing door. No blood. No lost fingernails. No broken bones. No more quick closing of doors.

Dateline: October 2002 (Babies' ages: 13 months)

Ahhh, lovely fall weather. Time to take the babies out for an after lunch stroll. Load Darren into the stroller. Load Sarah into the stroller. Lock door behind us. Lock keys in house. Thankfully, it was a stunning day, and fairly late in the afternoon. All of us slept like rocks that night from all the fresh air and exercise. Not such a bad thing. With hindsight 20/20, I'd consider a hidden house key a wise precaution.

Dateline: November 2002 (Babies' ages: 14 months)

Thanksgiving grocery shopping. Using the "push-double-stroller-with-one-hand-in-front, while-pulling-grocery-cart-behind-with-other-hand method," we complete our Thanksgiving grocery shopping on Thanksgiving Eve afternoon. The bag-man at Food Lion, in every effort to be helpful on this busy shopping day, offers to bring my cart to the curb once I have loaded the babies in the car. After his continued insistence, I go along. Pulling up to the front of the store, the bag-man is no where to be found. Not wanting to honk, I turned off the car to wait. Finally, realizing he has no doubt forgotten, I decide to pull directly in front of the automatic door, crack the back car windows for the babies, and run in the door quickly to signal the man for our cart. Better lock the car doors. Don't want the gifts for which I am most thankful to be at risk even for a few seconds. As I shut the car door, I see my keys. In the ignition. Ugh. Signalled for my groceries and for a call to the police, alerting them to my "two infants locked in the car" faux pas. The crew at Food Lion was fantastic, and far more panicky than I was. Needless to say, the babies were fine. We made goofy faces at them from the outside (as I usually do), so nothing seemed out of the ordinary to them. Another employee owned a similar model car, and offered to "break in" mine as he often did into his. After being told the wait was upwards of 45 minutes for the auto locksmith, this young, gallant Food Lion employee had us in our car within 5 minutes. Knowing the time, anguish, and money he had saved us by his feat, I was desperately trying to shove cash into the young man's hands. His response? "Buy something nice for the babies. They're cute." My faith in Generation X was thoroughly restored. However, upon recounting this tale to hubby, it took a while for his faith in mommy to be restored. When this car died a few months later, we purchased a used Volvo station wagon. In addition to the incredible safety rating, an undeniable selling point was that you cannot lock yourself out of the car.

Dateline: Early December 2002
(Babies' ages: 15 months)

Our day excursions are often to shopping malls, especially when the weather outside is frightful. As suits the season, a friendly mall Santa looking for midday lap-fillers kindly leaned over his North Pole fence to greet the twins. Thinking that this was a fantastic no-line opportunity, we went ahead and had the picture taken. My husband was justifiably crestfallen. Inconsiderately, I hadn't even thought for a minute that he might like to be there for the momentous "First Santa" experience. Mistakes don't necessarily mean one of your babies' being hurt; it could be your partner. Communicate actively with your spouse, especially regarding holidays and traditions that you each revere.

Dateline: March 2003 (Babies' ages: 18 months)

While unloading Sarah from the stroller into her car seat, I had Darren "parked" in the stroller near the hinge of the open car door. My fear had always been getting baby fingers caught in the closing end of a slamming car door. I never considered the possibility of teensy fingers getting caught in the hinge crease as it slams. In sheer horror, I watched as Darren extended his hand toward the narrowing crack of a hinged Volvo door slamming shut. He screamed in pain and disbelief as the tips of his three longest fingers caught. After smothering the freed fingers with kisses, I was brave enough to look. Creased and bruising, but no blood. No lost fingernails. No broken bones. No more quick closing of doors.

Dateline: April 2003 (Babies' ages: 19 months)

Part of our daily routine includes playpen time while I eat my breakfast. On this particular day, everyone was playing peacefully and happily, so I took advantage of the opportunity to go and check e-mails. As the old adage says, "Silence is Golden." With twins under two, silence is suspicious. I crept to the playpen to see a buck-naked Sarah holding her diaper over her head. A closer look revealed the "hat" was clean . . . thank goodness. Or so I thought. Creeping closer yet, Darren said, "Messy." Let it be noted, twins can assess situations quite effectively at 19 months. In the corner of the playpen (and across the mesh, in the toys, smeared on books . . .) was a puppy-esque pile of poo poo. No one to blame but myself. Sarah had long been able to free herself from the encumbrance of clothing. On this particular morning, I had neglected to include a crotch-snapping onesie under her PJs to foil the full-baby strip down. Additionally, too long a stray from eye line is never good, and quite often, unsafe, practice. Thankfully, the babies themselves were fairly poo-free. However, I wouldn't wish the clean-up that followed this escapade on my worst enemy. The experience truly solidified my theory that when consequences are unsavory, you avoid the causing action. Works for baby discipline; works for mommy discipline.

Dateline: May 2003 (Babies' ages: 20 months)

Baby baths are one of the joys of new parenting. Washing two babies simultaneously in the big tub (with two parents) is oodles of splashy fun. Watching naked babies trot around the room, dodging the big towel dry down is also oodles of giggly fun. Watching your son realize pee-pee comes out from his penis in an arc when no diaper is on is also good for lots of laughs. And lots of laundry. (The pee-pee parabola went right onto and through mommy and daddy's bedding.)

Dateline: September 8, 2003 (Babies' ages: 24 months)

Ah, irony. At two years to the day since the first documentable mommy faux pas, and alas, yet another. Winnie the Pooh was scheduled to make an appearance at our local Barnes & Noble. After a very rational discussion with my twosome, explaining how I was one mommy and they were two children, and that they would need to follow my instruction exactly or we would need to leave, I was somehow convinced that single-handedly, I could extract them from the safe confines of the double stroller. We could all hold hands and stay calm. We would quietly and gleefully reassume our seats in the stroller following our celebrity meet and greet. We would go happily home with a cute photo of twins with Pooh. Wrong. Yes, my facility in maneuvering Darren and Sarah has multiplied one-hundredfold since their birth. Their communication skills and ability to follow direction have blossomed similarly. So has their capacity and desire for independence. The photo bears witness to my delusion. In the shot, Darren's back is to the camera, after releasing Pooh's hand in order to explore the story-time stage. Sarah is pulling away from my clutches with such velocity, her pigtails are aloft. Pooh, bless his Hunny-lovin' heart, holds my free hand sympathetically and looks thoroughly befuddled.

My lessons learned? (1) Don't overestimate yourself, and (2) Don't set unrealistic expectations for your babies. And whatever you do, don't do both at the same time, in a public place.

Vanity prevents me from itemizing each and every mistake I have made in my first 2 years of motherhood. Let me assure you, this chapter, if not edited to some degree, would easily be the lengthiest in this book. Try not to fret over each and every mistake you make. Learn from them, laugh when you can, and move forward. Never assess your mothering capabilities based on what you do "wrong." And never berate yourself in front of your twins. Babies absorb an amazing amount of our behavior patterns before they can even speak. You don't want their first self-assessments to be self-condemning. Monkeys see, monkeys do. Be positive. Be proud. They'll do the same. And sooner than you'd think.

Note

1. Copyright © 1998–2005 Sesame Workshop.

VII

Your Special Situation

30

Twin Benefits

Beyond the special financial discounts and product offers, beyond the doubled savings of "kids eat free" night at your favorite restaurant, beyond the fact that they *will* eventually "entertain themselves," beyond the fun of composing the letter to explain that although you're currently breastfeeding twins, you'd happily serve your shift on jury duty (I was summarily released from my civic obligation), there are abundant other benefits to having your children arrive as a pair.

Twintensity

Throughout twin pregnancy, there are moments, sometimes lengthy ones, of intense discomfort, intense anxiety, and intense self-doubt. Fortunately, the eventual prize for your tenacity and tolerance through an often strain-ridden pregnancy is not one but two precious children. For those women (and there are many) who don't find pregnancy an enjoyable state, but rather one to be endured for the ultimate goal; what a tremendous benefit to have two babes to show for your labors and duress.

Of course, once the twins are born, for each stage of development, you can and should anticipate dual-injected intensity of each challenge. You may equally anticipate intensified triumph upon its completion.

Certainly, your twins are individuals, with moderately different rates of development. However, the time span for addressing and nurturing those maturation milestones is far narrower than for singleton siblings born in sequence.

Women who have two children closely born will regularly tell you, "My kids are 11 months apart, so I know how you feel."

While that comment is a notoriously annoying one for many twin moms, who are typically in the weeds of tandem public-place tantrums at the time, try not to take offense at the assertion. The fellow mommy is not trying to say she has done *exactly* what you are doing, but rather, she feels for your situation. She wants to offer whatever maternal empathy she can. Let her.

No, I don't believe anyone other than a twin mom can actually "know how it feels" . . . and even those other twin family experiences are as varied as the families themselves.

In truth, some aspects of having twins make it far preferable to having stair-step singletons.

Yes, you've double the crawlers, climbers, teethers, and diapers to coordinate. Yet when those double-strength obstacles are surmounted, you'll likely have a time reprieve to prepare parentally for the next level. Savor the achievement. Congratulate your twins. Enjoy the victory. Raising multiples is the extreme sports of parenting.

Our fellow parents with children born within a narrow, yet non-twin, span of time may have only half the difficulty during any single newborn developmental challenge, but their healing refractory window is almost entirely absent. The duration of each stage goes on twice as long. Stair-step families are the cross-country marathoners of parenting.

What of those families who have a singleton then twins? Or twins, then a singleton? You are the decathletes of parenting! Lend your empathy to all new parents you can. Your perspective should be universally respected.

Twindividual and Twinterchangeable

When a child is born singly, parents, through no fault of their own, often feel confident that they "know what babies are like" and how to handle them based on the personality and behavior of that single child. When baby #2 arrives, there is often shock when the child responds differently than #1 and requires adjusted parenting.

When kids come in twos, from the beginning it's glaringly obvious that despite their prenatal proximity and even if they are classified as "identical," they possess unique demeanors, reactions, and sets of personal needs.

If each twin is an individual, and surely they are, why would the word "interchangeable" even be mentioned? Isn't that twin parenting blasphemy? Not when it comes to sheerly superficial issues. Because of the simultaneity of their arrival and in the earliest of your twins' days, size, objects of interest, and physical care will be very similar. You will be able to buy a single size of diapers (while friends with stair steps need to keep two stashes of appropriate sizes), bulk packs of T-shirts and onesies, books, and other baby necessities—knowing two will benefit from the same supply. Two babies will also benefit from the fact they will likely have many sets of loving arms ready to hold them.

When I was plurally pregnant, a friend who'd recently had a singly born son declared excitedly, "How wonderful! You won't have to share your baby with your husband and family! There will be babies to go around!" She had a point. Of course in truth, you will have to share *both* babies, but you will likely always have your justifiably greedy new mommy hands on a twin. Interchange the twins periodically so the babes get equal mommy/parent time, as well as ample arm time from friends and family.

The Double Daddy Perspective

I'm a big believer in the "Two and Through!" philosophy. Sure it's double diapers and double the laundry, but unlike parents who do it one at a time, chances are we'll only be taking one trip through the land of 3 A.M. feedings, reflux, teething, and potty training. So I say laugh and enjoy the spit-ups and the blowouts because while the singleton parents may be more "relaxed" the second time around, you'll be done.

Twincentive

If you ask the parents of a newborn singleton are they fairly "relaxed," my guess is you will hear a resounding, "No!"

When a newborn enters a household, mom and dad are typically adrenaline-charged and at the ready to handle full-bore baby management. The goal of keeping baby happy and healthy by tending to each and every detail, however miniscule, will occupy 100 percent of their waking hours . . . waking hours which are far lengthier than before baby's arrival.

When twins enter a household, mom and dad are equally adrenaline-charged and at the ready to handle full-bore double baby management. The goal of keeping the babies happy and healthy by tending to each and every detail, however miniscule, will occupy 100 percent of their waking hours . . . waking hours which are far lengthier than before the babies' arrival.

With two newborns occupying 100 percent of parents' time and efforts, twin parents develop the incentive fairly rapidly to decipher what the nonimperative details of new baby management are for their specific family. For instance, coordinated clothing on a daily basis. For us? One of the first ideas sacrificed. Hyperscrutinizing a tiny non-bleeding scratch? We had other fish to fry and other diapers to change. (Of course we did do a cursory sharp fingernail check for both babies. No call to the pediatrician necessary.)

You may find yourself losing patience watching your friends with single children agonizing over what seem small concerns to your perspective. Especially since you have learned to quickly assess the dual "damage," perform twin "triage," and implement rapid priority management. Your incentive to do so was dictated by nature. Cut your singleton parent pals some slack.

You have equally inspired incentive to establish (and stick to) a daily family routine. With waking hours at an all-time high, the imperative of coordinating a predictable schedule for your twins so mom and dad get a modicum of much-needed rest supersedes the temptation (to which singleton parents often succumb) to "relax" the routine when convenient.

When my husband told a friend recently that he has 3-year-old twins, the friend replied, "You must be so grateful to be finally getting some sleep." Scott took great pride in saying, "Finally? We've slept since they were 3½ months old." The secret? Routine, routine, routine.

Twincessant Adoration and Offers of Assistance

Some afternoons, you feel whipped and overextended as a twin mommy. Against the reflexive tendency to sit and bemoan your exhausted state, try this. Load your cuties in the car, and drive to a well-populated park, playground, or shopping center. Unload the babies into the stroller and walk around a bit.

Watch people smile at your twins. Be sure to smile back at them. Let people open store doors for your double stroller, even though you can do it yourself. Thank them loudly enough for your children to hear. Listen to the people who tell you how they always wanted twins. Tell them you can understand why. Giggle to yourself when folks roll their eyes and say, "Better you than me!" They're right. Better you than them. Allow people to help you. Allow people to admire your twins. You'll feel better for it.

Twinkling Eyes—Four of Them!

Perhaps one of the greatest joys of parenting is the opportunity to vicariously enjoy the awe and beauty of our surroundings through consummately fresh eyes. As twin parents, you'll be privy to twice the wide-eyed wonderment. The inexplicable amazement provided by an exposed light bulb, the ticking of a watch, a flatulent dog, a fingertip touched to a nose . . . day-to-day sensory stimuli for which we've lost all novelty excite and fascinate newborns endlessly.

Allow yourself to be reintroduced to the pleasures of the "ordinary" world around you—you have not one but two enthusiastic tour guides to illuminate the way.

31

Adults Say the Darndest Things

A s you parade your new twins through public places, passers-
by will seem compelled to somehow acknowledge the fact
that you have not one but two infants in your care. Your outings will
always (not sometimes, *always*) be peppered with succinct little "salutes"
from well-wishers. Despite their undoubtedly kind intent, they may
become annoying when combined with the tens of other well-wishers
who've offered the very same greetings . . . over and over and over.
Adults do say the darnedest things . . . and they tend to plagiarize each
other, so be prepared. And try to be flattered.

"Double Trouble!"

If I've heard it once, I've heard it over two hundred times. That is no
exaggeration. Don't let this one get you all hot under the collar. The individual tossing out the world's shortest poem was probably grinning
jealously as he or she said it. Of course, your babies aren't "trouble."
Even if at the present moment you believe they are, you sure don't want
to reveal that to a stranger and certainly not in front of your children.

The reality is you're commandeering a special twosome. You have
a special role, one that not everyone has the opportunity to fill. Many,

if not most, are daunted and awestruck at the mere thought. Folks want to acknowledge you somehow. Let 'em do it.

As far as the literal meaning goes, ignore it. Let's face it, we all like rhymes. From nursery rhymes to off-color limericks to rap music, the aural appeal of rhyme is undeniable. Take solace in the knowledge you will hear "Twice as Nice" from the more thoughtful poets passing by.

"Better You Than Me!" or the Seemingly Synonymous, "My God, I Cannot Imagine!"

The folks that proclaim "they cannot imagine," despite their words to the contrary, are *actively* imagining . . . inaccurately. Try to be kind to those who dispense these two pithy, but empathy-implying, pronouncements. Whereas it would be much more pleasant to hear, "What an incredible responsibility it must be to have two infants. I truly admire you," people don't find quick "wit" in compliment. Try to listen between the lines.

"I'm So Sorry!" or the Seemingly Synonymous, "God Bless You!"

If there were any validity to these oft-doled expressions of sympathy, Hallmark would place "New Twins" cards in the "Get Well/Sympathy" aisle as opposed to the far more applicable "Congratulations" department. When someone consolingly extols God to bless me, I cannot resist responding with the obvious, "He already has . . . *twice!*"

"You Sure Do Have your Hands Full!" or the Seemingly Synonymous, "Bet They Keep You Busy!"

The accuracy of these comments is undeniable. You have two hands and two babies. Your hands *are* full! You *are* busy. (You are forced to wonder if these folks are the same individuals who make similarly obvious statements on the weather just to start up conversation. You know the type, "Hot enough for you today?")

"Instant Family!" or the Seemingly Synonymous "Got It All Done at Once!"

Suppose in our fast-food/immediate gratification-driven society, these stranger-offered sound bytes are proffered as genuine compliments. Accept them as such. If you are bothered by their double pregnancy-minimizing and twin delivery-ignorant assessments, go on your way with expedition exceeding the speed with which you acquired your "instant family"!

"You Are so Lucky/Blessed!" or the Seemingly Synonymous, "I Always Wanted Twins!"

You *will* hear this, hopefully often. When your double "blessing" feels more a yoke than a miracle; be grateful for the strangers who provide the reality-check reminder of the amazing gift that twins truly are.

The Double Daddy Perspective

Yes, people will do a double take when they realize that the stroller you are pushing through the mall contains twins. You will also be shocked at the number of women that will grant instant Sainthood upon a man when he rolls solo with his kids—as if we are somehow incapable or unwilling to go out with our babies! But it's amazing to note the number of encouraging smiles you'll receive from fellow fathers. Or, as one man put it as I wheeled the twins into our maiden journey to Lowe's, "Man . . . that . . . is . . . cool!"

32

The Best Advice I Ever, and Never, Got

Everyone wants to lend words of wisdom to a new mommy, especially when they realize she will be handling two new babies simultaneously. Advice will come at you from all corners. Here is the best advice I received. Included in the list is advice I never received, but sure wish I had.

When leaving the hospital, ask for any "freebies" or extra supplies they are willing to pass along. Formula companies usually have "gifts" for the new baby(-ies) waiting at the hospital for you. Don't be shy, ask for what's available. Knowing you'll have two babies to care for, maternity ward nurses are extra supportive and generous. We got lots of Vaseline tubes, alcohol swabs, snot-sucking syringes, formula samples, disposable changing pads, sterilized gauze pads for Darren's circumcision maintenance, and the list goes on and on.

Sleep when the babies sleep. Forget about your grown-up ritual of only sleeping when it is dark outside. Nighttime interruptions in the first few months will be lengthy and frequent. Learn to at least rest when they do, regardless of the time on the clock.

If valuable help is offered, accept it. If the "help" offered causes you to work harder, kindly decline. You will quickly learn the difference between genuine assistance and hangers-on who love babies and want to be near them. If someone wants to bring you food, clean your house, get your groceries, run a needed errand, those are priceless offers of true help. By all means, let them do it! However, if someone good-natured and well-intentioned, though they may be, offers to "come hold the babies" for you or "give you some grown-up conversation" time, hold off on those offers until the sleep-deprived early months are over. Ditto the folks and friends who want to "come see the sweet babies" within days after your arrival home. Decide and invite whom you want to visit in the earliest days. Then politely "get back" to the others when you are ready. Your biggest, and truly only, obligation is to your nuclear family in those challenging early days. Do not be guilt-ed into a houseful of nonstop visitors unless it is on your own terms . . . and certainly not at the expense of lost rest to a single individual in your household.

The Double Daddy Perspective

In the early days when you are living your life in 3-hour feeding cycles, always prepare for the next cycle! In other words, if you've just used the last diaper on the changing table, restock it. If you've just jammed the last diaper into the Genie, empty the Genie. If you've just used the last clean bottle, clean up a new pair so they are ready for the next round, because you never know if the next round may involve a cranky mom and two colicky babies with absolutely no patience for an overflowing Genie and no clean bottles!

With your pediatrician's directives in mind, develop, implement, and abide by a regular routine as soon as possible. (The Feed-Awake-Nap cycle worked very well for us; with each "Feed" beginning 3 hours apart in the first months. See the Routine, Routine, Routine chapter for details.)

If any of your new babies have a penis, be sure and tuck it "downward" toward the crotch of the diaper. Otherwise, the stream emanating from that penis will soak the baby's clothing more often than the diaper. You'll be doing enough laundry without adding to it that way. Trust me, this is one of the best tips you never hear.

Housework be damned. At least until they start crawling.

Laugh at your mistakes, but remember to learn from them.

Remember (and it will be hard to forget) that babies cry. It is what they know how to do, and they do it for all sorts of reasons. The primary three causes you can potentially remedy are hunger, gas, and wet diapers. You have addressed all three and they are still crying? It happens. Babies do not necessarily cry from sadness as adults do. They need to expend energy. They need to work their lungs. Do not project adult heart-wrenching sadness onto an infant who is not likely experiencing it. If you are truly concerned your infants are crying too much, or something is genuinely wrong, contact your pediatrician. Chances are, all is well. After one seemingly lengthy Sarah bawl session, we asked our pediatrician how long is too long to cry. Or more important, when should we truly worry. She said if a baby cries inconsolably, nonstop despite all efforts; go to the emergency room after 3 hours. Three hours. Our cry-fest had lasted 1½ hours, and the swing and back pats did calm her somewhat . . . which equals consolable to doctors. Again, if you are ever sincerely concerned, call your doctor. Chances are, all is well.

Side note: Grandparents have a notoriously difficult time hearing their grandchildren cry. It has been a while since they have experienced it in their household. If grandparents are staying with you in the early days, be ready for their input and opinions on how you are handling your children. Accept your parents' suggestions graciously. Realize they are coming from a place of love for both you and their new grandchildren. Whether you incorporate their advice into your childrearing repertoire or not, remember to be patient with your mom and dad and in-laws. Although it seems an eternity away now, you may be a grandma one day, too. The kindness you mete out will be returned to you, as no doubt will be the harshness.

Stock up on the daily necessities: diapers, baby formula/food, wipes, baby Tylenol, gas drops, etc. You don't need the stress of low supply when you are sleep-deprived. Better to have a big back stock, than no stock at all. Keep an eye out for sales, enjoy the savings of buying in bulk, and buy en masse. Know the location of a 24-hour drug store or grocery, just in case.

Remember to eat. Sure, it seems a silly reminder, but when you are caring so intently for others, it is easy to neglect yourself. You don't need your resistance to get down owing to insufficient nutrition, especially if you are breastfeeding. Continue to take your prenatal vitamins, and have healthy snacks and nutrition bars on hand.

Screen your phone calls. People will understand. Get back to folks when you are at a convenient point and can carry on a decent conversation. No one knows your schedule, but they do care and want you to know that they do. Consider e-mail updates. You may have a great window of opportunity and be wide awake at 4:00 A.M. They'll get a kick out of the fact that you want them "in the loop," and that you composed the correspondence at such a crazy hour.

Bibs. They're not just for sloppy eaters; they're for excessive droolers. The wee-est of babies can unleash an uncanny amount of slobber. So much so, that we found ourselves changing outfits frequently due to soggy neck and chest areas. Lo and behold, Grandma said, "Didn't you get quite a few cute tiny bibs at the shower?" Duh. From that day forward, the babies were both bibbed during waking hours. Much easier to change out a bib than a whole outfit. Reduces the altitude of the laundry pile as well. (And to think I thought it odd that newborn outfits had coordinated bibs. Infant fashion designers have not only accessory sensibility but comfort in mind. Kudos.)

When laundering bibs with Velcro closures, make sure they are fastened together before throwing them into the washing machine. Otherwise, you'll create snags and pills on other items in your wash.

Don't get upset if in the early days pacifiers go in each others mouths, bottles get confused, your mother-in-law dresses Twin A in Twin B's pajamas. If you decide to pick each and every battle, you'll be war weary well before your time. Accept the unavoidable switcheroos with grace, and raise the white flag on unimportant issues.

Likewise, once solid foods enter the picture, while mommy or daddy is administering each bite, use a single spoon and bowl to feed both twins. Unless one baby is clearly ill, don't bother trying to keep discrete sets going for both children.

Cameras will be put to use plenty in the first days with twins. Make sure that you have someone take a photo of the whole family, as well as daddy holding both babies, and of mommy holding both babies. Time flies quickly, so don't miss that fleeting opportunity.

Always carry with you a clean set of baby clothes that will fit either baby. Two sets of bodily fluid–producing orifices double your chances of an emergency full-wardrobe change.

If your husband is making every effort to help, for Heaven's sakes, don't criticize how he folds the laundry, puts away the groceries, or diapers the babies. Realize how blessed you are to have a teammate, and thank him rather than spank him.

33

Experience, Not Expertise:
The First Year, Month-by-Month

I am not a doctor, and I don't play one on TV or anywhere else. What I am is a new mother of twins, and I can share our family experience, freshly acquired. Hopefully, the summaries that follow will ease your mind about what you have already accomplished, what you are living through, and what to look forward to in the future. Obviously, every set of twins is different as are every mommy and daddy. Be sure to document your family's early history to share with others who may benefit from your story . . . especially your children.

Month One: Home at Last (Babies' ages: 0 month)

We were incredibly fortunate. Our babies were almost full term for twins and were breathing well at birth. After a few fluctuations and flare-ups, they managed to regulate their body temperatures well enough so that we were all permitted to leave the hospital together within 72 hours. I could have gone home in 48, but as I was trying to nurse them, a "rooming in" option was available to me for minimal cost, so long as the hospital didn't need the bed. The extra day of in-hospital lactation consult was extremely beneficial. If you have yet to give birth, check into this option at your planned hospital of delivery. Many, many sets of multiples are born and require a lengthier stay in hospital care. As disappointing (and challenging) as it may be to have your babies in the neonatal intensive care unit (NICU) upon your release, try to view their additional time there as investment in, and commitment to, their long-term health. Heaven forbid physical problems arise owing to a premature hospital discharge of one or both of your babies. Beyond the fact that doctors and nurses are caring people, the legal system being what it is, no one wants a malpractice suit. Your babies will only be released to your care when the medical staff feels they are healthy enough and stable enough to be cared for at home.

The pediatrician who "broke the news" to me that Darren and Sarah would need to stay an extra day was met with a very receptive spirit. The last thing I wanted was to rush their release and place my children at a distance from potentially life-saving individuals and equipment. So if one or both of yours need a bit more time, try to be patient. You all have the rest of your lives to spend together—or at least the next 18 years.

Our very first night home, the babies "slept" together in their crib, in the nursery. Well, at least for as long as we were permitted to let them sleep before the mandatory, scheduled feedings. A few days later, as soon as our twosome began demonstrating the spit-uppy symptoms of reflux, combined with nasal congestion typical for those born with tiny preemie nasal passages; our pediatrician exhorted us to have them sleep with their heads elevated. Our solution was to have them sleep in their bouncy seats, in our room. Bless their hearts, our two babies were *so* sleepy. We had to continually "jostle" their little jaws and rub their cheeks during nursings to keep them awake and sucking. My mother had an extremely difficult time believing that we needed to "wake a sleeping baby(ies)." Her thought was that biology dictates hunger as an imperative, and the babies would wake when they needed to eat. Our pediatrician assured us, sleep is also an imperative. For teeny babies, the energy required to eat is dramatic. Sleep, if uninterrupted, can triumph over hunger. If our babies had been much bigger, perhaps the rigorous nursing schedule would have been uncalled for. As things were, we did what we needed to do. Once the explanation was made, Mom was great with support, regardless of how horrifying she felt it was.

Since we were making every attempt to make breastfeeding work, and as our twins did not rapidly re-achieve their original birth weight, we were also giving bottled supplements of breast milk (and occasionally formula) following each nursing session. I was also using the breast pump (hospital-rented, double-funnel, electric super sucker) after each feeding/burping/diapering session to stimulate my breasts to produce adequate supply and to provide additional breast milk for the supplements needed.

After 2 weeks at home, we had an in-home lactation consultant visit. Without a doubt, that was one of the wisest decisions we made in those early days.

We were in and out of the pediatrician's office five times that first month to keep a close eye on the babies' weight gain. As a matter of fact, we had our first required weight check only 2 days after getting home. "Weight checks" are often a new twin fact of life. One of which I was totally unaware prior to their birth. If you are nursing, the likelihood your babies' weights will need to be monitored is even greater. Try not to let the frequency of the weight checks cause you to panic. As with everything, remember, safety first. At 2 weeks, Darren, our larger baby at birth, was still 5 ounces below his birth weight. Sarah was a mere 3 ounces over hers. Unless your baby loses 10 percent of his or her birth weight, it is typically not cause for alarm. Darren hovered right around that 10 percent mark for quite some time, so our trips to the doctor's office were numerous the first month. His skin was also somewhat "yellow," not quite jaundiced, so that was watched closely, too. (Funny side note: The substance that causes the yellowish tinge in newborns' skin is called bilirubin. For a while, we heard the word so often, the nickname Billy Reuben became very tempting.)

For the first month home, the babies' poo journal has all sorts of marginalia regarding my diet. Each time they were fussy, since I was breastfeeding, I was convinced something I had eaten provoked the discomfort. In retrospect, I am confident that it rarely, if ever, did. Try not to beat yourself up over every little thing. That first month home is full of self-questioning, feelings of inexperience/inadequacy, and perhaps most dangerous of all, sleep deprivation. Cut yourself some slack. With each passing day, things are getting easier. You may not feel it in that first month, but it is true.

Back to the actual experiences of that first month: At 2 weeks, the babies' gas discomfort was so pronounced (often demonstrated by arching their backs while screaming), our pediatrician recommended a mini-sized dose of adult Mylanta to ease their pain. Plenty of babies burp with ease, ours fought it like the plague. We even asked the pediatrician how long we should continue the burping back-thumping after each feed when it rarely produced the desired belches. (5 to 10 minutes was our doctor's suggestion.) Sometimes we got burps, sometimes we didn't. But thump 'em, we did, 5 to 10 minutes each, every time.

Diapers were monitored closely. By counting the dirty diapers, you can fairly safely determine if the babies are getting enough nutrition. Looking back at the Month 1 diaper tally, the smallest number of diapers we soiled in a 24-hour period was 17 (total for both babies); the most we dirtied in 24 hours was 25 (again, that's the two-baby total). An average day required about 20 to 22 diapers. Don't be surprised when the color of the babies' poo poo shifts dramatically in those first weeks. The first poo is tar-like blackish green and very tough/gummy. Then a stage of greenish output segues to a golden yellow, somewhat seedy looking BM. You can get specifics from your pediatrician if you have concerns, but don't expect your newborn twins' diaper contents to resemble what you have seen in older baby or toddler diapers.

Something we weren't expecting was the "hugeness" of Size 1 diapers. With twins, your babies will usually be smaller than the typical singleton. Have a big stock of newborn diapers on hand, or be ready for leaks. Bless my grandmother's heart. After I told her of the leaky diaper extravaganza, she rushed right out and purchased what used to be called "rubber pants." In generations gone by, the rubber pants were put on top of the (then, cloth) diaper, and leaks were minimized. The fact is, rubber pants keep the rash provoking urine (and potentially, poo) closer to the babies' skin. Sure, the clean-up process is reduced, but not necessarily without some discomfort to your babies, and of course subsequently, to you. Regardless, my Mamaw's thoughtfulness greatly warmed my then-exhausted heart. Her "jump in and do what I can to help" spirit, despite her age and frailty will be treasured as long as I live.

When the babies' umbilical cords are severed at birth, a dark brownish-black remnant remains at their belly buttons for a few weeks. Affectionately called the "umby" at our house, the perimeter around that projection needs to be swabbed with alcohol several times a day. We dipped a Q-tip in rubbing alcohol at each diaper change, and cleaned the umbies then. Establishing even the most mundane "routines" is very helpful in that first month. You do feel as though you are on auto-pilot at times. Believe it or not, that is a good thing. Sarah's umby fell off at 2½ weeks. Darren's lasted 3 weeks to the day.

If you have a boy (or boys) and decide to have them circumcised, at each diaper change you will need to gently slather the tender head of the penis with abundant petroleum jelly. After the peenie is suitably greased, you then wrap it loosely in thin gauze to protect it from the inside of the diaper (and its contents) while it heals. Hospitals are great about passing along extra "party favors" to twin families upon release, and we were given enough gauze pads to last the duration. At our two-week check-up, his penis was given the A-OK, and we discontinued the greasy-gauzy ritual.

Girl babies (Sarah included) usually have some creamy vaginal/labia excretions in those first days/weeks. The substance is not an indication of infection but merely a resultant of the hormonal overages passed along by mom. Keep the area clean, and you can expect the substance to dissipate in the early weeks.

Our babies were born two days early considering average gestational "term" for twins; but more than 3 weeks early considering "term" for singletons. Ideally, twins would stay in utero just as long as singly born babies. Do prematurely born twins look different physically for their reduced time in the womb? Most do; ours did. Our babies were born with loose folds of skin. In the last few weeks in utero, babies pack on fat to fill their little skin casings. Deprived of those weeks, Darren and Sarah's little arms and legs resembled wrinkly shar-pei puppy extremities. Don't be alarmed if your babies look similarly. As the babies regain their birth weight, and then rapidly surpass it, the little arms, legs, even bellies flesh out beautifully.

The other visible evidence of prematurity in our case was the preponderance of lanugo, especially on our daughter. Lanugo is the baby fine layer of hair that covers your babies' bodies during the last days of gestation. When babies are born "early," the lanugo hasn't fallen out. Our Sarah's shoulders, the hollow between her shoulder blades, and sides of her face alongside her ears had a fine covering of thin peach fuzz. Never fear, you haven't birthed a baby Bigfoot; it will fall out.

In the first days, you may be caught off-guard when you see your babies "twitch" or tremble erratically. The nervous system is developing rapidly in the last weeks in utero. Born early, your twins may have more than their share of newborn "tremblies." One particularly active episode of the "shakies" in Darren caused me to call the maternity ward nurses in the middle of the night. The nurses on-call kindly (and laughingly) alerted me to the completely normal phenomena. They re-assured me that the nursery ward always has a "whole lotta shakin' go-ing on," but medical staff is so used to it, they often forget first-time parents can be fearful when they see it. Even experienced moms whose first babies were born full term (or later) may never have seen the jit-ters of premature twins. Don't be as alarmed as I was. Keep your pedi-atrician in the loop, but keep your apprehension at a minimum.

Developmental and Physical Changes That May (or May Not) Occur in Month One:

- Umbilical remnants will fall off.
- Lanugo hair will fall out.
- Hair on heads may fall out.
- Bowel movements will cycle through a range of colors and tex-tures.
- Circumcisions will heal.
- Vaginal excretions will dissipate.
- Birth weights will be re-achieved, and surpassed. "Loose" flesh will be minimized.
- Eye colors may evolve.
- Legs that are bent and upheld (from long-term positioning in utero) will slowly begin to relax.
- Toes that splay outward will start to coalesce.
- "Pointy" heads and "crooked" facial features will assume a more "normal" appearance. (Vaginally delivered babies often experi-ence temporarily misshapen/shifted characteristics. The first "out" more so than the "second" . . . trailblazing the way "out" is rough work!)
- Yellowish skin tone will diminish and skin will become rosier.

Month Two: Settling In (Babies' ages: 1 month)

The frequent weight checks that had us feeling like "regulars" at the pediatrician's office tapered off in Month 2. As pleasant as it was to know both our babies had re-achieved and exceeded their birth weights, and that they were progressing normally, there was subcon-scious reassurance in those frequent visits to the doctor . . . the thought being that doctors know danger signs when they see them, and I didn't. As a first-time mom, I was unsure if I would "know" when something was wrong with one of my babies. In retrospect, it's clear *nothing* could have possibly escaped my maternal hypervigilance. Each and every movement and physical oddity was excessively overanalyzed. Yes, new mommy's attention is twin-divided and sleep-deprived. In that state, you can easily convince yourself that while you are tending to one baby, you will surely miss some earth-shatteringly important symptom in the other. Or, that while you are entrusting one baby to a helper's care that they aren't aware of what "normal" behavior for that baby is—and will miss something pivotally important. Just like in pregnancy, the best, and hardest, thing to do is *relax*. Your doctor is a phone call away. We learned quickly to keep a pad of paper handy and to jot down any minor issues or curiosities that arose. That way, when a call had to be made, or at our next scheduled appointment, we could remember what peculiarities had caused concern, and quiz our pediatrician (God love her) accordingly.

In the first month of our babies' newborn lives, we were monitoring their prolific post-feeding spit-up closely. By the second month, I was fearful that almost entire feedings of Sarah's were being rejected. Our pediatrician alerted me to a comforting "test." If we believed Sarah had ingested 2 ounces, and then had spat it up fully, here's what she suggested: Get a baby bottle and fill it to the 2-ounce calibration. Then pour onto a cloth diaper or towel an amount you believe is comparable to the circumference of the total spit-up. Rarely, if ever, did the simulated spit-up even come close to equaling the probable intake. I'd encourage you to do the same experiment if you find yourself anxious about feedings evacuating their intended destination.

Of course spitting up that often and so profoundly was a concern for our pediatrician. Our babies, especially Sarah our super-spitter, started out with low birth weights. The energy of crying, eating, and spitting might be burning off more calories than a healthy ideal. Sarah was also very angry whenever we burped her. The combination of voluminous spit-up after virtually every nursing and her reticence to be burped led our pediatrician to a diagnosis of early reflux. The acid coming back up with burps and/or spit-up was painful. Don't delude yourself for a minute; babies are very quick to learn cause and effect. If untreated, our pediatrician confirmed the spit-up pain could/would cause Sarah to limit her intake in efforts to avoid the following discomfort. Not what you want in a low-birth weight baby. She was prescribed a miniature dose of Zantac. Slowly but surely, her discomfort lessened. Whether it was the medication, the doses of Mylanta, or merely that she outgrew the reflux, we don't know. Wisdom dictated taking no unnecessary chances. Darren was placed on Zantac as a preventative.

Something you may want to consider in the first 2 (or more) months of your babies' lives is a pre-feed burping in addition to the post-feed burping . . . particularly if either or both babies have been crying vociferously in the minutes before their meal. Crying often causes babies to form a substantial gas/air bubble in their bellies. If a baby's feeding lands right atop the cry-induced belly bubble, you can rest assured the inevitable burping of that bubble will force the hitch-hiking meal out with it. Of course then panicky mommy will want to try and refeed an agitated baby and everyone loses. If you have completed a feed, and the meal is punctuated with a major spit-up, gauge the expelling baby's desire to resume eating. If a baby is uninterested, don't lose sight of the fact that another feeding is coming up in just a couple of hours. You can even pull the next feeding up 15 minutes or so if hunger rears its head prior to the next scheduled feed.

In our second month, I spent way too much time and energy obsessing over the "success" of each feeding. You will not let your babies starve. Your babies aren't gas tanks that require topping off at each feed. Relax a bit, and your babies will too. To this day I am convinced that my palpable stress about the twins eating enough at each and every feeding may have provoked, or at least intensified, our twins' digestive distress.

What about the moments of twin distress, digestive or otherwise? In the second month we started to get the feel of what each baby found soothing or calming. Now don't misinterpret, we didn't find a magical answer to halt crying immediately, but we did make some major headway. Darren and Sarah both loved their pacifiers. Sarah loved the side-to-side motion of her baby swing. Darren loved the vibrating bouncy seat. Obviously they both loved to be held, and we loved holding them. The tentative and overly cautious baby-handling typical of the first days/weeks rapidly develops into more confident and comfortable handling of the babies. The parental calm definitely has some contagious effect on the babies. You know how some people pick up a fussy baby and the baby immediately quiets? Those mommy-frustrating individuals are usually those who have well-practiced baby holding arms, and the babies sense their ease. The good news is that your arms are getting more and more practiced every day, and there is no one those babies would rather be held by than you. And whatever you do, don't assume that because one or both of your babies are crying that you are perpetually too stressed to hold them and will only make matters worse; you won't. You all can and should mutually comfort each other. Try lying down and placing the babies on your chest. Take some deep breaths. Your position and oxygen intake will calm you. Your breathing and the babies' familiarity with your heartbeat may very well calm them. Put the babies in bouncies or in Boppies and read to them quietly. Sing to them. Sometimes the quiet soothing quality of your voice can work wonders . . . even when you are convinced you cannot be heard over the din.

In our second month, we got permission to take the twins out for strolls. Seize the opportunities to pop your babies into a stroller and get some fresh air. Likewise, the subtle vibration of a moving car has soothed many babies. Grab the car-seat carriers and go for a ride. Play some classical music. Run the vacuum. Your uterus was a noisy place. Quiet may not always be the right solution for calming your twosome. Now, if you have been hugging and consoling and rocking your twins and there is no end in sight and if the chaos gets to be too much for you as mommy, place the babies somewhere safe—a crib, the bouncies, a playpen—and step away for 5 to 10 minutes. For their sanity and yours. You will return unbelievably refreshed, and the whole family will benefit.

A big achievement (and maternal sanity stabilizer) in our second month was that by month-end, we no longer needed to give Sarah a supplement of breast milk after each feed. Eliminating my mandatory meeting with the breast pump every 3 hours was invigorating. Adding that mere 10 to 15 minutes of sudden flextime into our routine was phenomenal. We could play a bit longer. More often, and more important for all of us, we could start naps a bit earlier. The second month will be filled with all sorts of seemingly small, but high-impact triumphs that will bolster you as twin parents.

Developmental and Physical Changes That May (or May Not) Occur in Month Two:

- Your twins may receive immunizations in this month's appointment. Be ready for some fussiness and mild fever/tummy upset. Your pediatrician will tell you how to handle and comfort your twins in the hours following shots.

- Babies can lift their heads and respond to sounds . . . especially voices.
- You may see some inklings of starter smiles on your sweeties' faces this month. Enjoy!
- In the first month of life, babies' eyes often move somewhat out-of-synch. In this month, you will likely notice their eyes moving more in tandem. Get close and enjoy the eye contact!
- Twins often start out slow in gaining weight. The babies will gain significant weight in their second month.
- The babies are less "shaky" and are slightly more in control of their movements.
- Your babies can likely hold objects for a short period of time. Instead of the constant "fist" position from the preceding month, you'll see evidence of fledgling hand control.

Month Three: The Whole World Smiles with You . . . (Babies' ages: 2 months)

By the third month, our poo log reveals a family that was clearly in a rhythm. Instead of a daily full-page document resplendent with florid details of every spit-up, bowel movement, and nursing idiosyncrasy, 3 days are now condensed on a single page in readily decipherable shorthand.

The parental dues we had paid in lost sleep paid off in smiles galore from our babies this month. Although we were still on a feed every 3 hours around the clock ($2\frac{1}{2}$ during a pronounced growth spurt) schedule this whole month, we were uncannily energized by happy responses from our twins. Creative ways to incite the smile patrol began to emerge. Peek-a-boo. Goofy faces. Flatulence sounds. It's no-holds-barred in attempts to get the grins. Have fun. You have earned it!

Our babies' social skills were blossoming profusely this month. Either their fussiness diminished significantly, or we were far more adept at handling it—maybe both. The twins' ability to follow voices, make lengthier eye contact, coo adorably, and of course to beam angelically at onlookers made them quite the attraction whenever we left the house . . . which we did far more often this month. Stroller walks to the local library and drug store enabled us to meet people, accomplish errands, get air, get exercise, and borrow some fresh reading material.

The babies' visual focus was much more honed this month, and they fixated on book illustrations throughout our reading times. Another object of fixation discovered quite accidentally was the television. All our nursing sessions occurred on our bed, and frequently, I'd put the television onto the local PBS station or the Arts Channel while the babies ate. After the double dining experience, one baby would be placed in a Boppy pillow alongside me as the first baby was burped. On this particular morning, Sarah was being burped first since her gas usually proved more uncomfortable. As I placed Darren in his Boppy to await his turn, he deliberately turned his head to enjoy the colorful spectacle of the Teletubbies. Clearly his ability to see for a greater distance, well beyond the 10 inches or so of the first month, was in evidence. Clearly I was grateful for apropos viewing selections made.

In this the third month, our babies made the major move from sleeping in our room with their heads elevated in bouncy seats all night to sleeping together in their nursery in their crib all night. They made the transition beautifully. We agreed Scott would be wise to continue sleeping in our guest room so he could dodge the midevening melees of the nursing bed. With the feeds at 1 A.M. and 4 A.M. lasting at least 30 to 40 minutes from positioning on nursing pillow to placing the last diapered baby back in their crib, there was no way he could function effectively at work if subjected twice nightly to the sleep interruption . . . especially since he is not one to fall back asleep quickly after awakening. As soon as the twins were placed in their beds and quiet, I could drop off to sleep immediately. (I'd encourage you to make your family specific decisions on the basis of your own personalities and collective needs. Don't feel obligated to incorporate any magazine/book psychology, or your girlfriends' well-intended directives, into your family's playbook.)

The twins' dexterity was on the rapid increase this month. A pacifier placed on Darren's chest, through some feat of baby contortionism, worked its way into his mouth. The babies' hands were far more mobile. We began to get indications that the twins could understand our words. For instance, when I would change Sarah's diapers, she always would start with her legs up in the air, bent at the waist. I'd gently push her legs downward so I could open the diaper tapes and say, "Put your legs down, Sarah." This month, when I said "Put your legs down, Sarah," without the physical reinforcement of the request, she'd do it on her own. No doubt a Mensa member in the making.

Joking aside, if you haven't already, you will probably start discovering unique attributes and skills in your twins this month. Keep your eyes open for them, and write them down. At the time, you may think there is no way you will forget a single accomplishment your twins make, but you are more tired than you realize. You have two babies who deserve to know who did what and when. Take notes; you'll be thankful you did.

Maybe less of an accomplishment in my daughter's eyes, but one that amazed me nonetheless, was Sarah's ability to physically process her intake. In this month, she went a full 48 hours with no poo. She displayed none of the usual unpleasantries affiliated with constipation, but I called the pediatrician's office just in case. Unbeknownst to me, breast milk is capable of being assimilated 100 percent into a newborn's body. Meaning every aspect of the milk is put to use, there is no waste; hence, no poo. Amazing! After 3 days, she finally pooed, but then she would regularly go 2 or 3 days with no BM at all. Darren on the other hand continued to poo daily without fail. Fraternal or identical, your twins are different children, and they may manifest their individuality in ways you have yet to imagine!

Developmental and Physical Changes That May (or May Not) Occur in Month Three:

- Smiles . . . potentially lots of them
- Some babies may laugh this month
- Neck muscles getting stronger, more head control
- Increased ability to grasp objects for longer periods of time
- The shakiness and "startles" of the first 2 months are almost entirely gone

Month Four: Sleep, Glorious Sleep! (Babies' ages: 3 months)

The babies were growing well. By midmonth, our pediatrician said we could eliminate the middle of the night feedings and attempt to get Darren and Sarah to "sleep through." Scott and I had done some reading on different techniques, and we were both strongly in agreement that the twins needed to be able to self-soothe and be put down awake in their cribs. Having seen many friends struggle in efforts to get their singly born children to sleep at night, we knew we wanted to set an expectation and develop a ritual as early as possible. Although flexibility is usually a quality I embrace, with two babies, you have less latitude in the flexibility you can exert in nightly practice if the family is going to be well rested. The temptation to "relax" routine would be great with one child, thinking you could "get back with the program" the next night. With two babies watching every parental move, consistency seems even more important. With their pacifiers and incrementally timed consolations when necessary, Darren and Sarah were sleeping $7^1/_2$ hours straight within three nights, and even longer in the days thereafter. My breasts adjusted remarkably well. Needless to say, the first few mornings after no middle-of-the-night nursings found me well prepared for the babies' breakfasts.

Well-rested mommy noticed a few anomalies appearing in Darren this month. His head was flattening from lying down on his back in the same position for each nap and now, for lengthy windows of night sleep. Apparently babies' heads are quite malleable (thankfully, when you consider the birthing process), and consistent pressure will actually mold/shape their little noggins. Our pediatrician suggested some side sleeping positions using soft supports to keep him from rolling onto his tummy (never advised for newborns, as tummy-sleeping is linked to SIDS). Sure enough, his head rounded back out within a few weeks. Since his birth, Darren's hips would pop occasionally when moving his legs during the diapering process. This month, I also caught his knees and shoulders adding to the popping cacophony. Our pediatrician had been alerted to Sir Pops-a-Lot's noisemaking earlier, and she did a thorough exam as part of this month's appointment. Hip clicking can be indicative of potential problems, but we were happy to discover Darren just had noisy joints. Bless him, Darren's issues this month didn't end there; his left eye was in a perpetual state of weepiness. Tear ducts for newborns (especially preemies) are sometimes very narrow or become blocked. With the doctor's advice, we began massaging the corner of his eye gently with a moist cloth daily in efforts to clear the duct and allow drainage.

Not to be outdone, Sarah showed symptoms of what we believed might be her first ear infection, 2 days before our first flight as a family of four. Ear pain and airplanes make unpleasant bedfellows, so we took Sarah in during weekend hours to ascertain if our home diagnosis was correct. We may never know. The doctor found her ear to be wax-filled. Once he extracted the candle's worth, he discovered her ear canals were so tiny, he couldn't see far enough to confirm an infection. Since she was able to sleep (and ear infection victims rarely can), he decided we should just try to keep her head more elevated while nursing and give her infant ibuprofen as needed for discomfort.

As if sleeping through the night wasn't accomplishment enough, our twins had a month of many other notable firsts. A personal and long-awaited/hoped-for favorite was a full 10 minutes of joint sibling discovery/fascination; they faced each other and sized one another up silently. Let the games begin.

Developmental and Physical Changes That May (or May Not) Occur in Month Four:

- Arms and legs may extend more fully
- Lots of coo communication
- Babies may emit squeal outbursts and will likely laugh
- Babbling with recognizable consonant and vowel sounds is on the increase
- Babies are more comfortable with tummy time and may try to hold themselves up
- Neck strength is more evident; head control is almost 100 percent mastered
- The babies may bat at or reach for toys
- Babies recognize mommy and daddy on sight, and perhaps by voice and scent

Month Five: Personality Times Two
(Babies' ages: 4 months)

With the rapid accomplishments of this month, it became difficult to fathom that these were the same two babies who were virtually immobile and uncommunicative only 3½ months earlier.

Our month started with the 4-month well-baby(-ies) appointment with companionate shots. The babies were holding steady on their growth curves, which pleased both pediatrician and parents greatly.

With the rest gained through our full-family, full-night, sleep-fests, our outings multiplied greatly this month. The double stroller conveyed our socially acclimating twins through malls (great smells and visual stimuli—none the least of which are homage-paying, twin-adoring strangers), book stores (mommy could get a cup of decaf and read fresh children's book purchases aloud to the twins in the café area), the fine arts museum (smooth marble floors, decorative high ceilings, and large sculptures and canvases), and even more frequent fresh air walks around the neighborhood. Our outings were limited only by time, as we were still nursing on a regular schedule, and the idea of tandem twin nursing in public did not seem feasible for me personally.

As a nursing mom, at long last, I stopped attributing each and every twin digestive upset to a poor decision made on my dietary intake. My breast ailments and challenges of the first months were in the distant past, and it seemed we would be able to achieve our goal of breastfeeding the twins for the first year of their lives.

The babies' intake was well-established and consistent, and their output took on a new consistency as well. Denser, well-formed poos worked their way into the twins' diapers this month. That is, after Sarah's first bout with profound diarrhea. Her diapers were so devoid of solid matter for a full week (following our airplane trip) that our pediatrician ordered a battery of tests to confirm no parasitic invasion. Sarah was fine. The new lesson for me was baby diarrhea can be extremely lengthy in duration . . . literally weeks. If you experience the same, as always, keep your pediatrician informed and updated.

Our poo log evolves again this month. Instead of 3 days worth of information consolidated onto a page, each page now represents a full month. Rather than a hypergraphic description of how each baby's pitch of screaming varied with my morning breakfast cereal selection, each entry line now notes a specific baby's achievement or amusing anecdote. The former "poo log" blossomed into nothing less than an achievement journal this month. Every line is preceded with an encircled "D" or "S," not because I was too tired to fully write their names but because the fun quotient had increased so, that I dare not waste time with unnecessary writing. This month's D's and S's were followed with these highlights: "can grasp and hold bottle," "follows voices with eyes and head," "squinchy faced smiles," "full open mouth smiles," "can put pacifier in mouth," "can make a raspberry sound," "loves to play with toes," "babbling constantly (the apples don't fall far from the tree)," "always puts a hand over eye when sleepy," "reaches out to touch mommy and daddy's faces," "can turn pages in a board book," "rolls from back to tummy," "can smile at someone from across the room," "likes to stand on legs with support," "passes pacifier back and forth between hands," and "fascinated by lights." The good thing? Some of these successes reveal "catching up" for the twins' ages. Others expose areas in which the twins have exceeded expectations for their age. Your twins will have the same balance.

Do remember to avoid assessing and assigning titles or vocalizing comparisons between your babies when you discover one twin's acceleration (or lag behind) in a particular arena. Reviewing these early triumphs of our twosome, I can see how easy it would be to declare one twin the "brain" and one the "athlete." With the benefit of time, I can see where both children have reversed and returned and abandoned and pursued different goals and interests repeatedly. Certainly praise and reinforce each twindividual upon every unique accomplishment but not to the detriment or accidental belittlement of the other. Sounds like a stating of the obvious, but trust me, it does take some concentration.

Developmental and Physical Changes That May (or May Not) Occur in Month Five:

- Either or both babies may start teething
- Babies may actively reach for desired objects
- Babies may start rolling; expect back to tummy first, and tummy to back shortly thereafter
- Babies "respond" to your eye contact and talking with eye contact and "talking"
- Babies may support themselves standing for a short time while you hold their hands

Month Six: Rice Is Nice and Pictures Paint a Thousand . . . (Babies' ages: 5 months)

At our 4-month appointment, our pediatrician suggested we add solids to the twins' menu at 5 months. We were to nurse the babies first and then offer the highly diluted rice cereal at one "meal" a day until an affinity (or at the very least, acceptance) developed. Be ready for your twins to respond differently to the sudden substance in their mouths . . . and have a camera nearby. Also have a Diaper Genie or Diaper Champ or some sealed receptacle nearby for the more fragrant diapers that result from solid food feeding.

The personalities that began to reveal themselves in earlier months were unabashedly on display by 5 months. Gamely, I decided to take the babies out for a first "professional" photo. Dressed in two of my favorite outfits, the twins were in good spirits and were as ready as they would ever be. The Picture People in our local mall was inordinately quiet, so we wheeled the double stroller right on in. Unphased by the unannounced arrival of infant twins, the high-school aged photographer cleverly threw a satin sheet over a beanbag chair. Placing them both centrally, he began to shoot. Following only the fourth click of the shutter apparatus, Sarah erupted in a cry-fest that would clearly dictate the conclusion of her (and her brother's) first modeling gig. Apologetically, I thanked the hard-working photographer, and told him not to bother developing the few photos he was able to take . . . that we'd certainly have better luck next time. As if I had hurt his feelings, he was insistent that he got "at least one good shot or two," and forcefully encouraged me to return in the promised hour to view the session's results. The motion of mall-walking calmed Sarah immediately, so we strolled leisurely and let people compliment my precious cargo for the hour's wait.

Not since the babies' births had my eyes confronted such a miracle. Temporarily framed and propped against the wall when we returned to Picture People was a memory-searing image of Darren and Sarah. In black and white, the picture assumed a timeless quality. Through their own initiative, not by photographer posing, their inner arms had crossed. "Big" brother Darren somehow appears seated a bit higher than his "little" sister Sarah, and they are staring knowingly into each other's eyes. Not one to place too much emphasis on the "in-born" connectedness of twins, this photo visually refutes my casual dismissal of twin myths. Barely able to contain my still-easily hormonally provoked tears, I whipped out my credit card in order to purchase a few copies beyond the freebie my coupon provided. At every stoplight the whole way home, I extracted the free 10-by-13-inch from its protective envelope as if to confirm it wasn't a fantastic mirage. How grateful I am for the spur-of-the-moment decision to have a photo taken that day. Consider doing the same.

Developmental and Physical Changes That May (or May Not) Occur in Month Six:

- Babies may be able to support themselves sitting up for a short while
- Rolling, rolling, rolling . . . back to tummy, and then tummy to back

- Physical manifestations of personality traits may be in evidence; for fun, compare your twins' sleeping positions
- Babies may protest when mommy is out of sight (early separation anxiety)
- Babies recognize/know their names
- Toes and fingers become ever-present and fascinating playthings

Month Seven: Double Babies, God Bless 'Em!
(Babies' ages: 6 months)

Since the babies were 4 months old, I began alternately taking one a week to church with me. My two-pronged goal was to resume attendance in my adult discussion group while one twin at a time acclimated to the idea of spending an hour with another (nonparent) caregiver. The nonchurch attending twin would get some one-on-one time with daddy at home. Embarrassingly, with each attempt to depart the church nursery, the plaintive cries swayed me from the "Bye-Bye Sweetie, I love you, and will see you soon," partings I had planned. The nursery/Sunday School supervisor has performed her role superlatively for 40-plus years. I had complete faith in her and her team. Regardless, I still couldn't bring myself to leave. Finally, after spending a few weeks with each baby in the nursery for the full hour, I mustered the fortitude to depart. The process of "leaving" the babies in another's care proved a classic example of my maternally "knowing" what I wanted to do, and with what approach. When the opportunity came to actually *enact* my parental plan, it was far tougher to act than it was to develop my philosophy.

This month, we had a dedication service for Darren and Sarah. To hear a congregation of individuals voice their collective commitment to support us as parents and to love and nurture our children was more meaningful than words can describe. In the months that have passed since that ceremony, those individuals have not only lived up to their words in happy times but exceeded them in tough times. A testimony to the proliferation of twin births: our minister had been at our church less than a year when we asked him to bless our babies publicly. His only other baby dedicatory prior to ours? Another set of boy/girl twins.

Food fun was on the increase this month. Applesauce, a roundly heralded favorite amongst the newborn solid-food set, was not so well received by our dear daughter. Her response resembled a cat expelling a hairball. To witness distinctly varied responses to the same stimuli, as you inevitably do with twins, is one of the most entertaining aspects of parenting two infants simultaneously. The differing reactions truly helped us solidify the individuality of each child. For instance, this month, both babies were clearly exploring their senses of touch and texture. Sarah's hands were always at her eyes; she would blink her eyes and graze her fingertips across the span of her eyelashes. In contrast, Darren loved to scratch his fingernails against pillows, car-seat armrests, and corduroy pants.

Fussiness almost seemed a thing of the past by this month. Gas issues were either outgrown or well medicated. The babies were regularly waking happy and often giggling. Humor actually seemed to emerge in Darren this month. When reading the tear-jerking, adult-geared book posing as a children's book, *Love You Forever*, at one of the most emotional moments, Darren broke the teary tension with an impressive raspberry.

Sarah displayed obvious pride whenever we would say, "Good job, Sarah!" Needless to say, we rapidly learned to verbally reinforce the behaviors we wished repeated. We did the same with Darren.

Developmental and Physical Changes That May (or May Not) Occur in Month Seven:

- The babies' 6-month appointment will be a fun one to discuss progress made with your pediatrician. Shots will follow the well-baby(-ies) visit.
- Some babies may begin sleeping on their tummies after mastering the "roll." (Still place them in cribs on their back.)
- Twin interaction may be on the increase this month.
- Babies may sit up with no assistance for longer periods of time.
- The babies' vocalizations may start resembling words.
- Babies may figure out how to "scoot" themselves to reach objects. Let them! Don't immediately place the desired plaything in their hands. Better yet, put some fun toys just out of reach and applaud like crazy when the baby retrieves them.
- Babies may be putting everything in their mouths. Make sure no toys have small removable parts.
- If they haven't already, babies might be put on solid foods this month.
- Babies are rolling pros at this point.

Month Eight: Getting Back in a Groove
(Babies' ages: 7 months)

Sarah and Darren had gotten rave reviews from the doctor at their 6-month appointment. Only one "concern" arose. Sarah had dropped from her consistent location on the 3 percent weight curve down to the 1 percent weight curve; meaning out of every 100 infants her age, 99 weighed more than she did. As a result, for the first time since the days immediately following her birth, we had a scheduled weight check for Sarah at the onset of this month. We may never know what caused her "drop," but this month she reclaimed her position on the 3 percent weight curve.

Socially, we started meeting friends more often for Food Court lunches, hosting more "playgroups," and "talking/babbling" more with visitors. A visit to BabiesRUs provided a chance meeting with a couple and their new son from our Prepared Childbirth classes. Our babies seemed far less-impressed with the occasion than we adults did!

On a less-socially acceptable topic, we were grateful to see and hear our twins burping and tooting with apparent ease this month. After all their gas discomfort of earlier months, audible expulsions were music to our parental ears . . . and provided plenty of giggle fodder for the kids. Late-night check-ins on the babies often revealed them sleeping with booties in the air . . . a position that naturally eases (and releases) gas bubbles.

Major mobility seemed imminent this month as both were rocking and scooting on their backs. Each day we were sure we'd have "crawlers" soon. (It didn't happen this month.)

Our bath time locale shifted from plastic baby tub to kitchen sink. Each baby could sit stably for a while. We'd place one baby in their high chair facing our kitchen sink, while two adults bathed the other. Then we'd switch infants. Bath time was so entertaining; it was no small factor in our decision to purchase a camcorder the following month. (In retrospect, I wish we'd done it sooner. It was 100 percent worth the investment.)

Darren's sense of humor continued to be on the upswing this month. Reading a book that repeated the word "Ooops!" over and over sent him into gales of laughter. He and his sister also derived giggles galore from pulling pacifiers from their sibling's actively sucking mouth. The "pop" of suddenly halted suction, plus the sibling heckle factor, proved one of the month's greatest entertainments. With twins, somehow the act didn't seem "mean" . . . perhaps because the babies were on a level playing field.

Physical achievements included the emergence of Sarah's first tooth and her ability to stand while holding onto a chair or table.

Developmental and Physical Changes That May (or May Not) Occur in Month Eight:

- The babies' "conversation" sounds more conversation-like . . . more utterances that resemble words.
- Babies may begin to crawl or develop a non-crawl/body-drag method of getting from place to place.
- Babies may be able to wave "bye-bye."
- Babies like to thoroughly examine objects.
- Babies may clearly know the meaning of words frequently used: bottle, pacifier, sister, brother, mommy, daddy, etc.
- Babies may be able to support themselves while standing beside a table or chair.
- Babies may be able to point to the correct objects when asked.

Month Nine: Twin Talents and Tendencies Emerge (Babies' ages: 8 months)

The precrawling well-practiced wiggles allowed our babies to travel impressively this month. No longer was it "safe" to leave one baby briefly unattended while I changed the other in the adjoining room. Traveling as a group in-house became a constant. Mommying twins is a fluid process of modifying daily routines and practices as the babies grow and develop. Our routine by Month 9 now incorporated three "solids" meals and a snack nursing. We were down to two daily 1½- to 2-hour naps and a 12-hour nightly sleep.

Unfortunately, despite daily tear duct massages and eye drop medications, Darren's blocked/narrow duct was not clearing. Our pediatrician recommended a pediatric ophthalmologist, for the minor (but traumatic for all) surgery. Fortunately, despite the eye doctor's prediction that a second follow-up procedure would be necessary to finish the job; one operation proved sufficient, and we said good-bye to the "Darren has a goopy eye" era.

The benefits of having a musically gifted daddy are innumerable. From the twins' earliest days, their daddy has serenaded and surrounded them with music. Darren has undoubtedly inherited his daddy's musical interest. As of this month, it became a fairly safe bet that not just interest but daddy's musical talent is stirred into Darren's genetic cocktail. With the "ba–ba–ba's" so prevalent in 8-month old infant-speak, Scott casually started playing the Beach Boys' "Barbara Ann" for the babies. Right on pitch and with correct timing, Darren "sang" along. Late in the month, as Scott was changing his diaper, Darren babble-worded to the tune of "The Blue Danube Waltz" . . . the melody played by one of the twins' favorite toys. Scott was justifiably agog and impressed.

Sarah's future with Cirque du Soleil seems somewhat assured with her graceful hand gestures, effortless ascension from sitting to standing, yogic acrobatics and elegant-beyond-her-months natural poise. Even in her soundest sleep, as her daddy likes to say, "With Sarah, every move is a picture."

Many mental pictures of our babies' first days are blurred in my maternal mind's eye and ear. The jotted notations of each baby's accomplishments and special stories have been a God-send in triggering visual memories of some of the more hazy events. However, a few unforgettable moments are forever imprinted in my mind and heart.

Case in point, my first Mother's Day: We had invited my parents to spend the day with us. We were all sitting in the den, which in recent months had evolved into our baby-proofed and well-stocked play area. As I sat on the floor, the babies were being held (and adored) by Grandma and Grandpa. Suddenly, and without known provocation, Darren enunciated with perfect diction while looking straight at me, "Mama." Overwhelmed by the miracle of the moment, I rudely plucked my beloved son from whichever grandparent's arms held him and squirreled him upstairs for cuddly crying and bonding. You'd think my freakishly sentimental overreaction would have terrified him into "Mama"-free silence. Thankfully, he's been a "Mama"-sayer ever since.

Developmental and Physical Changes That May (or May Not) Occur in Month Nine:

- Scooting, crawling, cruising around the perimeter of tables, along the edges of sofas . . . however they choose to do it, you've got movers!

- Babies may say "Mama" and "Dada," maybe even "Bye Bye" (more like "Ba Ba").
- Babies can pass items from hand to hand (their *own* hands . . . don't get prematurely excited for twin sharing yet!).
- Greater indications of the twins' personalities, interests, and abilities may either surface, or be solidified this month.

Month Ten: Now They've Been out as Long as They Were in (Babies' ages: 9 months)

The 9-month well-baby(-ies) appointment and accompanying round of immunizations proved no challenge for the twins. All fared well and continued to show appropriate growth and development.

The twins were fortunate enough to be born in the same town where their maternal great-grandparents reside. Fully aware of the remarkable blessing this multigenerational proximity is, Darren and Sarah have weekly visits with their "Mamaw" and "Papa," on their turf and ours.

This month we experienced our first confrontation of "fear." The catalyst? A bouncing Tigger toy that had previously been a favorite. Whether caused by the mechanized leg springing or the somewhat hysterical-sounding "Hoo Hoo Hoo!" in Tigger-ese, we needed to remove the toy from the babies' sightline in order to insure a restful evening.

Both twins began using "Mama" and "Dada" with regularity that fully warmed (more like microwaved) our parental hearts.

Developmental and Physical Changes That May (or May Not) Occur in Month Ten:

- Babies may learn to clap and maybe play patty-cake.
- Babies enjoy banging objects together; haul out the pots, pans, and wooden spoons . . . you've got a percussion ensemble!
- Babies spend more time and energy "pulling up," or trying to.
- Babies may "fight" you as you change diapers or get them dressed.
- Fine motor skills become more refined, and the ability to pick up small objects improves.
- Babies may start crawling

Month Eleven: Outgrowing the Fancies of Youth (Babies' ages: 10 months)

Having served valiantly as impromptu bassinets during our first weeks home, our "big kids" no longer had any use for our beloved bouncy seats, so we consigned them this month. Having spent the post-bouncy seat nights sleeping together in the same crib, this month we graduated each baby to their own crib . . . butted against one another perpendicularly so they still could see each other and "communicate."

Don't despair, all our "baby" entertainments and practices weren't abandoned this month. We still used exersaucers, our playpen, and the double stroller on a close to daily basis. Our babies were still on the smallish side, so on occasion we still used the swing and Johnny Jump Up . . . but we knew their time was drawing to a close.

A favorite memory this month was catching Darren smile and laugh while he contently watched Sarah having fun.

Developmental and Physical Changes That May (or May Not) Occur in Month Eleven:

- Babies may master waving good-bye.
- Crawling may start this month, or speed up, or change how they do it.
- Babies may walk this month.
- "Mama" and "Dada" are likely in use this month (not necessarily always directed to the corresponding parent).
- Babies may start to (or already) understand the word "No." (Twins may understand it earlier for having heard it twice as often!)
- Some babies may get the hang of a sippy cup this month.
- Babies may point to objects they would like to have.

Month Twelve: These Booties Are Made for Walkin' (Babies' ages: 11 months)

Sarah did it. Before bed, at 11 months, in her crib. Three consecutive steps. As parents, it was shocking to discover that even though she *could* walk, she did not gravitate to walking as her selected method of loco-motion for many weeks to come. Crawling was well practiced, and un-believably fast. At 11 months, Darren still had not "mastered" tradi-tional crawling on all fours. He preferred his own elbow-driven, knee-propelled, and uncannily fast modified "crawl." Walking was months in his future.

His spirit of generosity however was well developed. He would of-ten extract the pacifier from his own mouth and place it in daddy's or Sarah's.

Rather belatedly this month, we decided to make our first full-family visit to a restaurant. (We had done plenty of Food Court meals but none in restaurants.) Keeping our babies in their car-seat carriers instead of using the restaurant high chairs, we placed a baby alongside each adult in the booth where we were seated. Everyone did *great*. As their "reward" for good behavior (although I am quite certain they don't withhold "rewards" from the poorly behaved), our kids were given their first helium balloons as a parting gift from the family-friendly restaurant.

We began weaning the twins off the breast this month, knowing we planned on discontinuing nursing at their first birthday. As part of the weaning process, with our pediatrician's okay, we offered sippy cups of cow's milk along with meals instead of preceding each meal with an increasingly shortened nursing session. Darren slurped it up. Sarah took longer to acquire the taste. Using the plan our nurse practitioner sug-gested, the process went smoothly and with minimal to no discomfort for any of the parties involved.

Developmental and Physical Changes That May (or May Not) Occur in Month Twelve:

- Many babies begin giving up the breast or bottle in this month before their first birthday.
- Babies may practice a lot of "monkey see, monkey do" mimicry.
- Babies may be able to put objects into a container; putting blocks into a box and the following "dump out" can prove entertaining for a surprisingly long period of time.
- Babies may be able to follow simple single command directions (e.g., clap your hands, wave "bye bye").
- Babies can probably stand without support for a fairly significant period.

Month Thirteen: Happy Shared Birthday, Dear Babies . . . (Babies' ages: 1 year)

So much (too much) has been written on how to approach the first birthday and ensuing party. We decided upon a family-only function, with only one other child in attendance, a cousin. It was the perfect decision for our family to keep it small and intimate. Your family's decision may be very different and equally perfect for you. Bow to no birthday party pressure but your own.

Enjoy your one-year well-baby(-ies) visit to the pediatrician's office. Immunization discomfort aside, the appointment is a great occasion to acknowledge the dramatic progress your twosome has made in a single calendar year. So much has been accomplished, and so much more awaits. Celebrate your success. Toast to your future.

Developmental and Physical Changes That May (or May Not) Occur in Month Thirteen:

- A word or two may be added to your babies' vocabularies this month.
- Let your babies play with crayons . . . they might be ready.
- Hair is probably thickening.
- Babies may start climbing on furniture, toys, and tables.
- Babies may be able to stack, and happily demolish, a short block tower.
- Babies may initiate games like peek-a-boo or patty-cake.
- Babies may walk this month.

If you have absorbed this chapter as a checklist for what *should* happen and when, rather than what *could* happen and when, please rethink your point of view. Your two babies are two individuals who will achieve milestones at the timing that is correct for them. If you ever have concerns that either or both of your twins are "behind," talk to your pediatrician. He or she will undoubtedly provide the reassurance of the broad range of "normal" for various key developments and achievements. Taking twin prematurity into consideration, the "normal" span for twins is broadened significantly. Reviewing our month-by-month experience, undeniably my notations focused on the dramatic "early" accomplishments. Yours will, too. You *should* take pride in your babies' triumphs. We certainly did. However, in our house, the achievements that occurred *after* the web-touted and highly publicized "norms" were often cause for unnecessary maternal concern in those early months.

No preschool enrollment form asks if your babies rolled over at 6 weeks or 2 months and then administratively places them in academic cubby holes accordingly. If one twin walks at an awe-inspiring 9 months and the other crawls until 15 months, don't assume one twin will lag behind the other in all arenas. By the twins' second birthday you'll be unable to empirically determine who has been walking longer. If (or when) you find yourself obsessively comparing your twins' development with other children's, or even comparing one twin's progress with the other's, put down that mommy magazine, log off the parenting website, put aside that pediatrician-distributed pamphlet, put down this book if you must. Step back, and work hard to keep a big-picture perspective.

34

Frequently Asked Questions: Everything You
Wanted to Know about Conceiving/Delivering/
Raising Young Twins but Were Afraid to Ask

From moms and dads expecting twins, to your family and friends, to strangers on the street, everyone seems to have questions about what it is like to have new twins in your belly, or in your home. The questions that follow are the ones we were asked most often. The answers that follow are ours and ours personally. In a broader scheme of things, answers are surely as varied as those who have experienced the situation. Please bear in mind our singularity of viewpoint when reading this chapter. Start composing your family's answers now. Trust me, the questions will be asked.

More important, try not to be offended by those queries that seem to have a "question(s) behind the question." Sometimes the asker has subliminal (and nosy) need to know your innermost feelings. Sometimes you are already sensitive about areas of your twin motherhood. Other times the asker is merely making conversation. Since you will rarely be able to know the difference between the types of questioners, do the American thing, and assume innocence . . . or ignorance. Neither of which should be met with condemnation, however tempting. Keep conversation civil in front of your highly impressionable children.

Question: Were you on fertility drugs?

Answer: No . . . well, not really. We had seen a fertility specialist and had taken a single rotation of the prescription drug Clomid since my period went AWOL for months after many years on the pill; but we were not undergoing official treatment. My obstetrician believes our twins occurred spontaneously . . . as a result of my "advanced maternal age."

More modest folk will take incredible offense at the personal nature of this question. The questions behind the question being: "Were you desperate for children? How much money did you spend to get them? Do you and your husband have reproductive issues making pregnancy "naturally" an impossibility? Get used to the fact that you will be asked. This is a question for which you may want to prepare an answer. Remember that your babies are a gift. It doesn't matter how you "got them"; you got them. Share information if you wish. You never know the intent behind the curiosity. You could unknowingly be providing hope, reassurance, or comfort.

Question: What do you do when both babies are crying?

Answer: Very rarely do both twins demonstrate equal duress at the same time. I'm not saying they don't cry at the same time, they do . . . but usually you can decipher fairly quickly if one is grievously, legitimately provoked, and then you tend to that baby first. When both are equally angsty, I pick one to be consoled first, try to do so expeditiously, then try to pick the other the next time.

Of course the tempting answer when this question is asked is to reply, "I cry, too!" And in truth, sometimes you may. It's okay, and totally normal. Don't feel like you have to share such intimacies with inquisitive strangers.

The questions behind the question being: "Don't you feel terrible having to divide your attention between two children?" "Are you going crazy?" "Do you feel thrust into a situation for which you are ill-equipped?"

The answers to any or all of those questions are your business alone, and your answers are subject to change at any moment. Let it go.

Question: Do you ever get out? Just you and your husband?

Answer: When we want to, we do. But honestly, the entertainment level in our household has increased exponentially with the arrival of our twins. We're less interested in the restaurant meals and movies that filled our social calendar pre-twins.

The oft-assumed (and highly irritating) question behind the question: "Is your marriage suffering for the additional stress/strain?" Again, no one's business but yours and your spouse's.

Question: Is one [twin] smarter than the other?

Answer: Of all the questions we're asked, this is the only one that really does provoke me. Largely because it is asked in the twins' presence! Sadly, many adults seem to think that if a child cannot speak, they cannot understand. My method of subtly "enlightening" the asker (without resorting to overt condemnation) is to physically bring the twins into the conversation. Lovingly rubbing both heads, I tend to respond, "I'll bet if you ask Darren, he'll say he is. No doubt Sarah thinks she is. Personally, I think they are both *very* smart."

Questions behind the question: "Twins aren't completely alike, are they?" and "How will you deal with the varied skills between them?"

Question: Do you find yourself "favoring" one over the other?

Answer: Again, this is a rather horrifying question to be asked in your twins' presence. Usually I have used these occasions to clearly delineate that there are certainly *behaviors* I favor, but both twins are loved equally.

As a mom, sometimes you may need to remind yourself that when you feel particularly frustrated with one twin for behavioral reasons, it is not that you *favor* his or her sibling. When you are exasperated and exhausted, remember to separate the act from the actor. Don't guilt yourself into believing you "favor" one of your twins.

The question behind the question for this one is similar to the preceding question: "Maternally, is it worse to compare twins than other siblings?" Some "comparison" is inevitable; but so is a mother's love for her children, whether born within minutes, months, or years of each other.

Question: Do they have a special "twin language" only they understand?

Answer: They certainly have their own indecipherable nonsense words they have created and reused; but those words seem to have no communicated meaning. Not to minimize or cast doubt upon those parents whose twins actually *do* have their own twin-speak, I think a lot of same-age non-twin infants/toddlers, if in constant presence of each other, might have some level of unique "language" or communication between them.

The question behind the question: "Are your twins the 'extra con-nected' variety, or just 'regular'?" Whether your twins communicate via idioglossia (the medical term for "twin-speak") or English, they *are* spe-cial and have an undeniable connection.

Question: Are you done? (Real question: Are you going to have any more children?)

Answer: Yes, we're "done." We had always hoped to have two chil-dren; we just had no idea they would arrive within 7 minutes of each other!

Many moms of same-sex twins find themselves very frustrated with this question; the question behind the question implication being that they need to "complete" their family by having a child (if they don't already) of the opposite gender. Again, try to be merciful with the ig-norance of strangers. You and your partner dictate and define what "complete" is for your family.

Question: My friend/wife/sister/daughter is expecting twins. What can I do to help?

Answer: For some inexplicable reason, new twin moms are reluc-tant to ask for, or even accept, help when it is offered. Perhaps there is an underlying desire to prove to ourselves that single-handedly we can indeed meet all the expectations and demands of multiple-mommying. If you genuinely want to help, you may need to just "jump in," rather than ask what it is you can do to be of assistance. What were some of the invaluable "helps" we received (or would have appreciated)?

- Prepared meals delivered (homemade, store-bought, restaurant carry-out, or pizza delivered . . . all were a God-send!)
- "Visits" that weren't adult social occasions but timed to allow me (and ideally the babies) to nap while the "visitor" would do a load of laundry, empty the dishwasher, or clean a bathroom, while tending to any waking babies
- Gift certificates/gift cards for baby product providers like BabiesRUs, Target, Wal-Mart, or the grocery store
- Loans/hand-me-downs/pass-alongs of infant clothing
- Diapers left at the door with a note of support (If the family is bottle feeding, a formula gift would be equally apropos. Do con-firm the type of formula the family needs/uses.)
- A pre-paid visit from a maid service
- Flowers or cards voicing congratulations and providing a phone number to call anytime (24-7) for support or help. (Granted, I

never took advantage of the offer, but knowing I could was very reassuring)

- A gift membership to the local Mothers of Multiples club
- A gift subscription to *Twins Magazine*

If you are a friend committed to helping, make your availability known early; but you may actually wait a bit prior to "jumping in." The family help in-house for those first weeks with twins is more abundant than it ever will be again. When the babies are 1, 2, 3 months old, the twin household acclimation/sleep deprivation is still intense, but the offers of help come less and less frequently. Friends that brought a surprise lunch or diaper supply months into our twin parenthood were greatly appreciated.

Refreshingly, there is rarely an ulterior subquestion behind the question when this inquiry is made . . . just a heartfelt desire to do something genuinely helpful for a twin-expectant loved one. When you are asked this question when out-and-about with your twosome, be sure to share the ideas that you found most helpful.

Question: Are they identical?

Answer: No. They do resemble one another, but our twins are boy-girl, so they are fraternal.

Question(s) behind the question: "Does looking alike equal 'identical' twins?" "What is the true meaning of 'identical' twins?" Identical twins share the same genetic DNA makeup. Subsequently, identical twins are the same sex. (Note: A worldwide total of three cases have been documented in which one of the gestating identical boy twins "lost" a Y-chromosome, in essence, creating a girl who lacks the usual second X-chromosome. The cases of this occurrence are so rare, it is statistically accurate to say identical twins are of the same sex.)

Question: Do you miss your job?

Answer: No. I don't. I keep in touch with my former coworker friends, but I don't miss my actual job at all. My new stay-at-home-mom career utilizes many of the talents/skills that made me a formidable force in my professional role: multitasking, attention to detail, working capably within deadlines, strong interpersonal and diplomacy skills, and the ability to function effectively amidst perceived chaos. The benefits in my new profession supersede my former benefits package. The pay? Well, that's a different story, but I *can* wear my pajamas to work!

Question(s) behind the question: "Are you *truly* satisfied/fulfilled by your decision to become a stay-at-home mom?" Or for the working twin moms: "Do you regret your decision of returning to work, knowing someone else is caring for your twins?" Regardless of which 9 to 5 decision a new mom makes, others (usually women) are often unconvinced that they would be happy making the same choice. True and honest feminism should encourage, trust, and support every woman's ability and competence to make the decision that is best for her and her family. If you wish to convince the frequently inconvincible, develop your testimony now. Otherwise, trust yourself and save your breath. Don't be swayed or insulted by those whose preferences are different than your own.

Question: Why don't you dress them alike? (Or: Why do you dress them alike?)

Answer: For the occasional holiday or photo opportunity, I'll coordinate their attire. To dress our children alike every day is more effort than I need to add to my plate . . . especially in the early days—when errant spit-up or diaper malfunctions force frequent wardrobe changes.

Question behind the question: "Do you have concerns about their individuality?" My feeling is that the vast majority of twin parents are hyperattuned to the fact that their twins are often viewed as a singular unit. Whether you elect to dress your twins alike or not, do everything you can to reinforce their individual *personality* differences. Despite the old cliché, clothes don't make the man, nor the child. What they wear is merely superficial. When your twins are old enough to express their displeasure (or desire) regarding dressing similarly, then reconsider your stand on the duo's daily duds.

Question: Do twins run in your family?

Answer: They didn't, but they do now!

Question behind the question: "Can you substantiate the statistics that twins indeed run in families?" The current belief is that identical twins occur fairly randomly. Fraternal twins do tend to run in families. Have fun doing some informal genealogical exploration. You may discover twins so distantly related they may not even "count," but enjoy looking. If you don't, excited relatives probably will.

Question: Do they sleep at the same time?

Answer: They go to bed at the same time every night, and we get them up at the same time every morning. Whether they actually *sleep* simultaneously each hour of the evening, I don't know. As parents, we're trying to sleep too; so unless we get a loud midevening indicator that one (or both) isn't using the time to actually sleep, we assume they are at least resting quietly. Daddy and I certainly make every effort to give them a predictable, conducive environment to do whichever they can.

Question behind the question: "Are you perpetually exhausted?" This question always warms my heart a bit, as it seems the asker has either had sleep challenges with their children or can vividly imagine (and sympathizes with) the difficulty in trying to get parental rest with two infants in-house. If the questioner seems truly interested in more detail, I will reveal that in those very early days/weeks, even with a regimented schedule, getting rest was tough. With each passing day, with continued consistency of routine, and with two great kids (cue to rub the twins' heads) it does get much, much easier.

Question: How do you do it?

Answer: You just do! You don't have the luxury of time to deliberate or overevaluate each twinstance that needs addressing. In reality, that is a blessing. By virtue of the fact you have multiple demands on your personal resources, you're typically forced to "go with your gut." Often, those reflexive, instinctual responses are the best.

Question(s) behind the question: How in the world can you do it all? Aren't you in a constant state of feeling overextended, overstressed, and underequipped? Clearly there are times when you feel poorly prepared, poorly suited, and extremely poorly rested for the task at hand. Never say it in front of your twosome; but in truth, you have no choice in the matter. You do what situations demand, and with two newborns, demands *are* plentiful. Commensurately plentiful will be your sense of accomplishment, your confidence in your ever-improving parenting skills, and your growing feelings of gratitude for your double blessings.

VIII

Celebration

35

Your Graduation Speech, Congratulations!

Believe it or not, your perception of twin pregnancy and parenting is all in your mind . . . although your body may still feel huge. As is pretty much the case with everything in life, how you elect to look at your situation is going to make all the difference. This is especially true during twin pregnancy and the first year of your babies' lives.

The truth is you have received a tremendous gift. You got the advertising world extolled "two-for-one"! One pregnancy; one labor and delivery session. Sure, your pregnancy, labor, and delivery might prove a bit more daunting than in a single baby scenario, but you are up to the challenge. Not only can you *do* this but you can *flourish*. The power of positive thinking and speaking is an unstoppable force. Convince yourself of your competence. These babies are yours, and no one can love them and raise them better than you.

Everyone will have advice. Many will offer help. Take the good stuff. Laugh at the silly mistakes you feel you have made, and know that tomorrow is a fresh day. Each day that passes, you are a more experienced parent. Accept the kudos of strangers for the undertaking you are handling. Smile and lavish praise on your babies . . . others will, too.

Before you know it, your newborns will be toddlers, and "babies" no longer. You will officially graduate from "new mommy" to "experienced mommy." In the instance of twins, most will regard you as "Mommy Summa Cum Laude." Congratulations!

Glossary

AAP: Abbreviation for the American Academy of Pediatrics.

Adjusted age: The age your twins would be if actually born on their 40-week-based due date. (*See also* Gestational age.)

Advanced maternal age: Classification for pregnant women aged 35 and older.

AFP test: Acronym/abbreviation for alpha feto-protein prenatal screening (not "test") also called "Triple Screen."

Amniocentesis: Prenatal extraction (by needle) of amniotic fluid to detect chromosomal abnormalities in the corresponding baby.

Amniotic: Referring to the amniotic fluid sac in which a developing baby floats prior to birth. Monoamniotic twins share a sac; diamniotic twins each have their own.

Anesthesiologist: The doctor/angel who administers the epidural.

Apgar score: Tests administered to newborns at both 1 minute and 5 minutes after they are born. With scores that range from 1 to 10, the tests measure babies' heart rates, breathing, muscle tone, overall color, and reflexes.

Areola: The darkened circular area surrounding the nipple.

Aversions: The absolute antithesis of pregnancy cravings—foods that inspire nausea in pregnant women.

Axillary temperature: Method of measuring temperature by placing a thermometer in the armpit of an infant over 3 months of age.

Baby A: In a twin pregnancy, the baby closest to the vagina/birth canal.

Baby B: The next in line.

Bed rest: Doctor-prescribed limitation/confinement of mom-to-be's physical activity in order to prolong a multiple pregnancy.

Bilirubin: A chemical created as red blood cells break down; often evidenced by yellowish-jaundiced tinge in newborns when the liver function is not fully developed.

Bouncy seats: Small, low to the ground chairs (with safety belts to secure young infants) that provide soothing vibration via battery power.

Braxton-Hicks: Tightenings of the uterus experienced during pregnancy, but not in a painful or consistent pattern. Often a result of over-exertion, pregnant women with numerous Braxton-Hicks contractions are advised to drink a lot of water and lie down when they become uncomfortable.

Breech: The position of a baby heading booty-first toward the birth canal.

Brethine: A drug administered to women experiencing the symptoms of preterm labor to slow or halt the process.

Butterball effect: The popping outward of twin mommy-to-be's belly button—resembling the "done" timer on the Thanksgiving turkey.

Car-seat curls: Twin mommy biceps building.

Cerclage: An OB-GYN "stitch" to stabilize a strained cervix.

Chorion: Referring to the placenta and the membrane(s) that line the uterus encasing the amniotic sac(s) and baby(-ies). Monochorionic twins share a placenta; Dichorionic twins each have their own.

CIO: The acronym often used on computer message boards indicating "Cry It Out" . . . a method of getting an infant(s) to sleep through the night.

Clomid: The pet name for clomiphene citrate—a drug used to stimulate ovulation.

Co-bedding: The practice of having your twins sleep together in the same crib in their first few months of life.

Colic: An umbrella diagnosis often used to describe very fussy/crying babies with no discernable medical condition. Colic can be particularly frustrating for new parents who are concerned by their babies' apparent discomfort.

Concordant: Parallel/congruent. Used in a sentence? Our twins' growth was *concordant* until our last perinatologist appointment, whereupon we learned our Baby B was no longer experiencing proportionate growth to our Baby A.

Conjoined: Term describing twins who are physically joined together at birth. The politically incorrect term often used is Siamese twins.

Contractions: Tightenings of the uterus that when they occur rhythmically, regularly, and uncomfortably predict the pending arrival of a baby. Braxton-Hicks contractions may occur throughout pregnancy and are milder and nonthreatening.

Co-sleeping: The practice of parents sleeping with twinfants (and occasionally other siblings) in a full-family bed.

Craving: An increased desire (bordering on uncontrollable compulsion) for certain foods during pregnancy.

Crib divider: Designed especially for use by twin families, a foam pillow approximately 6 inches high that fits horizontally across the width of the crib. The divider ties onto the crib slats, creating two sleeping areas, one per twin, in the same crib. Appropriate for use once the babies can roll over and "mess" with each other but are not yet capable of vaulting/crawling over the low obstruction.

C-section: Commonly used term that refers to cesarean sections: births that occur surgically via abdominal incision and extraction of the infant(s).

CVS: Acronym/abbreviation for chorionic villius sampling, a prenatal test.

Dilated: Word that describes the degree to which the cervix is "opening." Dilation occurs commonly (and ideally) in the latter weeks of pregnancy.

Discordant: Unequal/incongruent. Used in a sentence? When we learned at 36 weeks and 4 days that our twins were suddenly experiencing *discordant* growth, we were subsequently scheduled to have an induction that evening.

Discrepancy: Variance in size or development between twins.

Dizygotic: Twins (fraternal) that have developed from two separate eggs.

EDD: Abbreviation for estimated due date.

Effaced: Word that describes the "thinning" of the cervix. Occurs in tandem with the dilation of the cervix, in preparing for the vaginal delivery of a child(-ren).

Epidural: An anesthetic spinal injection that reduces/pain numbs the abdomen and nether regions.

Forceps: Oversized tongs used to aid in guiding a vaginally lodged baby out of the birth canal.

Fraternal: Twins developed from two separate eggs and two separate sperm fertilizations. Genetic similarity between fraternal twins is no more alike than any other siblings.

Full term: The recommended 40-week (measuring from start of last menstrual period) duration of pregnancy. Many consider 36 to 37 weeks full term for twins.

Fundal height: The measurement between pubis bone to the top of the uterus. Obstetricians will take regular fundal height measurements throughout pregnancy.

Gestational age: The age your twins would be if actually born on their 40-week-based due date. (*See also* Adjusted age.)

Gestational diabetes: Diabetes that develops in an expectant mother. Typically, the diabetic condition disappears following the babies' births.

Hallucihearing: The audio mirage that your babies' are crying even when they are not.

Hyperemesis: Excessive nausea/vomiting sometimes experienced in morning sickness.

Identical: Twins that have developed through the division of a singly fertilized egg and share genetic pattern—identical twins are same sex, share same eye color, hair color, etc.

Idioglossia: Term to describe what is commonly called "twin language" that some twins develop and speak between only themselves.

Incubator: A warming box often used to keep newborns (especially preemies) in a safe, temperature-regulated environment.

Indigestion: One of the most universally experienced symptoms of twin-pregnant women, particularly in the third trimester.

Induction: The process of medical intervention to "kick-start" a labor and delivery.

In-line stroller: A stroller that has two (or more) babies placed linearly rather than side-by-side.

Irish twins: An affectionate term referring to children born sequentially, but within 12 months of each other.

Isolettes: The warming "boxes" used to regulate temperature in newborn babies. (*See also* Incubator.)

IUGR: Abbreviation for intrauterine growth retardation; evidenced by suddenly slowed or poor growth in utero.

Journal: A record kept during pregnancy or as a mother of newborns to record experiences that might be forgotten otherwise.

Kangaroo care: The practice of placing a premature baby (wearing only a diaper) upright upon the bare stomach/chest (with the baby's ear on the heart) of a parent/caregiver. The benefits of this practice to preemie newborns have been well documented since the 1980s. Likewise, the parents appreciate the intensified closeness while their babies are in NICU.

Lactation consultant: An individual skilled in assisting women as they begin to nurse their newborns.

Lanugo: Baby-fine hair/fuzz covering areas of newborns' bodies.

Latching: The process of an infant effectively placing mouth to nipple/breast and suckling.

Left-side sleeping: Doctor-recommended positioning for sleeping or resting/regrouping during pregnancy.

Let down: The pre-feed surging of mother's milk toward the nipples in preparation to nurse . . . sometimes characterized by a tingling.

Lochia: The term describing the maternal vaginal bleeding/discharge output in the weeks immediately following childbirth.

MOM: Abbreviation for Mother of Multiples.

Magnesium sulfate: A drug administered to women experiencing symptoms of preterm labor to slow or halt the process.

Mastitis: An illness/infection in a lactating new mother's breast(s) requiring medical intervention, often in the form of antibiotics.

Milestones: Word used to describe key achievements/accomplishments of pregnancy or baby/newborn development.

Mirror image: Identical twins whose genetic similarities are manifested in an "opposite" fashion—one twin is left-handed, the other right-handed, one has a birthmark on left cheek, the other right, etc.

Monozygotic: Twins (identical) formed by the division of a single fertilized egg.

Mylicon: A brand name of baby gas relief drops.

Nasal syringe: A handheld plastic bulb used to siphon excess mucus from babies' nasal passages.

Neonatologist: A doctor specializing in the care of newborns—especially those who are premature.

NICU: Abbreviation for neonatal intensive care unit.

Nipple confusion: When a newborn "confuses" or prefers a nonbreast nipple (e.g., an easy-flow bottle or pacifier).

Nipple shield: A plastic device that allows the nipple to project out further by pushing back the encroaching milk-filled breast . . . allowing a newborn greater access.

Non-stress test: A test administered late in pregnancy to monitor the babies' heart rates onto a "ticker tape"-style reading.

Pacifier: A nippled soother used to satisfy the suck urge in newborns/infants.

Palpate: Method employed by OB-GYNs to examine by feel the surface of a pregnant woman's abdomen.

Pediatrician: A doctor specializing in the care of newborns/children.

Perinatologist: A doctor specializing in high-risk pregnancies.

Pitocin: A drug administered to spur the onset and intensity of labor.

Placenta: The organ(s) that develops to provide oxygen and nourishment to the babies in utero via their umbilical cords.

Plugged ducts: A situation in which milk gets "backed up" in the breast and forms an uncomfortable lump/swelling.

PPD: Abbreviation for postpartum depression. A severe mental state of maternal sadness following childbirth that needs to be treated immediately.

Preeclampsia: A potentially dangerous high blood pressure and protein in the urine combination that may be experienced late in pregnancy. Doctors monitor twin-pregnant women closely to detect any signs of preeclampsia.

Preemie: Refers to a baby born prior to his or her estimated due date. (Even though "term" is considered between 36 and 37 weeks for twins, many will still refer to twins born in that range as "preemies" as they did not reach the full 40-week mark.)

Preterm labor: For twin-pregnant women, the onset of labor prior to 36 to 37 weeks. Although many OB-GYNs will not attempt to slow or halt a twin labor after 34 weeks.

Pump and dump: If nursing mom ingests a questionable substance (e.g., shellfish or alcohol), this term refers to the practice of expressing the breasts on schedule but not offering the resultant potentially contaminated milk to the infants.

Rear-facing: The car seats for babies need to be in the back seats and facing the rear windshield until babies are 20 pounds *and* 1 year old. After both those milestones are attained, the seats may become front windshield facing (still in the back seats).

Reflux: A condition sometimes experienced by newborns in which acid comes up with belches and spit-ups, making them uncomfortable.

RSV: Acronym/abbreviation for respiratory syncytial virus. RSV in adults and older children manifests merely as a cold. For infants, it can lead to bronchiolitis. Premature infants are particularly susceptible, especially in the months of October to March. Many pediatricians recommend preventative shots for RSV for their premature-twin patients.

SAHD: Acronym/abbreviation for Stay-At-Home Dad.

SAHM: Acronym/abbreviation for Stay-At-Home Mom.

Singleton: Term used by doctors and parents of twins to describe a baby that is born solo.

Sleeping through: Term that describes regular evening sleep consisting of at least 6 consecutive hours without a feeding or major interruption.

Soft spot: The location on newborns' heads where the skull has yet to fuse. A baby's pulse is often visible via their soft spot.

Sonogram: *See* Ultrasound.

Stadol: Drug offered to women midlabor to ease the discomfort.

Steroid shots: Injections offered to women at risk for premature labor to speed the development of babies' lungs in utero. (Breathing difficulties are a primary concern for premature babies.)

Stretch marks: Silvery scar-like skin markings that occur as a result of rapid skin expansion. Most often occur on pregnant abdomens, but thighs and breasts may get stretch marks as well.

Swaddling: The practice of wrapping a newborn snugly in a receiving blanket to retain warmth and mimic the enclosed sensation of the womb.

Tandem: Word applied to describe any action done simultaneously (e.g., tandem nursing).

Transverse: Rather than "head down" toward the birth canal, a baby positioned side-to-side—as if perpendicular to the birth canal.

TTTS: Abbreviation for twin-to-twin transfusion syndrome. A complication in which twins share the same placenta but with abnormal/unequal blood flow, resulting in a donor twin (with too little blood) and a recipient twin (with too much). Medical monitoring and extensive prenatal care is imperative for families amidst a TTTS pregnancy.

Twincandescence: The intensified pregnancy glow experienced by twin-pregnant women, caused by increased blood flow under the skin.

Ultrasound: System that bounces high-frequency sound waves off an object in order to produce a visual image . . . usually how you will discover you are carrying twins (also known as a Sonogram).

Viability: Term used to describe the likelihood of survival at a point of early delivery.

Water breaking: The vaginally departing gush of water (actually amniotic fluid) that indicates the onset of labor.

Weight checks: Upon twins' discharge from the hospital, their pediatrician will want to confirm they are gaining weight appropriately and will require numerous office visits to monitor your twins' progress. Weight checks are often conducted using the same in-office scales to eliminate the possibility of misinterpreted growth problems based on measuring apparatus discrepancies.

List of Helpful Web Resources

www.AllAboutMoms.com
www.AmericanBaby.com
www.AMBA.org.au (Australian Multiple Birth Association)
www.BabyCenter.com
www.BabyCentre.co.uk
www.BabyZone.com
www.Birth.com.au
www.Childbirthsolutions.com
www.Christian-Mommies.com
www.DoubleBlessings.com
www.ExpectingMultiples.com
www.IntlTwins.org
www.JustMultiples.com
www.LaLecheLeague.org (Breastfeeding support)
www.MarchofDimes.com
www.MarvelousMultiples.com
www.Mom2Many.com
www.MommyGuide.com
www.MOPS.com
www.MoreThanOne.com
www.MOSTonline.org (Mothers of supertwins—triplets or more)

www.MultipleBirth.com
www.MultipleBirthsCanada.org
www.Multiples.about.com
www.NOMOTC.org (National Organization of Mothers of Twins Clubs)
www.ParentCenter.com
www.PreemieMagazine.com
www.PreemieParents.com
www.ProactiveGenetics.com (Services for determining identical or fraternal twins)
www.SheKnows.com
www.Sidelines.org (Support for expecting moms on bed rest)
www.StorkNet.com
www.TAMBA.org.uk (Twins and Multiple Birth Association, United Kingdom)
www.TTTSFoundation.org
www.TwinAdvice.com
www.TwinlessTwins.org
www.TwinsandMultiples.org
www.TwinsClub.co.uk
www.TwinsDays.org
www.TwinsFoundation.com
www.Twinshock.net
www.TwInsight.com
www.Twinsights.com (author's website)
www.TwinsList.org
www.TwinsMagazine.com
www.TwinsNetwork.com
www.Twinspiration.com
www.TwinsToday.com
www.Twinstuff.com
www.TwinsWorld.com
www.Twinteresting.com
www.YourBabyToday.com

Various "Twins and Multiples" groups on www.Yahoo.com

Index

abdominal pain, 56–57

acetaminophen, 187

achievements: logging of, 269–70; pride in, 219

A-Child, 47–48, 61; assessment of, 219; sensor attached to, 107; and use of buddy system, 76

adoration, of twins by others, 244–45

adult reactions to twins, 232

advanced maternal age, 6, 12, 23, 37, 284

aerosol fumes, 22

AFP. *See* alpha-fetoprotein (AFP) screening

ages of twins, growth and experiences during: 3 days, 229–30; 4 days, 230; 6 days, 231; 0 months, 255–60; 1 month, 231, 260–64; 2 months, 264–66; 3 months, 266–68; 4 months, 232, 268–70; 5 months, 270–72; 6 months, 272–73; 7 months, 274–75; 8 months, 275–77; 9 months, 232, 277; 10 months, 232–33, 278; 11 months, 278–79; 12 months, 280; 13 months, 66, 233; 14 months, 233–34; 15 months, 234–35; 18 months, 235; 19 months, 235; 20 months, 236

air travel, 18, 191, 232; airline miles and credit card use, 189; awareness of regulations, 192–93; layovers, 194, 195; preboarding option, 192; preparation for, 193–97

alcohol, 18

allergic reactions, 204, 205; and introduction of solid food, 210; and non-allergic twin, 214; and restaurant food, 213

alpha-fetoprotein (AFP) screening, 40–41, 42

American Academy of Pediatrics, 151

amniocentesis, 41, 42
anesthesia, 107–8
anesthesiologists, 109
anger, 225
anniversary observations, 77–78
answering machines, 100
antibacterial soap and wipes, 97,
    172–73, 232
antibiotics, 148, 149
Apgar test, 110, 111, 112n1
appetite, loss of, 54–55
applesauce, 272
areolas, 32
aromatherapy oils, 21
artificial sweeteners, 19
aspartame, 19
assessments: avoiding, 217–20; of
    mothering capabilities, 237
assistance. *See* support systems
attentiveness of mothers, 122
audible stimulus, 44
au pair, 69, 71
Avent nipple, 139

babies: descending of, 58;
    movement in utero, 55; neural
    development of, 20. *See also*
    multiples
BabiesRUs, 274
baby food, 87–88
baby product manufacturers,
    186–87
baby proofing, 162
baby showers, 80
back pain, 56–57
balloons, 279
Barnes & Noble, 165, 169, 236
bassinets, 70
bathing, 175, 236; from baby tub to
    kitchen sink, 274; bath bubbles,
    175, 178n1; bathtubs, 85;
    postpartum, 118; while twins in
    bouncy seats, 177
bathroom, trips to, 34

batteries, 95
B-Child, 47–48, 61; assessment of,
    219; and use of buddy system, 76
Beach Boys, 276
bed rest, 61; and fundal height
    measurements, 45; in third
    trimester, 54
bedtime rituals, 133–34
belly buttons, 59, 258–59
benefits of twins, 241–45
beverages, 212; to consume prior to
    breastfeeding, 146; cow's milk,
    150–51, 212, 279; items to avoid,
    31, 34; juices, 146, 212; sodas,
    212; thrown off high chair trays,
    214–15
bibs, 79–80, 213, 254
bilirubin, 257
binkies, 89–90, 100
biological urges, 231
birth announcements, 50, 109
birthday parties, 280
birth defects, 40–41
birthing experience, father's
    perspective, 111
birth routes, 26–27
birth weights, 18, 261
bladder, 30
blood clots, 118
blood flow, byproducts of increased,
    12–13
blood pressure, 43–44
bloodshed, 30, 118; bleeding gums,
    20; from nail clippings, 230
blood sugar levels, 43, 204, 205
bonding, 122, 152
books, 86, 90
Boppy pillows, 97–98, 133, 163, 164
botox injections, 22
bottles and bottle feedings, 155,
    164–65; and air travel, 194;
    bottle feeding vs. breastfeeding,
    65–66; bottle-plus-breast feeding
    method, 152, 257; supply of

clean bottles, 252; use of fast-flow bottles, 90

bouncy seats, 71, 95, 133, 164; consignment of, 278; sleeping in, 256; used while doing kitchen chores, 177

bowel movements, 34–35, 57, 266; after solid foods, 270; color of, 258; constipation, 57, 266; culture tests of, 232; and diaper counts, 94, 156; diarrhea, 57, 232, 269; disposal systems, 82. *See also* poo log

bowls for babies, 215, 216

brand name products, 188

bras, supportive, 11

breakfast, 215

breastfeeding, 87, 137–44, 253; advice concerning, 145–46; and air travel, 193–94; and Boppy pillows, 97–98, 133, 163, 164; bottle-plus-breast combination, 152, 257; choosing not to, 151–52; and diaper counts, 94; diet while, 24–25, 31, 142, 269; ending of sessions, 155–56; holds for, 140; in-hospital, 139; journal of, 153–55; logistics of, 147; and nipple confusion, 89–90, 115; rejection by babies, 114–15, 144; schedule for, 143, 147, 256; tandem, 142, 162–64, 194; and use of pacifiers, 89, 90; vs. formula feeding, 65–66; weaning from, 150–51

breast milk, 87–88, 266

breast pumps, 149–50, 193, 194, 257

breasts: blocked ducts in, 148–49; breast form, 32; postpartum care of, 119–20; and skin stretching, 32; supportive bras for, 11; tenderness of, 10–11, 117; washing of, 118

bruises, 120

buddy system, 76

budgets. *See* finances and financial preparations

burping, 65, 261, 262; burpie cloths, 89, 163; length of time to produce results, 258; pre-feeding, 262; routine of, 164

butterball effect, 59

calcium, necessity for, 212

cameras and camcorders, 85, 111, 254

caregivers, 272

cars: fingers getting smashed in, 233, 235; getting to/from/in and out of, 166–69; keys locked inside, 234

car seat carriers, 164, 166–67, 263

car seats, 48, 88; and air travel, 192; and rear-view mirror systems, 99; and ride home from hospital, 229–30; stress test for, 229

cats: and crib tents, 98; and litter boxes, 23

CDC. *See* Centers for Disease Control and Prevention (CDC)

CDs, 85

cell phones, 99

center of gravity, 56

Centers for Disease Control and Prevention (CDC), 5

cerclage, 25–26

cervix, 42–43, 106

Cesarean. *See* C-section

changing tables, 82, 84; in airports, 194, 232; and air travel, 193; use of antibacterial soap on, 97

Cheerios, 212, 232

childbirth classes. *See* Prepared Childbirth classes

childcare, stay-at-home parent vs. daycare, 69–70

childhood illnesses, 200–201. *See also* sickness

childrearing, 253
choking, 71, 232
chorionic villius sampling (CVS), 42
Christian, Lori, 68. *See also* pediatricians
chromosomal abnormalities, 40, 42
chronic conditions, relief from, 35
cigarettes, 19, 31
circulation of blood, 12–13
circumcision, 204, 205, 259
Clomid, 284
cloth diapers, 94
clothes: crotch-snapping onesies, 235; dressing twins alike, 288; for emergencies, 254; maternity, 13; for photographs, 271; for twins, 79–80, 235, 288; while breast pumping, 194
co-bedding, 81, 133, 256, 265
communications, 76, 78; concerning discipline, 74; concerning holiday traditions, 235; with other multiple moms, 188; overcommunication, 11; with spouse, 222–25
comparisons, 270, 281; avoiding of, 217–20; favoring one twin over the other, 285
complications, late-pregnancy, 61n1
compliments, 219, 248
compromise, 76
consignment stores, 188, 278
constipation, 57, 266
Consumer Reports, 83
containment of twins, 162, 203
contractions, 107, 109; postpartum, 119–20
coordination, 233
costs, formula, 66
couple time, 223
coupons: baby product manufacturers, 186–87; for diapers, 88; for formula and baby

food, 87–88, 210; for later use, 188–89; for photographs, 175
cradle hold, 140
cravings for food, 25, 31–32
crawling, 279
credit cards, 189
cribs, 51, 70–71, 81–82; co-bedding, 81, 133, 256, 265; placement of, 278; use of as part of bedtime ritual, 134; vinyl mattress covers for, 203; waterproof pads for, 134
crib tents, 98, 195
crying, 284; controlled, 134–35; as energy expender, 252
C-section, 107, 118
CVS. *See* chorionic villius sampling (CVS)

danger signs, awareness of, 261
Darren Jacob, 120, 159, 160, 232; adult reactions to, 218, 285; allergic reactions, 204, 205; birth, 114, 163; breastfeeding, 140, 142, 150, 153–55; circumcision, 204, 205, 251; the first year, 255–79; illnesses, 200; journal for, 153–57; mistakes made concerning, 230–36; naming, 124; picking up, 161; solid food consumption, 211; tear duct problems, 204
daycare, 66; vs. stay-at-home parent, 69–70
dedication services, 272
defecation. *See* bowel movements; poo log
delivery, birth routes, 26–27
dentists: dental appointments, 20; and sugary liquids, 212
depression, postpartum, 114–15, 117
developmental characteristics, 87–88, 281; month one, 260; month two, 263–64; month

eating and diet (*continued*)
forbidden foods, 31; junk food,
21; and morning sickness, 10; as
part of routine, 253; postpartum,
120; and twins' bowel
movements, 257; and use of
aspartame, 19; while
breastfeeding, 24–25, 31, 142,
269. *See also* beverages; solid foods
EDD. *See* estimated due date
(EDD)
edema, 57, 61n1
effacement, 43, 106
e-mails, 253–54
emotions, 122, 225; dual, 60–61;
and hormones, 11; postpartum
depression, 114–15, 117
employment, vs. stay-at-home
moms, 287–88
energy level, in third trimester, 54
epidurals, 107–8, 109
episiotomy, 114
errands, 171–74
estimated due date (EDD), 48
exercise, 31, 100
exersaucers, 84, 96, 278
exhaustion. *See* fatigue
expectations, setting high, 219
experiences, and childhood illnesses,
200–201
eyes: twinkling of, 245; variation in
strength of, 204; visual focus, 265
EZ2 Nurse Twin Nursing Pillow,
98

fall prevention, 33–34
false labor, 14
family issues, 77–78
family size, 286
FAQs. *See* frequently asked
questions (FAQs)
fast food, 21, 99, 174
fathers, 254; assistance in labor, 108;
assistance with feedings, 65–66;

and strollers, 83; support for
breastfeeding, 143. *See also*
Double Daddy Perspectives
fatigue, 10, 15, 221, 289
favoring of one twin, 285
FDA. *See* Food and Drug
Administration (FDA)
feeding schedules, 125, 132–33,
139; setting alarm clock for, 231
feet, elevation of, 31
fertility, 5
fertility drugs, 284
fertility treatments, 5, 37
fetal alcohol syndrome, 18
fetal heartbeats, 39, 44
finances and financial preparations,
71–72; elimination of budget
expenses, 185–86; estimation of
budget for twins, 183–84;
evaluation of spending patterns,
185, 189–90; expenses for
formula, 143; need for monetary
safety net, 189; savings
opportunities, 186–89; stay-at-
home parents vs. daycare, 70
fingernails, clipping of, 230
fingers, 233
first trimester, symptoms during,
9–16, 29
flexibility, postpartum, 124
food: aversions to, 21, 32; to avoid
during pregnancy and
breastfeeding, 24–25; cravings for,
25, 31–32; fast food, 21, 99, 174;
junk, 21; safety issues, 31; scents
of, 12. *See also* eating and diet
Food and Drug Administration
(FDA), 19
Food Lion, 234
football-hold position, 140
forceps, 110
foreskin, 204, 205
formula, 87–88; developmental
information from manufacturers,

93; gifts offered by companies, 251; length of time on, 212; samples from pediatrician's office, 187. *See also* bottles and bottle feedings; breastfeeding
fraternal twins, 287, 288
freebies, 251
frequently asked questions (FAQs), 283–89
full term, 225
fundal height measurements, 44–45
fussiness, 273; logging of, 153–55

gassiness, 71, 89, 257–58; from foods eaten by mother, 146; outgrowing of, 273; and sleeping position, 274; and sleep location, 134
gastrointestinal problems, 56, 71; constipation, 57, 269; diarrhea, 57, 232, 269; indigestion, 56, 120; intestinal infections, 232. *See also* gassiness
gauze pads, 259
gender of twins, desire to know, 40
gestation, 259
gestational diabetes, 43
gifts, registering for, 149–50
The Girlfriend's Guide to Pregnancy (Iovine), 107–8
glossary, 295–302
glow of pregnancy, 35
glucose tolerance test, 43
Goldfish, 212
grandparents, 253, 277
greetings, by other adults, 247–49
grocery carts, 172, 233–34
grocery shopping, 233–34
groin pain, 56–57
Gymboree music classes, 165
gynecologist. *See* OB-GYN

hair dye, 22
hair spray, 22

handicapped access, 101–2
harnesses, 98–99
heartburn, 56, 120
hemoglobin, 43
hemorrhoids, 33, 114
herbal remedies, 21
high chairs, 90, 164, 214–15
high-risk pregnancy, 37
hip clicking, 267
holidays, 77, 223, 233–34
home-based businesses, 189
homeopathic practitioners, 21
honey, 22
hormones, 11, 231
hospitals: care in, 256; packing bag for, 51–54, 106; postpartum in, 113–15; stays in, 25; and transition to motherhood, 117–24
household expenditures, 71–72
household management, 176–78
household renovations, 20
house keys, 233
housework, 252
humor, during pregnancy, 4

ibuprofen, 268
identical twins, 287
immunizations, 263, 268, 277, 280
incentives, to establish routines, 243–44
independence, desire for, 236
indigestion, 56, 120
individuality of twins, 243, 288
individual needs of twins, 159–60
inducement of labor, 106
infections, 117–18, 232
insurance information, 106
intelligence, 285
intensity of twin pregnancies, 241–42
Internet: and e-mail, 253–54; and home-based businesses, 189; for information on multiples, 18,

Internet (*continued*)
93–94; searching for baby
product manufacturers, 186–87;
and telecommuting, 189
intestinal infections, 232
in utero, health of babies in, 27
Iovine, Vicki, 107–8
itching sensation, 32

jaundice, 257
jogging strollers, 96
Johnny Jump Up, 84, 278
joints, 267
juices, 146, 212
juniper leaves, 233
jury duty, 241

Kegel exercises, 121
keys, 233, 234
kick counts, 55
Kool-Aid, 212
Krispy Kreme, 100

labor and delivery, 105–12; labor-
slowing drugs, 25–26; postpartum
in hospital, 113–15; preterm, 14,
25–26; and sexual relations, 23–24
lactation, 119
lactation consultants, 138, 141;
advice to use, 146; in-home
visits, 142, 257; in-hospital visits,
162, 255–56
lanugo, 259
latching on, 139, 141, 145; routine
for, 163; and use of pacifiers, 89,
90
laughter, 225, 274; parental, 215
laundry: during sickness, 203;
facilities at vacation spots, 195;
getting out stains, 101; of Velcro
bibs, 254; washing baby clothes
prior to wearing, 80
layette requirements, 80
La-Z-Boy recliners, 34

library story time, 165
lifting, 118
limping, 33
linea nigra, 57–58
liquids. *See* beverages
litter boxes, 23
Love You Forever (Munsch), 273
low birth weights, and reflux, 261

magnetic resonance imaging (MRI),
5, 6n1
malpractice suits, 256
manicures, 22, 230
marital relations, 221–27
martyrdom, 124
massages, 20–21; postpartum, 113
mastitis, 117, 148
maternal wisdom, 200
Maxi-pads, 118
mealtimes, accessories for twins,
215–16
meconium, 157
medical history and records, 38–39
medical reference texts, 199–200
medical staff, and release of twins
from hospital, 256
medications: acetaminophen, 187;
antibiotics, 148, 149; Clomid,
284; dispensing of, 202, 203;
labor-slowing drugs, 25–26;
over-the-counter, 23, 202;
Pitocin, 107, 109; prescription
drugs, 23; Zantac, 155, 262
memory lapses, 126
mental health, 46, 225; mommy
brain, 59–60, 61; and personal
time, 77; postpartum depression,
114–15, 117
message boards, 93
microwave ovens, 22
milk: allergic reactions of babies to,
147; cow's milk, 150–51, 279;
daily intake of, 34; demand
created for, 138; need for in

breastfeeding mothers, 146; pumping breast milk, 143; whole, 100

mirrors: rear-view mirror systems, 99; for watching birth, 110

mistakes: at different ages of development, 229–37; learning from, 252

mobiles, 134

mobility, and professional photographs, 175

mommy brain, 59–60, 61

Mommy and Me, 165

Moms of Multiples Club, 187–88

monitors, 71, 96–97, 107

Montgomery glands, 32

monthly cycle: and breast tenderness, 10–11; irregularity of, 5–6

morning sickness, 9–10, 14–15, 38

motherhood, transition from hospital to, 117–18

mothering capabilities, assessment of, 237

Mother's Day, 276

MRI. *See* magnetic resonance imaging (MRI)

multiples, maneuvering of: bath time, 175; child-centered outings, 165–66; double strollers into stores and malls, 169–71; during mom's time, 176–78; during photo sessions, 175; during storytime, 176; getting to/from/in and out of cars, 166–69; grocery shopping, 171–74; picking up at same time, 161–62; running errands, 171–74; tandem nursing or bottle feeding, 164–65

museums, 169

music: during labor, 110; exposure to, 85

musical talent, 276

My Brest Friend Nursing Pillow, 98

Mylanta, 258, 262

name selections, 49

nappie-sacks, 179

nasal congestion, 256

nasal passages, 86

nausea, 9–10; dry heaving during delivery, 110–11; and eating tactics, 31–32; and food aversions, 21

navels, 59

necessities, stocking up on, 253

neck muscles, 230

negotiations, 224–25

neonatal intensive care unit (NICU), 50, 81, 109, 256

nervous systems, of premature twins, 259–60

nesting, 55–56

neural tube defects, 40

NICU. *See* neonatal intensive care unit (NICU)

night sweats, 121

night-teeters, 34

nipple confusion, 89–90, 115, 138

nipples, 32; bleeding of, 149; for bottles, 138–39, 155, 156; choice of, 156; munching on by infants, 150; shields for, 119; soreness of, 119

non-stress test (NST), 43–44, 108

nosebleeds, 30

nourishment, and use of pacifiers, 90

NST. *See* non-stress test (NST)

nurse practitioners, 279

nurseries: preparation of, 51; and sleeping arrangements, 70–71

nurses: advice on baby care, 115; advice on "shakies" of premature twins, 259–60; and decision to breastfeed, 137–38; labor and

nurses (*continued*)
delivery, 108–9; postpartum care, 114
nursing. *See* breastfeeding
nursing pillows, 97, 98, 140, 142, 163; and breast rejection, 144; tandem, 140
nutrition: and breastfeeding, 253; and diaper changing, 88; and diaper counting, 94. *See also* eating and diet

OB-GYN: and bleeding, 30; communication with, 55; and daily routines, 31; first trimester visits, 12; and morning sickness, 10; phone-diagnosis of preterm labor, 14; pregnancy confirmation visit, 3–4, 38–39; questioning of, 17–18; screening tests, 40–42; six-week postpartum visit, 226; on use of aspartame, 19
off-brand products, 188
Once Upon a Child, 84
onesies, 235
open-mouth-and-let-food-roll-out routine, 211
oral syringes, 202
outings, 171–74, 264, 268–69; child-centric activities, 165–66; and diaper bag contents, 180–81; and house key, 233; husband and wife, 284–85; meal-focused, 216; snacks for twins during, 212–13
over-the-counter medications, 23, 202
Oxi-Clean, 101
oxygen, 110

pacifiers, 89–90, 100, 115, 163, 254; leashes for, 100; placed in dishwasher, 97
Pack 'n Play, 84, 177
panties, maternity, 34

panty liners, 34
paper towels, 97
parental work roles, 185–86
parking places, 101–2
paternity leave, 159
pediatric allergists, 204
pediatric endocrinologists, 204
pediatricians, 66; advice on babies' crying, 252–53; advice on babies' gas discomfort, 258; and concerns about BMs, 258; and hand washings, 204; and release of twins from hospital, 256; on routines, 252; savings opportunities in office of, 187; selection of, 67–69; suggestions on sleeping arrangements, 81, 256, 267; visits to, 200, 201, 261, 268, 280; weight checks for babies, 257
pediatric ophthalmologists, 204, 275
pediatric orthopedists, 204
pediatric urologists, 204
pelvis, pressure on, 30
penis, 236; care after circumcision, 259; and urination arc, 236
peri-bottle, 114
personal appearance, postpartum, 123
personal hygiene for moms, 176
personalities, 219, 270–71, 288
personal time, 77
pesticides, 20
petroleum jelly, 88, 157
pharmaceutical company samples, 187
photographs, 254; coupons for, 188; professional, 175, 271; with two year olds, 236
physical characteristics: month one, 260; month two, 263–64; month three, 266; month four, 268; month five, 270; month six, 271–72; month seven, 273;

rooming in option, 255
routines: at 8 months, 275; for
    breastfeeding, 143; incentives to
    establish, 243–44; pediatrician's
    advice on, 252; preparation times
    for, 90–91; setting up and
    maintaining, 131–35
rubber pants, 258
rubbing alcohol, 258

safety: and assessments of twins,
    219; and baby swings, 96; and
    personal modesty, 101; and
    vacation spots, 195
salves, 88
Santa Claus, 234–35
Sarah Jane, 120, 159, 160; adult
    reactions to, 218, 285; birth, 114,
    163; breastfeeding, 140, 150,
    153–55; broken wrist, 204; crying
    sessions, 253; diabetes, 204, 205;
    the first year, 256–79; illnesses,
    200; journal for, 153–57; naming,
    124; picking up, 161; rash, 210;
    solid food consumption, 210, 214
savings accounts, 189, 190
sciatic pressure, 33
screenings, 40–42
secondhand smoke, 19
secondhand stores, 84
second trimester, 29–36
self-assessments, 237
self-calming by twins, 134
self-care, 124
self-diagnosing, 30
self-fulfilling prophecies, 218–19
sense of texture, 273
sense of touch, 273
sensor pads, use in labor and
    delivery room, 107
September 11, 2001, 231
sexual relations, 23–24, 119; after
    birth of twins, 225–27
shoes, 80

shopping, 171–74
shopping malls, 234
shortness of breath, 60
showers, 14, 19, 177
showing, 12
sickness: attitude of parents
    during, 201; documenting of,
    201–2; and medicine
    dispensing, 202, 203; of
    mothers, 204; symptoms
    displayed, 200–201; use of
    antibacterial cleaners during,
    203–5; and use of dry erase
    board, 201–2; and use of high
    chairs, 203; and use of vinyl
    mattress covers, 203
SIDS. See sudden infant death
    syndrome (SIDS)
silence is golden, 235–36
sippy cups, 97, 279
sitting, 161
sitz baths, 114
skin stretching, and itching
    sensation, 32
skin tags, 59
sleep, 177; deprivation of, 125–26,
    221; interruptions in, 58;
    methods to induce, 135; need
    for, 114, 231; as part of routine,
    132–35; taking opportunities to,
    251; vs. feeding schedule, 256
sleepers, 141
sleeping, 288–89; arrangements for,
    70–71; with Boppy pillows, 98;
    in bouncy seats, 95; co-bedding
    twins, 81, 133, 256, 265;
    rooming in option, 255; through
    the night, 133, 266–68
smell: of aerosol fumes, 22;
    secondhand smoke, 19; sense of,
    11–12
smiles, 264, 266
smoking, 19
snack foods, 212–13, 215

weight: checks for twins, 257, 274; monitoring of, 43–44; postdelivery, 66, 121

weight gain, 12, 35, 61n1; month two, 264; recommendations for, 33

weight loss, 54–55; maternal, 142; postpregnancy, 66

well-wishers, 247–49

Winnie the Pooh, 236

wipes, 88, 94, 232

wipe warmers, 94

working moms, 287–88

worry, 15

www.morethan1.com, 81

www.twinslist.org, 94

www.twinstuff.com, 93, 224

X-rays, avoidance of, 20

yard sales, 187–88

yoga, 20–21, 165

yogurt, 212

Zantac, 155, 262

Ziploc baggies, 212

About the Author

Cheryl Lage, a lifelong Virginian, was raised in Alexandria, a suburb of Washington, D.C. After receiving her B.A. in art history from the College of William and Mary, Cheryl embarked on a career spanning fourteen years in TV/video post-production.

Production of quite a different kind began in early 2001, when she and her husband, Scott, learned they were expecting twins.

Since Darren and Sarah's conception, Cheryl has fully embraced the MOM (Mother of Multiples) experience. Her twin-centric perspectives have appeared in *TwinsMagazine*, *Pregnancy*, and *Richmond Parents Monthly*. On the web, Cheryl's articles can be found at www .twinstuff.com, www.storknet.com, her "Ask a Twin Mommy" monthly column on www.christian-mommies.com, and via her own website, www.twinsights.com.

When not expounding on the adventures of twin parenting, Cheryl enjoys reading, giving museum tours, and participating in her church discussion group. Above all else, she prefers hanging out with her family.